THE CLASSIC WINE LIBRARY READER

THE CLASSIC WINE LIBRARY READER

A TASTE OF THE WORLD'S BEST WINE WRITING

FOREWORD BY JULIAN JEFFS

infiniteideas

First published in 2023 by
Infinite Ideas Limited
www.infideas.com

A CIP catalogue record for this book is available from the British Library

ISBN 978–1–913022–32–7

Printed in Great Britain

Picture credits
Page 10 courtesy of the Wellcome Collection; page 14 Richard Semik/Shutterstock;
page 28 courtesy of Monty Waldin; page 37 courtesy of Caroline Gilby MW; page
42 © AWMB/Komitee Kamptal; page 63 courtesy Sadie Family; pages 70, 71, 233,
236 © Anthony Rose; pages 83, 85 courtesy of Ricardo Diogo Freitas of Barbeito;
page 90 © BIVB/Benoit France; page 107 courtesy of Domaine Roulot; page 106
Mark Davidson; page 123 courtesy of Dean Mackenzie; page 129 Courtesy of Ralf
Kaiser; page 137 © Lisa Granik MW; page 147 © Archivi Masi; page 157 courtesy of
Mas Amiel; page 162 courtesy of Leo Duff; page 164 courtesy of Symington Family
Estates; page 177 © Matt Walls; page 186 courtesy of Gary Macdonald; page 193
Wines of Portugal; page 203, 205 maps created by Darren Lingard, page 205 based
on an original © José Hidalgo; page 213, 214 Ktima Sigalas; page 223, map by T. J.
Tucker; page 225 An Pham; page 251 Jon Chica/Shutterstock; page 260 courtesy of
Inniskillin Niagara Estate Winery; page 272 © BNIC/Gérard Martron.

CONTENTS

WINEMAKING

REGIONAL PERSPECTIVES

SOME WINES OF NOTE

FOREWORD

The story begins a long time ago. In 1956 I graduated from Cambridge as a scientist but I was not a good one, not nearly good enough to do any serious research, which I had wanted to do as a schoolboy, nor did I work hard enough. My principal pleasure had been debating in the Union and I thought of becoming a barrister. After passing the preliminary papers I faced the Bar Finals. It was a cold, bleak English winter. A friend had just got back from Alicante and he told me what a perfect climate it had, and that it was very cheap to live in, so I packed my books in a bag and went there. I read them sitting on the beach and, until recently, when I looked at them sand would fall out from between the pages.

My father was a wine lover and gave me my first lessons in wine. He had an enthusiastic pupil. Having decided to go to Spain I asked him to get me introductions from a wine merchant friend to some sherry shippers. He got me three, all of which became and were to remain my friends. Being a very slap-happy young man, I did not look at a map and did not realize how far Jerez de la Frontera was from Alicante. Having rejected the train journey as tedious, I decided to take a boat from Alicante to Cádiz. I embarked on a rolling, sea-sick coaster to Cádiz by way of Melilla and Ceuta in North Africa. It put me in mind of the line 'The night we went to Bannockburn by way of Brighton Pier', in Chesterton's 'The Rolling English Road'. Having arrived, I was amazed to find that Cádiz was at the end of a peninsula. No one had told me this when I was taught at school about the singeing of the king of Spain's beard. I disembarked and set off to explore the city only to find in a couple of minutes that I was on the other side. I caught a bus to Jerez and, as it laboured up from the salt marshes to the city, I had the odd sensation that I had come home. One of my introductions was to Williams & Humbert where I met the legendary Don Guido – Guy Williams – who was the British vice-consul and ran the bodega. I told him I adored it and wished I could live there. We got on. He told me his English assistant was about to leave and offered me his job. I went for five days and stayed eight months. I often wish I were there still.

I read everything I could lay my hands on about sherry and found much of it inadequate or wrong, so I took a year off and wrote *Sherry*. In 1961 when Faber & Faber created their wine series, *Sherry* was their first book. I became the out-of-house series editor, a role I filled until 2002. I was delighted when, ten years ago, the series was recreated by Infinite Ideas. I have been pleased to see it grow and new wine lovers share their expertise on wine. I wish the Infinite Ideas Classic Wine Library every success for the future.

Julian Jeffs
East Ilsley, 2023

INTRODUCTION

I always say that there is no better moment in the day than sitting down with a good wine book, preferably accompanied by a good glass of wine from the same region. The Classic Wine Library now has thirty books in the series and, to my mind, that means an almost infinite number of glasses of wine to choose from! *The Classic Wine Library Reader* celebrates ten years of wine writing and is the first book in our series that is not constrained by geographical boundaries. It covers the whole world of wine. It is an anthology of some of the best prose from some of the most accomplished wine writers, whose expertise spans the world.

It has been a pleasure to act as one of the series editors for Infinite Ideas for the past decade. The Classic Wine Library emerged at a time when the concept of a book seemed old fashioned and under threat from new technology and means of communication. As someone who still likes to handle a proper book I find it reassuring that, far from being in decline, there are ever more titles to choose from, and online shopping can bring a physical book straight to your door. Our books are not formulaic: we trust our writers and like to see their individuality show through. Along with a passion for their subject, as editors, we value our authors' idiosyncrasies and opinions. I hope that all these valuable traits show through in this wide-ranging anthology on wine.

The Classic Wine Library is far from static. All our titles are regularly revised and updated by our authors, covering the evolution of wine-making, new producers, changing fashions and the latest vintages. To illustrate the point, my book *Port and the Douro* was first published in 1999 and is about to go into its fifth edition. The first edition of my book was edited by Julian Jeffs, whose 1961 book *Sherry* is now in its sixth edition. As editors with a background in wine we are acutely aware of our heritage and are honoured that Julian has agreed to write the Foreword to this anthology.

It would be invidious for me to single out another author from the Classic Wine Library but I would like to pay tribute to my co-editors on the Editorial Board, Sarah Jane Evans MW (also the author of a book in the series) and James Tidwell MS, who looks after our interests in the US. We all enjoy wine and words and the three of us are constantly on the look-out for new authors and titles for this expanding series. Rebecca Clare has been on hand from the start and has been meticulous in her role as Editorial Director for every title published so far. I can honestly say that she has been a pleasure to work with. She knows the series better than anyone and it is her selection from nearly three million words written over the last decade that forms this unique anthology. *The Classic Wine Library Reader* is a mark of posterity. I am thoroughly looking forward to sitting down with it, accompanied of course by one or more glasses of wine. It is, after all, a taste of the world's best wine writing.

Richard Mayson, Series Co-Editor
Ashford in the Water, 2023

PREFACE

The Classic Wine Library has a long and distinguished heritage, stretching back more than sixty years, to the first edition of *Sherry* by Julian Jeffs, in 1961. In 2013, when Infinite Ideas published *Port and the Douro*, by Richard Mayson, little did we know that in ten years' time we would be the proud publisher of thirty wine titles. As we celebrate a decade as custodians of the Classic Wine Library we publish this anthology to offer a taste of the best from each of the books in the series.

When that first manuscript landed on my desk I knew very little about wine beyond the enjoyment of drinking it. Now, having read thirty of the most erudite books available on the subject, my knowledge and understanding have both grown considerably. Putting this book together has been both a challenge and a delight, and I hope that reading this anthology not only expands your knowledge but also has you seeking out some of the less mainstream titles in the series. All the chapters are of around ten pages in length and can be enjoyed in any order and completely independently of one another. So pour a glass of wine and dip in wherever takes your fancy.

The book begins by exploring the historical background. Before looking into any particular region, it seemed appropriate to investigate the history of vineyard cultivation itself, with an extract from Rod Phillips' social and cultural history, simply entitled *Wine*. Next, the late Nicholas Faith's characteristic wit imbues his chapter on the achievements that 'inventor of sparkling wine' Dom Perignon really deserves to be remembered for. We are then given a history of the increasingly popular, and environmentally significant, practice of biodynamics, by Monty Waldin, before Caroline Gilby MW, Stephen Brook and Stephen Skelton MW each offer us an aspect of the history of a region close to their hearts. The section ends with a look, by Jim Clarke, at how South Africa's wine industry is involved in attempts to make amends for the country's historical treatment of its black and coloured population.

Next we head into the vineyards. Anthony Rose begins by explaining the effect of terroir on sparkling wines and asks what impact climate change might have on fizz of the future. We are then given detailed descriptions of the vineyards of Madeira, by Richard Mayson, and of two sets of burgundy vineyards – first Chablis, by Rosemary George MW and then Raymond Blake on Côte d'Or. In a brand new chapter from his forthcoming book, *The wines of Australia*, Mark Davidson explains the history and importance of Australia's collection of old (some very old) vines. If you often find profiles of grape varieties a bit dry then I urge you not to pass over the two at the end of this section. First up is a lively and in-depth study by Rebecca Gibb MW of Pinot Noir and how it expresses itself in New Zealand's wines, and then Anne Krebiehl MW turns her attentions to the distinctive aromatic variety Riesling and its long connection with German wine.

The third section provides four chapters on the winemaking process, examining how some historic wines are made. Lisa Granik MW takes us to Georgia to look at the very special traditional winemaking vessel the qvevri, and how it is made and used to make wine. The region of Verona, in Italy, is home to several wines made by first drying grapes, a traditional, but sometimes tricky, process described by Michael Garner. In a chapter on Roussillon's Vins Doux Naturels, Rosemary George MW lets the region's winemakers explain how they are made and asks why these wines are not more widely drunk. Richard Mayson rounds off the section with an atmospheric chapter on the development of young Port wine into its various styles.

Our selection of regional overviews begins in the Old World. First, Matt Walls gives a detailed account of Côte Rôtie, explaining the geography, soils and grape varieties that combine to make the wines of this northern Rhône appellation. We then travel south, to the Languedoc, where Rosemary George MW explores what it is that defines one of her favourite appellations, Faugères. On the Iberian Peninsula we are guided by two series editors, Richard Mayson and Sarah Jane Evans MW, as they highlight the key features of the Portuguese appellation of Vinho Verde (increasingly fashionable for its lower alcohol wines) and the prolific northern Spanish region Rioja. Konstantinos Lazarakis MW takes us into less familiar territory in his chapter on the volcanic Greek island of Santorini, with some unusual growing conditions and, says Lazarakis, some of Europe's most distinctive wines. The US state of Arizona is a region few of us will have tasted wines from – yet – but Jessica Dupuy is convinced that the quality on display means they will soon be making their mark on more wine lists. Here, she summarizes the regional conditions and the challenges affecting the state's wine industry. Finally, in this section, Anthony Rose explores the wine history and recent rapid winemaking progress of Japan.

The final section of the book gives us the chance to learn about some notable wines. Rosé expert Elizabeth Gabay MW begins by uncovering the history of Tavel and finding out what makes these age-worthy rosés special. Julian Jeffs makes a charming guide to the Spanish coastal town of Sanlúcar de Barrameda and its distinctive dry sherry, manzanilla, before Rod Phillips transports us to colder climes to provide the inside story on Canada's most famous wine export, Icewine. We conclude, naturally, with a little brandy, as Nicholas Faith invites us to enjoy a glass of cognac.

We are now looking forward to the next ten years of The Classic Wine Library. We still have many more regions and countries to explore, particularly in North and South America as well as emerging regions in southern Europe and Asia. I am looking forward to expanding my wine knowledge and working with expert wine writers to bring you more of the best informed wine books around.

Rebecca Clare
Editorial Director, Infinite Ideas

THE HISTORICAL BACKGROUND

THE BEGINNINGS OF VITICUTURE

In this extract from his 2018 book *Wine: A social and cultural history of the drink that changed our lives*, Rod Phillips outlines the history of wine grape cultivation, explaining how a wild tree-climbing species was domesticated to become the orderly vineyard plant we know today.

In 1584 the French philosopher and essayist Michel de Montaigne was travelling with a party of companions near Mulhouse, in Alsace. He noted in his diary that one day 'in the morning we came across a fine, broad plain, flanked on its left side by slopes covered with vines that were beautiful and very well cultivated and so extensive that the Gascons [people from the Bordeaux region] who were there said they had never seen the equal'. The vineyards he was referring to were in what is now the Haut-Rhin region, home to most of Alsace's Grand Cru vineyards. But what struck Montaigne and his companions was not the quality of the wine (which they had not tasted) but the sheer extent of the vineyards that covered the slopes. It impressed even his travelling companions from Bordeaux, where the area planted in vines had increased dramatically in the previous centuries – largely to meet foreign demand for clairet, the light red wine that was then Bordeaux's signature wine, and which became popular in England as 'claret'.

Unlike Montaigne and his company, who were so impressed by vine-covered slopes, anyone who visits many of the world's wine regions today will very likely soon become blasé at the sight of vineyards covering hundreds of hectares and stretching far into the distance. These are the landscapes of wine regions as diverse as Champagne in France, La

Mancha in Spain, the Barossa Valley in Australia, and the Central Valley in Chile. In these and many other regions, viticulture has become the dominant and even the sole form of agriculture as it has progressively taken over land that had been used for other agricultural purposes. In Paso Robles, in central California, much of the land now in vines was formerly dedicated to farming beef cattle, while in many parts of New Zealand sheep and dairy cattle have been shunted aside to make room for grapes. (In New Zealand it is not only sheep that vastly outnumber people; vines now easily outnumber sheep.) In yet other cases, vineyards have been extended to areas that had not before been cultivated. Some grow where the land is too steep for other forms of cultivation, as in the Mosel Valley, where slopes can be as steep as 70 degrees; some vines are planted at altitudes that are too high for other crops, as they are in the foothills of the Andes in Argentina; other vineyards have been planted in areas that were previously forest or scrubland, such as the vineyards in plots cleared from garrigue in Languedoc; yet other vineyards, such as many in Bordeaux's Médoc district, are located on previously marshy areas that were drained specifically for viticulture.

While these developments were and are based on calculations by landowners that producing wine would be a more profitable way of using their land, it is likely that not everyone was happy about the disruption to the landscape that planting vines led to. People who are not interested in wine were probably not thrilled to see vines displace other forms of agriculture or encroach on forests, woodland, or marshes that were home to game and other wildlife. In his witty and perceptive book on Germany, *Germania*, Simon Winder notes that German wine producers 'battle constantly against a cold, rough climate and short summer', but he continues 'Germany does have some fabulous wine areas. The train trip from Koblenz to Trier down the Mosel Valley is a hymn to grapes, with every tiny jut or near-vertical slope stuffed with vines. For non-drinkers it might seem a rather depressing monoculture – the Mosel must have looked very pretty before wine wrecked it – not unlike driving through an oil-palm or rubber plantation. But for those, like me, in favour, it is a grapey Angkor Wat.'

Whether or not it has been universally welcomed, the result is that, over time, vines have occupied an increasing part of the land surface in many parts of the world, although the world's total viticultural area peaked in about 2003 and has declined somewhat since. Even so, vineyards occupy only a small part of the earth's cultivated surface. The world's total vineyard area is about 7.5 million hectares, which is a small but significant decline from the almost 8 million hectares recorded in 2003. These 7.5 million hectares represent about twice the area of land dedicated to growing tea (3.7 million hectares) but are somewhat less than the 10.5 million hectares devoted to growing coffee beans.

Despite the recent decline in world vineyard area (which is almost certain to be slowly reversed in the coming decades) there are many more hectares of vines today than at almost any time in history – despite the fact that some national vineyard areas have shrunk dramatically, including those of Europe's two biggest wine producers. The vineyard area of Italy declined by half between 1970 and 2015, going from 1.3 million to 680,000 hectares. In France there has been a staggering decline in vineyard area in the last 150 years, from 2.5 million hectares in the 1870s to about 780,000 hectares today, a decline of about two-thirds. The area occupied by vines in France continues to decline steadily, year after year. In contrast Spain, which is Europe's other major wine producer, has seen its vineyard area stabilize since 2011, after some significant shrinkage in the preceding four years (2008 to 2011).

The steady overall contraction of Europe's vineyard area since 2000 largely accounts for the decline in the area under vines worldwide because of the importance of European wine to world production. Although some wine regions outside Europe have expanded, they have not yet done so enough to counteract the decline of Europe's vineyards. The most important driver of growth is China, which now has almost 850,000 hectares of vines, making it second only to Spain (with a little over a million hectares) in terms of the size of its vineyard area. Between 2012 and 2016, China's vineyard area grew by a fifth, by far the fastest rate of increase anywhere. If China's vineyard area continues to expand as it has in the last decade or so, it will begin to compensate for losses in Europe. It is quite easy to foresee China becoming the world's biggest producer of wine, as vineyards extend their presence across the regions suitable for viticulture.

It is a dramatic understatement to say that the extent and the dynamic state of the world's vineyards today is far removed from the early status of grape vines. Growing wild, as members of the genus *Vitis*, grape vines were part of the landscapes of much of Asia and North America for millions of years. But only in the last few thousand years, when they have been domesticated and cultivated, have they in any way stood out from other flora. Instead, for most of their history, grape vines were integrated into their biodiverse environments. The approximately sixty species in the genus *Vitis* grow in various ways and in diverse contexts. Some grow up trees, seeking the sunlight needed to ripen their fruit, while others trail along the ground; some flourish in forests, others thrive along riverbanks.

One species, *Vitis vinifera sylvestris* – the forest-dwelling, tree-climbing species that now produces the great bulk of the world's wine today and includes varieties such as Chardonnay, Riesling, Merlot, and Pinot Noir – stands out, because it is the main species to have been domesticated and widely planted for wine production. A few other species are used for raisins and currants, and for products such as grape juice and jelly. But grape varieties other than *Vitis vinifera* are also used for wine, even though in very small volumes. Some varieties of the *Vitis labrusca* species, such as Catawba and Niagara, are used to make wine in some regions of the United States, as is Scuppernong, a variety of the *Vitis rotundifolia* species. Non-*vinifera* varieties have also been employed to create hybrids when they possess desirable characteristics such as cold-hardiness or resistance to phylloxera. At the same time, dozens of species of *Vitis* that are not used for wine or any other produce continue to grow wild in North America and Asia, largely ignored by humans.

When people began to use grapes to make wine, they undoubtedly at first picked the grapes from the vines as they grew wild without any human intervention. Very likely they initially picked the same grapes to eat fresh and – although this is all speculation – the first wine was made by accident when grapes intended for eating were crushed under their own weight and the juice fermented. At this early point, whether grapes were for eating or making wine, the species and variety must have been unimportant; people picked any grapes that were to hand. What eventually became important was the suitability of the grapes to make wine, no matter what the volume or quality, and the reasonable proximity of the vines to human settlements. An archaeologist who helped excavate the oldest known winemaking facility, dating back 8,000 years and located in the South Caucasus region of Georgia, speculated that the grapes that were processed in it had been growing wild on the nearby hillsides and were harvested and brought to the community to be fermented.

With the development of settled communities in the Neolithic period and the spread of cultivation and agriculture, some species and varieties of grapes were clearly found to be more suitable than others for winemaking – perhaps because they had a better flesh-to-seeds ratio or smaller seeds, or simply made better-flavoured wine. These varieties were transplanted into designated plots – the earliest vineyards – and over time, as varieties were even more carefully selected and bred, they became the grape varieties used to make wine today. Many of these varieties, such as Chardonnay, Pinot Grigio, Merlot and Cabernet Sauvignon, are familiar to wine drinkers, but most are not. The standard reference work, *Wine Grapes* by Jancis Robinson, Julia Harding and José Vouillamoz, lists more than 1,300 varieties used to make wine throughout the world. It includes not only the couple of dozen varieties familiar to most wine drinkers, but also such little-known varieties as Gamaret, Maligia, Prunesta and Shevka.

A critical underpinning of the success of *Vitis vinifera* was the evolution of the wild species, *Vitis vinifera sylvestris*, from being dioecious to hermaphroditic. Dioecious vines have male flowers on one plant and female flowers on another, so that pollination is needed for fruit to form. Hermaphroditic vines have flowers that are both male and female. They thus produce fruit spontaneously, which makes them far more reliable as producers and enables them to be used commercially. How and at what point in the process of domestication this change took place, we do not know, but it was after vines were taken from their indigenous habitat in forests and woods, and transplanted in the biodiverse gardens that were the earliest vineyards.

Needless to say, we have no information on the size of these vineyards, how the vines in them were spaced and organized (in rows or randomly), and how they grew – whether they trailed along the ground, grew up the trunks of trees, or were trained up dedicated stakes driven into the ground to stand in for trees. Among early depictions of vines, a relief from the royal palace at Nineveh (about 650 BC) shows King Ashurbanipal and his queen drinking wine from shallow cups, while seated under a bower of grape vines. This suggests that vines were trained in a way that is similar to a pergola system where the grapes hang down from a trellis supported by vertical posts. This method of training vines provides some protection from birds (the bunches of grapes are hidden from birds as they fly over the vineyard) and it also enables farmers to grow some shade-tolerant crops under the pergola.

Even earlier Egyptian representations of viticulture and winemaking, dating from about 1450 BC, also depict vines trained the same way. The vines are shown growing vertically from the trunk, running overhead, and then down the other side. With the vines planted side by side in a straight line, the arbour effectively became a tunnel of vines. These Egyptian paintings show big bunches of grapes hanging from the sides and roof of the tunnel, with a few stray, untrained canes hanging down to give these idealized images a touch of verisimilitude. The grape harvesters are shown in the middle of the arbour, picking grapes from the sides and roof. Sometimes the trellis is high enough that the harvesters are able to stand upright, but sometimes the roof of vines is so low that the pickers have to crouch.

Despite the suggestion that vines were planted in straight lines and on trellises in Egypt, we have little information on the patterns of planting in most other parts of the ancient world. Were vines planted in rows or were they planted randomly, like trees in a forest? Spaces between rows are needed when animals and machinery are used in vineyards, but not when grapes were harvested by hand or when animals were simply let loose to graze at will among vines. We might expect patterns of planting to show some consistency as knowledge and techniques of viticulture were transferred from region to region. If the Egyptian vineyards looked the way they are depicted in wall paintings, we might assume that the Egyptians learned to train vines in an arbour from the regions to the east (such as Mesopotamia) where wine was produced earlier, and that the Egyptians in turn passed this technique on to vineyard owners in Crete and the Greek mainland.

To judge by images of vineyards, there seems to have been no standard consistent system of planting vines during the Middle Ages. An illuminated illustration from the Khamseh of Nizami, now in Iran, dating from the sixteenth century, clearly shows vines growing on an overhead trellis system. The vertical stakes that support the trellis have forked tops in which the cross-beams are secured, and the vines are trained along the roof of the trellis. But an illumination from the *Très Riches Heures du Duc de Berry*, dating from the early 1400s and showing the grape harvest in northern France in September, equally clearly depicts bush vines (without any external support, such as stakes or trellis) growing randomly. A third image, from a book on distilling published in 1500, shows several techniques of training vines. There are vines growing on flat-topped and inverted U-shaped trellises, vines trained up trees, and vines growing up stakes that are evenly spaced in rows. But vines growing randomly are not shown.

In the Early Modern period, from about 1500 to 1800, we continue to find various patterns of planting. A manual on viticulture written in the 1620s by a native of Languedoc to guide English settlers in Virginia recommended planting vines equally spaced in rows. It suggested laying a length of rope along the ground to make sure the rows were straight. The vines were to be planted directly into the soil, but the author also suggested training them up trees or poles stuck in the ground. Training vines up trees growing in woods and forests would have led to a random pattern of planting. While touring France in the late eighteenth century, the English agronomist Arthur Young noted several patterns of planting vines. In general, he noted 'The vines are planted promiscuously, three or four feet or two and a half from each other' and were 'tied to the props [stakes] with small straw bands'. But near Toulouse he also saw vines being trained up trees: 'Here, for the first time, see rows of maples, with vines, trained in festoons, from tree to tree; they are conducted by a rope of bramble, vine cutting, or willow. They give many grapes, but bad wine.' The account books of Burgundy vignerons in the eighteenth century show purchases of stakes and ties, indicative of the method used there at the time.

Despite scattered evidence that vines were in some places trained up trees or planted in rows, the overall weight of evidence suggests that throughout most of Europe until the late nineteenth and early twentieth centuries, the straight rows of vines that are the rule today were rare. Instead, vines were generally planted randomly in vineyards, largely because instead of being planted individually, vines were propagated by a method known as *provignage*. This involves taking a cane from an existing vine, stretching it out and burying the end of it. The part of the cane that is buried grows roots and becomes a new vine, after which the piece of cane linking it to its parent can be cut – although that is not necessary.

As far as planting patterns are concerned, vines in such vineyards were spaced as far apart as the regenerating cane would extend. In principle it is possible to position vines in what would probably be ragged rows, but it would have been easier to bury canes wherever they did not interfere with existing vines. There was, after all, no reason at that time to plant vines in straight rows. Randomly planted they might have been, but French vineyards were well looked after, as Arthur Young noted in the late 1700s: 'their vineyards are gardens; the turnips of Norfolk, the carrots of Suffolk, the beans of Kent, and the cabbages of an English gentleman are not so clean as the vines of France'.

We have spotty and incomplete information on the extent of vineyards over time, whether it is of the size of individual vineyards or the area planted in vines in specific districts, regions, or later in entire countries. But it is clear that there was no smooth, linear increase in the area of land planted in vines. Rather, because vineyards were the basis of a wine business – whether at the smaller scale of an individual vigneron's household, the substantial holdings of a monastery, or at a big-production corporate level – financial and economic calculations underlay decisions to increase or decrease the area planted in vines. Decisions to extend the size of vineyards might result from a shortage of wine, increased demand, rising prices, or all three, while a fall in demand and prices might result in decisions to allow vineyards to fall into decay or to pull out the vines and replant the land with more profitable crops.

Vines fill the landscape in a harvest scene,
probably from the sixteenth century. Engraving (no date)

In some cases we can only guess at motivations. During the last millennium BC, the Assyrians embarked on a massive vine-planting programme. In what Patrick McGovern refers to as the 'Assyrian Domesday Book' they recorded tens of thousands of grape vines in the upper Balikh Valley. More were planted, some up hillsides as high as 1,500 metres – rather like many high-altitude vineyards in Argentina today – in the eastern regions of the kingdom north-east of Nineveh. But the Assyrians also destroyed vineyards. When they crossed into what is now Azerbaijan in about 700 BC, they noted the extensive vineyards at the fortresses of Urartu. Practising a scorched-earth policy, the Assyrian armies 'came down like the wolf on the fold', as Lord Byron put it, but their aim was not to kill sheep but to destroy the vineyards of their enemy – while at the same time helping themselves to the wine stored in the buried ceramic jars (*kvevris* or *qvevris*) in which it had been made.

As for the initial spread of vineyards in Greece and Italy, it was almost certainly a response to demand, probably from the elites who had become accustomed to drinking imported wine from places such as Crete and Egypt. When vineyards were planted in Greece (at first close to centres of population) the supply of wine increased, and it in turn stimulated additional demand. In both Greece and Italy, wine was by far the most common alcoholic beverage – in fact, it was for all intents and purposes the only alcoholic beverage, because beer was not produced and mead was made in very small volumes. As virtually the sole alcoholic drink in Greece, wine was such an important product – with cereal and olive oil, it was one of the three most-traded commodities in the Mediterranean region – that vineyards soon spread beyond the mainland to the islands of the Aegean Sea. As for the Romans, wine became fundamental to their diet, and they planted vineyards throughout their European empire in the first couple of centuries AD.

The expansion of vineyards in Europe seems to have stalled when the Roman Empire broke up and much of western Europe was dominated by the migrant populations from eastern Europe (the so-called 'Barbarian invasions') but there was another surge of vine planting at the end of the first millennium AD. There is some evidence that around the year 1000 the climate warmed in a number of regions, enabling grapes to ripen on a regular basis in areas where viticulture had been marginal or impossible. Just as important, Europe's population increased, and clusters of large towns (with relatively prosperous wine-drinking middle classes engaged in business and the professions) developed in northern Italy and northern Europe.

All these conditions encouraged the expansion of vineyards in order to provide wine for the new and growing markets. Some regions, such as Tuscany in north-central Italy, supplied wine to nearby population centres that included Florence, Venice, Genoa and Milan. Others, such as vineyards in Germany's Rhine and Mosel Valleys and in northern and western France, shipped their wines to London, Ghent, Brussels, Bruges and other markets in northern Europe as well as in the Baltic area. As Paris grew, so did the area in surrounding regions that was planted with vines.

The number of vineyards along the Rhine and Mosel rivers seems to have increased appreciably at about this time. One study shows that along the Rhine between Bonn and Bingen and along the Mosel between Koblenz and Trier, about seventy vineyards were mentioned in documents before 900 AD but another sixty-five were first mentioned between 901 and 1050. In other words, it could well be that as many vineyards were planted in the 150 years after 900 as in the preceding 700 or 800 years.

Bordeaux's vineyards also expanded at this time. In the early 1100s, viticulture was largely confined to the gravel soils around the town itself, but as the wine trade with England grew, vines extended as far as 4 or 5 kilometres from the town walls, until they encountered the small communities of Bordeaux's hinterland. Here vines were planted with other crops and generally took up no more than a fifth of the land. In some areas – north of the town of Bordeaux and on the right bank of the Garonne – marshes were drained so that vines could be planted. Some of the region's vineyards were surrounded by hedges or marked off by ditches, but most were not. Bordeaux's viticultural landscape throughout the Medieval and Early Modern periods must have had an open and rural appearance quite different from that of today.

But the growth of vineyards was neither steady nor constant. Throughout much of Europe in the late 1300s, the Black Death killed a third or more of the population, reducing demand for wine (and all goods and services) as well as cutting into the labour supply needed to tend the vines. Many vineyards were simply abandoned and effectively disappeared, but as population and markets began to grow again, there was another surge of vine planting, part of a general recovery of agriculture. It was at this time, at the end of the 1400s, that the Florentine humanist and agronomist Michelangiolo Tanaglia encouraged the expansion of vineyards in his verse treatise *De Agricultura*:

> *Now is the time, in my opinion,*
> *On the open hills to never tire,*
> *Of planting vines, of the best kind,*
> *Or of attending the plant of Bacchus.*

THE REAL PERIGNON, AND THE MYTH

In this excerpt from *The story of Champagne* (2016), Nicholas Faith looks beyond the myths surrounding Dom Perignon to relate the true story of how a seventeenth-century monk revolutionized winemaking and vineyard management.

The Abbey of Hautvillers provides one of Champagne's most effective theatrical experiences. The site has an unequalled view over Epernay and the valley of the Marne, source of the *vins de la Rivière* already famous in the mid-seventeenth century. Ecclesiastical man was already exploiting the site before the turn of the millennium, and although most of the original abbey was destroyed during the French Revolution, enough remains to convey a sense of eternal consecration to a devout purpose. The ruins are genuine enough to inspire a suitable sense of historical awe – a feeling intensified by the archaeologists still painstakingly examining the stones to determine the exact size of the abbey in the early Middle Ages.

Art and nature combine to seduce the visitor into the delusion that sparkling champagne was invented here during the near half-century between 1668 and 1715 when Dom Perignon was procurator of the abbey. The myth also introduces an agreeable paradox – that so hedonistic a wine should have been invented by a monk. For its apparently holy origins greatly help legitimize a drink originally associated exclusively with dissipation and seduction. Even today so reputable a publication as the *Encyclopaedia Larousse* names Perignon as the creator of sparkling champagne.

In reality Dom Pierre Perignon, the *procureur* – all-powerful administrator – of the Abbey of Hautvillers for nearly fifty years after his appointment in 1668 was revolutionizing the wine itself, but emphatically not providing the sparkle. Indeed, even within Champagne the revolution consisted of a number of evolutionary developments over a period of nearly two centuries. Dom Perignon was simply one of the most distinguished 'evolutionaries' in developing the region's wines. In the words of the French writer Fernand Woutaz: 'If Dom Perignon did not "invent" champagne, all the same he was its "*inventor*" in the legal sense of someone who uncovers buried treasure … during forty-seven years of unceasing and methodical work, Dom Perignon lifted to the highest possible level all the stages of making white wine, from the cultivation of the vine to bottling the wine, so uncovering a "treasure" which was soon to make the fortune of everyone connected with the wines of Champagne.' He was – no mean achievement – the pioneer in producing the still wines we know today. But there was nothing he, his rivals and successors, and sophisticated wine drinkers in general for up to a century after his death, disliked so much as the mere thought of sparkling champagne. To Dom Perignon's generation of winemakers, wines which sparkled were not, as the mythologists would have it, the final and deliberate result of the whole careful process. They were a problem, pure and simple. Making a still wine was a sophisticated process, but making a sparkling wine emphatically wasn't. For sparkling champagne was not invented. It just happened, partly because of technical inadequacies, rather than technical innovations. In the words of the French wine writer Raymond Dumay, 'he knew of no enemy more dangerous than wine which "worked", that is to say wine which, despite everything, was determined to bubble for the whole of its life'.

The fact that a wine fizzed was simply proof that there was something wrong with it. Its only advantage was that the carbon dioxide released as fizz separated the wine from the oxygen in the air and thus stopped it from oxidizing and turning into vinegar.

The abundant loose talk over the centuries of Perignon's 'secret' is ridiculous, he merely imposed a firm and detailed discipline at all stages of the grape growing and winemaking. He used grapes from the right sites and the right varieties and while he certainly didn't 'invent' sparkling champagne he introduced proper winemaking techniques – ones still recognizable today – for the first time. There were few other winemakers as sophisticated as him elsewhere in France. Among his most important innovations were that of making white wine from black grapes and blending wines from different *coteaux*. Careful harvesting, ensuring that the grapes didn't burst, combined with constructing presses nearer the vineyards, ensured the freshness of the juice. The quality of the wine was improved because he selected the first pressings.

Like every other reputable winemaker in Champagne, Perignon knew that the wines of Champagne were peculiarly prone to fizz once in the bottle. As André Simon explained 'owing to the calcareous nature of the soil on which the grapes grow, Champagne wines contain a large proportion of carbonic acid gas. They always had such a marked tendency to effervesce that the greatest care had to be taken to check their effervescence, which, for a long time, was considered as impairing the quality of the wine.'[1] Obviously the less ripe the grapes, the more acid the wine, the colder the temperature at which it was fermented – and all three conditions were present to a much greater extent in Champagne than in warmer, more southerly vineyards – the less likely it was to have completed its fermentation before winter stopped the yeasts' work.

Dom Perignon had a number of advantages over other abbatial winemakers. For one thing his abbey was more important. For several centuries its wine had been mentioned as one of the finest *crus* in the region. But the abbey had been devastated during the Fronde so there were only twelve monks when he arrived (the number had doubled by the end of

1 Simon, André, *History of the Champagne Trade in England*, Wyman Brothers, 1965.

the century). To rebuild the abbey he needed money, and the most obvious source of income was the wine for which it was already well known.

But he was not the only clerical winemaker to be improving wines. The firm of Taittinger put forward the claims of Dom Jean Oudard who occupied the same role as Dom Perignon at the abbey at Pierry, a subsidiary house of Hautvillers. Dom Oudard, like other *procureurs*, was a fine winemaker. After browsing through a major collection of original seventeenth and eighteenth-century documents a nineteenth-century writer, Armand Silvestre, was left exclaiming: 'O noble Jean Oudard, O precieux Dom Perignon.' Oudard, sixteen years younger than Dom Perignon, outlived his master by twenty-seven years, well into the age of sparkling wine. The vineyards he supervised included a number in choice communes on what is now the Côte des Blancs, at Pierry, Chouilly and Cramant, and the wines from Pierry are often mentioned in the same bracket as those from Hautvillers. When he died in 1742 he was given the unusual honour of burial in the nave of the abbatial church, and a delegation from Hautvillers (including Dom Perignon's successor) came to the funeral and signed the register. Nevertheless, Perignon rightly remains the symbol of the winemaking revolution of the late seventeenth century.

Perignon took every possible opportunity to increase the size of the abbey's vineyards and the quantities of wine and grapes passing through its hands. A great deal of land had been left fallow, apparently ownerless, as a result of the widespread misery and destruction caused by the Fronde and France's war with Spain which ended in 1659 with the Treaty of the Pyrenees. It helped that pious locals left the abbey considerable sums of money while he also increased the landholdings by lending money to the peasants (apparently at around 5 per cent), and then seizing their land if they could not repay their debts. He inherited 10 hectares of vines, an estate which had increased to 21 hectares by the time he died. He was pretty ruthless, and not only with the peasants, for he appropriated as much as he could, taking disputed cases right up to the King's Grand Conseil. His other achievement as treasurer was to increase the value, as well as the quantity, of the wine sold by the estate. By 1700 the wines from Hautvillers, like those from Sillery and a handful of other ecclesiastical estates, were worth four times that of ordinary wines from Champagne and twice as much as a superior Champagne wine. Improving the still wines of Champagne was a full life's work for anyone even if he had had the inclination to induce the fizz.

The wines of Hautvillers came partly from the abbey's own vineyards, partly from the *dime*, the eleventh or twelfth part of the tenants' crop to which the abbey had the rights, notably at Pierry, Avize and Mesnil-sur-Oger, famous vineyards then as now. The abbey also had many other agricultural holdings, as well as windmills and fishing rights. The *dime* could be paid either in money, in grapes taken *au pied de la vigne*, or in wine. As always in pre-revolutionary France local habits were utterly confused even in the same village. In Aÿ and Dizy, two key parishes, most landowners paid in cash, but the Hautvillers estates had always made every effort to get their rights in wine.

As a result, in the words of Emile Roche: 'Taking the dime in kind provided the Abbey of Hautvillers with a quantity of wine infinitely greater than could have been produced by its own vines – a fact which explains why throughout the ages the ecclesiastics had blended their wines and why what was known as "vin de Hautvillers" was simply the wine blended at and sold by the Abbey but not necessarily coming from its immediate neighbourhood.'[2] Roche estimated that just before the Revolution, only an eighth of the 1,025 *pièces* of wine – enough to fill 280,000 bottles – sold by the abbey came from its own estates, the rest came from the *dime*. So Hautvillers, like Sillery, was a brand name for a blend of wines, only part of which came from the village of the same name. In selling the wines Perignon had the advantage that under the incredibly complicated internal tax system prevailing in pre-revolutionary France wines from ecclesiastical estates paid lower dues on their entry into Paris than those from private citizens, who themselves paid less than merchants.

Thanks to Dom Perignon and other clerical winemakers the Champenois mastered the art of making white wine from black grapes in a matter of a few decades, although they were probably red rather than truly black. They remained alone in their mastery for centuries. As a late eighteenth-century author put it: 'Except for Champagne, all the white wines made elsewhere come from white grapes.' A few old-timers, like St Evremond, deplored any attempt to interfere with natural colouring, or lack of it, particularly where the *vins de la montagne* were concerned for he was none too keen on the successful attempts by Perignon and his successors to make a white wine from black grapes.

2 Roche, Emile, *Le Commerce des vins de Champagne sous L'Ancien Regime*, Chalons-sur-Marne, 1908

Commercially, white wine was more profitable than red. Unfortunately, the white wine made from white grapes by Dom Perignon's predecessors didn't last: it often went yellow by the spring after the vintage, whereas the tougher, redder wines from the Montagne de Reims lasted five or six years. One of Dom Perignon's achievements – and one which we rather take for granted now, although contemporaries clearly didn't – was to make a white wine which stayed white. To confuse matters, however white the wine, it was called *vin gris* because it was made from black grapes. It could thus easily be confused with the previous, tinted, *vin gris* – indeed, the fact that two different wines shared the same name has masked Dom Perignon's achievement in developing a new wine.

In trying to remove the colour from the wine Dom Perignon had the advantage that he was dealing with grapes from the *rivière*. In the words of Nicolas Bidet, 'There are two types of vineyards in Champagne, those of the Montagne de Rheims and those of the River of the Marne. The first produce a red wine with lots of body as well as straw-coloured wines, but these are so strong and cloudy that one can scarcely drink them except after several years. The latter produces fine and elegant vins gris, a direct result of the nature of the terroir … the wines from near Rheims … are more capable of producing red wines … while those from Ai, Epernay and others from the river produce red wines only with the greatest difficulty.' Nevertheless, there was a considerable gap between making a rosé wine, and the discipline and skill required to make a truly white one, untainted by the colour in the skin of the grape.

*

The myth that Dom Perignon was the inventor of sparkling wine did not start in his lifetime. As so often with similar legends, it originated well after the death of the man concerned, and this one was created by Dom Grossard, Perignon's last successor before the Revolution swept away the monastic order. In 1821, at the height of the Bourbon reaction against the Revolution and all its works, the aged Grossard, by then reduced to a simple parish priest, was naturally not averse to exaggerating the achievements of his most distinguished predecessor. Grossard arrogated to Dom Perignon all the many advances in viticulture and winemaking which had occurred in his lifetime. But in a letter the aged Grossard added one crucial point: 'It was the famous Dom Perignon who discovered the secret of how to make both sparkling and still wines properly; before him people knew only how to make wine which was "gris", or straw-coloured.' The letter was published by the historian Louis-Perrier in 1865 with the warning note that: 'If the quality of the wines of Hautvillers consisted exclusively in an intelligent blend or marriage of the wines, all that would remain of Dom Grossard's assertion would be the points concerning fining and clarifying the wines' – in reality he seems to have tasted the grapes before they were fermented.

Grossard piled on the fantasy by claiming that Perignon went blind. His affliction had not been mentioned by any of his contemporaries, but was instantly accepted by popular writers and commemorated in the painting of the aged monk, so miraculously accomplished that he could tell the source of grapes simply from their flavour. The contemporary evidence removes the foundations for both the mythomanes and their opponents, for theirs is an argument based on an unsustainable thesis: that a winemaker as distinguished as Dom Perignon would *want* to make sparkling wine in the first place. Although sparkling champagnes were first made and sold during his lifetime, until well into the eighteenth century, a generation after his death, *mousseux* champagne was despised as a decidedly inferior beverage. Neither he, nor any other contemporary winemaker proud of his wine would have been willingly associated with it.

Normally the 'secrets' of distinguished winemakers were written down shortly after their death. At Hautvillers this role was performed by the Abbé Pierre, Dom Perignon's immediate successor. But his memoir was lost for nearly two centuries and only retrieved by Paul Chandon-Moët[3] at the end of the nineteenth century. So most of our information about the methods used by Dom Perignon and his colleagues derives from a memoir first published in 1718, three years after his death, entitled 'Manière de cultiver la vigne et de faire le vin en Champagne' – 'How they cultivate the vine and make wine in Champagne'. The work was obviously popular, for it ran through three editions in four years and emphasizes just how much modern winemaking in Champagne owes to Dom Perignon and his contemporaries. The memoir was anonymous, although it is now generally attributed to Canon Godinot, a priest in Reims probably connected with the monastery of Saint Thierry a few kilometres to the north.[4]

---

3 His collection of books and manuscripts, now in the public library in Epernay, forms the single biggest source of information on the history of *la Champagne viticole*.

4 Saint Thierry, a few kilometres north-west of Reims, was famous for its Benedictine monastery, founded in the ninth century. Its wine was not normally listed as one of the great wines of Champagne, yet the author claimed that it had 'been for a long time one of the most renowned and sought-after' of Champagne's wines.

Unfortunately for the Dom's disciples, it does not mention him – or any other winemaker for that matter – by name. This rather startling omission is explained by the fact that the author came from Reims, already a jealous rival of Epernay's. But the anonymity of the winemakers in Godinot's memoir emphasizes that the 'Perignon revolution' was not confined to his work, nor to Hautvillers, although it is invariably mentioned as one of a group of two or three sources of fine wine.

The only contemporary advice on actually encouraging *mousse* is a short addition tacked on to the end of the third edition of the memoir. This talks of the 'famous secret of Dom Perignon', confided to the author by 'a credible witness'. It was the first recipe for encouraging *mousse*, and although it comprises a great many rather curious ingredients – including peaches and nuts – these do include the crucial *sucre de candi*, the sugar, required, then as now, to encourage the formation of the *mousse*. The recipe was probably tacked on to the memoir to try and associate the generation of *mousse* with the mainstream of winemaking in Champagne, for the first edition is concerned rather with the prevention than the creation of *mousse*.

Dom Oudard, who continued making wine for twenty-seven years after Dom Perignon's death, had to bow to the times. This was the more inevitable because the vineyards from which he drew his grapes, at Pierry, Chouilly and Cramant, are in what we now call the Côte des Blancs, planted exclusively with white grapes. And for up to a century these, supposedly inferior, grapes were virtually the only ones used to make sparkling wines. One customer even asked Bertin de Rochelet for a 'good sparkling wine from Pierry produced according to Dom Oudard's methods'.

The memoir was reproduced by the author of a treatise called the *Nouvelle Maison Rustique* and by the two other authors on whom we depend for most of our information on the period, Abbé Pluche and the army officer Nicolas Bidet, whose family owned vines at Aÿ. Although Pluche was a friend of Godinot's, both he and Bidet pay repeated tribute to Perignon's work. The memoir makes clear that Perignon's technical innovations, however important, were less crucial than his role in instilling the primordial fact about champagne then as now: the painstaking, scrupulous and disciplined care required in making it. The discipline he imposed applied not only to the abbey's own lands, but also to tenanted land farmed by sharecroppers.

THE ORIGINS OF BIODYNAMICS

Monty Waldin sets out the principles underpinning biodynamic agriculture and argues that adopting this methodology not only produces better wines but has become essential for both sustainable wine growing and the health of the planet. This appears in *Biodynamic Wine*, published in 2016.

Biodynamics dates from 1924 and is the oldest alternative agriculture movement. Biodynamics pre-dated the global organic agriculture movement whose founding organization, the UK's Soil Association, dates from 1946. In fact the very word 'organic' was derived from the biodynamic ideal that each farm or smallholding should always work towards becoming a self-sustaining *organism* in its own right.

The particular feature of biodynamics – and where biodynamics differs from organics and indeed all other forms of alternative agriculture – is the use of nine so-called 'biodynamic preparations'. These are made from cow manure, the mineral quartz (also called silica), and seven medicinal plants: yarrow, chamomile, stinging nettle, oak bark, dandelion, valerian and *Equisetum arvense* or common horsetail. These nine preparations are applied to the land or crops either by being first incorporated into a compost pile or by being diluted in water as liquid sprays.[1]

Biodynamic preparations are used in homeopathic quantities, meaning they can produce an effect in extremely diluted amounts, but they are not homeopathic treatments per se. Their purpose is to make the farm and farmer, its crops, animals and wild habitat, self-sufficient,

---

1 Note the common horsetail 508 (*Equisetum arvense*) tea or liquid manure is not considered a true preparation by some biodynamic practitioners, even though they use it. Here, I have considered it such, and assumed therefore there are nine preparations in total.

self-sustaining and socially, economically and spiritually robust. These concepts may seem woolly in our world of smartphones and space exploration, but would have seemed less so to 1920s Europeans coping with the ravages of both the First World War and then its even deadlier successor, an influenza pandemic.

The methods used to make some of the preparations may seem strange initially but are neither high tech, expensive, costly to the environment nor potentially harmful. Anyone, from children to grandparents, can (and do) make these preparations. The biodynamic preparations are not patented so they can never realistically be made purely for profit, and they seem to get good results for farms and vineyards.

Sceptics, however, claim the biodynamic preparations produce no measurable changes to either farm health or crop quality; thus there is no 'biodynamic effect'. Such sceptics argue that biodynamic winegrowers owe the high quality of their wine either to having a top-quality vineyard *terroir* in the first place, or that vineyards which improved after 'going biodynamic' did so because the winegrower learned to become extra attentive in the vineyard by following a biodynamic 'prevention rather than cure' mindset (for example, better pruning, recalibrating spray machinery so sprays are more effective), and not because the vines were treated with biodynamic sprays or composts. Nevertheless, increasing numbers of winegrowers are using these preparations which are essential to biodynamic agriculture. Their regular use is the fundamental requirement of Demeter, the non-profit organization which has overseen and certified biodynamic agriculture worldwide since 1928.

The biodynamic preparations were created by an Austrian called Rudolf Steiner (1861–1925) shortly before he died. His motivation was to remedy what he sensed was the arrested spiritual development of his contemporaries. Steiner believed the forces people needed to kickstart their spiritual development would come from digesting food imbued with these desirable and necessary forces, and that getting these forces into food required a new way of growing food: biodynamic agriculture. For this Steiner developed nine biodynamic preparations to moderate and regulate biological processes in nature. This is the 'bio' part of biodynamics. The 'dynamic' part comes by understanding the preparations' role in enhancing and strengthening forces that form or shape material substance, both on the farm and within both the farmer and the crops. These forces are referred to in biodynamics as 'etheric formative forces'. Like gravity, they are unseen but have a tangible effect on both soil and on crop plants as well as on the animals or humans who digest those plants. Steiner's nine biodynamic preparations can therefore be thought of as spiritual remedies for the human being which are administered indirectly through the healing process of the Earth.[2] Biodynamic farmers accept that there is no substance or matter without spirit, and equally no spirit without matter. So the point of growing biodynamic food and drink is not only to provide the substances (vitamins, carbohydrates, protein, fats, minerals) to nourish the human body but also to provide the forces needed to form and nourish the human spirit.

The spiritual side of biodynamics is the one most open to misinterpretation, misrepresentation and ridicule. One common misconception is that apart from encouraging you to start wearing sandals and paying less attention to personal hygiene, growing or eating biodynamic food will also turn you into a religious fruitcake. I discovered biodynamics in 1993 but had struggled to find many redeeming features in organized religion from the age of seven (1974) onwards. I am not a fan of sects. I do consider myself spiritual in the pantheistic sense of feeling my spirit lift palpably when I feel a connection with the natural world. This can happen when standing euphorically on the top of a mountain or, more mundanely, when looking at pigeons fluttering around under the eaves of the railway station my train is about to depart from.

In my experience winegrowers – be they biodynamic or conventional – who come across as fundamentalist proselytizers tend not to make the best wines, often because they are inflexible and unwilling to compromise. This may be fine when churning out widgets on a production line but is not adapted to a product like wine, dependent on the vagaries of nature. Fortunately, the fundamentalist proselytizers tend to be in the minority.

Most winegrowers newly adopting biodynamics start by seeing it as I did initially: as a sensible, doable, interesting, inexpensive tool to produce tastier grapes to nourish the human palate – and if they also provide the formative forces to nourish the human spirit, so be it. Biodynamic ultras argue that this purely 'substance rather than forces' way of looking at biodynamics means missing the real reason we should be biodynamic. I would argue that materialistic and only vaguely spiritual people like me – meaning exactly the kind of people Steiner developed his biodynamic preparations for – first have to understand and accept how the

2   Stevens, Joseph A., *Applied Biodynamics* 33/2001, p. 3

biodynamic tool works, and only then can we perhaps appreciate that our spiritual development may have lacked something to begin with after all.

*

Steiner first described the biodynamic preparations publicly between 7 and 16 June 1924 during a course on agriculture consisting of eight lectures and four discussion sessions. This series of lectures was published in English (various translations) as *Spiritual Foundations for the Renewal of Agriculture* but is more usually referred to in biodynamic circles simply as the *Agriculture* course.

The *Agriculture* course was held at Count Carl von Keyserlingk's estate at Koberwitz near Breslau in what was then Silesia in the eastern part of Germany but is now Wroclaw in Poland. More than a hundred farmers, vets and others whose livelihoods depended on the land attended. They had asked Steiner to give the 1924 *Agriculture* course partly because their livestock was suffering ever more frequent outbreaks of foot and mouth disease, but also because they could see small, diversified family farms being swallowed up seemingly inexorably into much bigger, more mechanized and overtly monocultural ones. The area around the Koberwitz estate had been especially affected by this trend. The attendees were all members of the Anthroposophical Society, which Steiner had founded in 1912.

Anthroposophy or spiritual science is a view of life that includes both spirit and matter. It sees plants in a slightly unusual way, as having four organs to their development: the root, the leaf/shoot, the flower and finally the fruit, meaning the part which contains the plant's reproductive seed. These archetypal four organs also relate to the four elements (or ethers): the roots to the earth, the shoots and leaves to water, the flowers to air/light, and the fruit/seed to fire or heat.

Thinking of individual vines or farm crops as being made up of four organs is the first step in understanding entire vineyards or farms as being individualities or organisms in their own right. When anthroposophical farmers picture the agricultural individuality or farm organism they do so as though it were a person standing with his/her head in the soil.[3] Weleda, a German-based pharmaceutical company (www.weleda. com), pioneered the development of anthroposophical medicines from

---

3   Courtney, Hugh, 'Biodynamic Preparations', *Applied Biodynamics* 3/1993, pp. 3–4

1921 by following Rudolf Steiner's advice, selecting specific plant 'organs' to treat specific human conditions. Plant roots, which compare to the human head, provide remedies for problems in the nervous (senses) system. Leaves and stems provide remedies to treat the human rhythmic organism (heart, lungs, circulation), while the fruit or flowers serve the sexual and metabolic (digestive) system. Healthy farm organisms should be resilient, self-sufficient and produce not just healthy crops but farmers of healthy mind and body too – as though the farmer and his animals are running around in the belly of the farm.[4]

This anthroposophical way of thinking about plant organs and the farm organism was developed by Rudolf Steiner. He was born in 1861 in Kraljevec, then part of the Austro-Hungarian empire and now part of Croatia. His father Johann was a station master on the newly constructed Vienna–Trieste railway; his mother Franziska was maid to the local count. During his early childhood Steiner developed a strong connection to nature via local smallholders, peasants whose feudal existence had remained essentially unchanged for centuries. Steiner's connection with the natural, physical world around him was matched by the connection he sensed with an unseen, spiritual world that lay behind it, a world he felt a need to explain or codify in some way before it slipped inexorably away forever from both him and his contemporaries. Steiner believed he had a clairvoyant ability to connect with the natural world but was well aware that modern methods of communications, like the newly installed telegraph his father used daily for his job on the railway, would soon render anyone like him, who claimed to sense an inner perception of the non-physical world, ridiculous.

By his eighteenth birthday Steiner had moved with his family closer to Vienna, where he studied science at the city's Technical Institute, then considered one of the world's foremost scientific universities. Steiner's humanistic, spiritual side may have risked being extinguished in this increasingly science-oriented world but for a chance meeting on the train taking him to school with Felix Kogutski, a herb-gatherer who sold medicinal plants both to the city's pharmacies and the botanical department at the medical school. Steiner felt the course of his life changing because he believed Kogutski represented 'an instinctive clairvoyance of an earlier era'. Kogutski provided Steiner with the opportunity to talk with a like-minded person about the spiritual aspect of reality.

---

4 Lovel, Hugh, *A Biodynamic Farm* (Acres USA, 2000), p. 53

Steiner switched from science to arts, leaving Vienna for Rostock in Germany where he studied literature and philosophy, entitling his dissertation 'Truth and Knowledge'. After publishing an introductory book called *The Theory of Knowledge Implicit in Goethe's World-Conception* in 1886, Steiner was invited by the Grand Duchess Sophie of Saxony to edit the scientific writings of Johann Wolfgang von Goethe (1749–1832), Germany's most famous writer and poet. Goethe's pioneering work in phenomenology and the organic sciences provided Steiner with what he had yearned for, the bridge between the seen physical world and the unseen spiritual world.

Goethe's phenomenological approach held that through regular observation of plants, animals or other living organisms in all stages of their growth, inner and outer pictures of their processes of movement and their changes of form can be developed, and that insight into natural laws and processes could be gleaned.

Goethe's approach asks us to think about how plant growth is affected by intangible but identifiable 'nitrogen processes' rather than merely by how much nitrogen a plant has been fed with, which is the approach of physical chemistry. While working on Goethe's archives in Weimar, Germany from 1890 to 1897, Steiner published his own seminal work called *The Philosophy of Freedom* (1894). Its anti-materialist thrust, that humans become spiritually free only through the conscious activity of thinking, was the basis of Steiner's own theory of spiritual science or 'anthroposophy', from the Greek *anthropos* or 'wisdom of man'.

As well as biodynamic agriculture, anthroposophy embraces diverse fields. Waldorf education is one example, Steiner having been asked in 1919 to formulate his educational theories by Emile Molt, a representative for workers in the Waldorf-Astoria cigarette factory in Stuttgart. An offshoot of Waldorf education is the Camphill Movement of schools and villages for children with severe learning disabilities, founded in 1939 by Dr Karl König. With his wife Marie von Sivers, Steiner developed eurythmics, a human art form with therapeutic uses sometimes referred to as 'visible speech'. In the field of medicine Steiner collaborated with pharmacists and physicians in creating Weleda (mentioned above), whose plant-based medicines paid homage to Kogutski, the herb-gatherer on the Vienna train. Steiner also conceived an organic form of architecture when creating his school for spiritual science in 1913, the Goetheanum in Switzerland, in honour of Goethe.

What Steiner had understood from Goethe and his own intuition was the flaw he saw in modern scientific methods: science was limited when it came to helping man understand nature and, by implication, farming because it overlooked the spiritual aspect of reality. The most obvious examples of concern to Steiner were the inorganic soluble fertilizers popularized by Baron Justus von Liebig (1803–73), the German chemist regarded as the father of so-called 'chemical' farming. It was von Liebig who put forth the 'Law of the Minimum', the idea that whichever essential inorganic plant nutrient was least available to a plant would dictate or limit its growth potential.

The consequence of von Liebig's idea was the development of soluble nitrogen, phosphorus and potash (or 'NPK') fertilizers. Via the Haber-Bosch process, named after its German inventors, chemists Fritz Haber and Carl Bosch, nitrogen in the atmosphere could be converted under high pressure and high temperature to ammonia (nitrogen comprises nearly 80 per cent of the atmosphere, oxygen making up most of the rest). The process was initially used to make explosives during the First World War to compensate for the loss of saltpetre whose supply from British-owned mines in Chile had been blocked by the Allies.

Steiner argued that using these artificial fertilizers weakened crops by forcing plants to expend some of their own life energy or vitality in raising these lifeless chemical substances from the inert mineral state to an alert one capable of carrying life force.

However, artificial fertilizers – although expensive – conveniently boosted farm yields at a time of rapidly rising and shifting post-industrial populations, as small rural communities were superseded by large cities. Artificial fertilizers were there to stay despite unwelcome side effects, like producing bigger, more persistent weeds. They were also detrimental to the balance of key soil micro-organisms, making it harder for plants to feed as normal via the fungi on their roots and for the soil to maintain a viable, healthy structure. This, coupled with the increased use of steel ploughshares pulled quickly by machines rather than more slowly by animals, exacerbated soil erosion – the 1930s dust bowl in the American Midwest becoming the prime example. As crops weakened, so did the animals and humans fed on those crops, as Steiner had predicted. Steiner said water-soluble or mineral fertilizers as he called them would encourage excess fungal activity in the topsoil, and that this would result in the migration of the excess spores on to crops which would then became more prone to disease.

Even before he died von Liebig had begun to rue his attempts at playing chemical god to the soil and the negative effect his work had had on farming. Were he alive today, von Liebig would have realized how plants are able to assimilate only about 10 to 15 per cent of the nitrogen provided by soluble fertilizers, and that the excess free-nitrogen leftovers contribute significantly to global warming (via nitrous oxide, a more potent greenhouse gas than carbon dioxide, and one which hangs around for longer), ozone-layer depletion and acid rain. Phosphorous, potassium and nitrogen run-off from fertilizers also stimulate algae to breed frenetically, causing algal blooms which create so-called 'dead zones' in rivers, lakes and the sea. The dead zone in the Gulf of Mexico, caused by run-off from Midwestern farms, is now larger than the state of Connecticut.

The farmers of the Anthroposophical Society who came to hear Steiner's *Agriculture* course at Koberwitz in June 1924 knew that the anthroposophical plant-based medicines Steiner had developed with Weleda provided ways of using wild plants to heal humans. What they wanted to know was whether Steiner could describe a way of reversing the declining health of their livestock, crops and soil too. Steiner made it clear from the outset that rather than provide a Liebig-like way of farming by numbers his aim was to provide a new way of thinking about farming, food and nutrition. His message was that we are what we eat, certainly, but we must not think of food by simply calculating how much we consume in terms of grams or calories, especially since most of what we eat we then excrete anyway. We must think about whether our food contains the forces we need to nourish our spirits, and maintain both our vitality and that of the planet we live on.

Steiner's precise words were, 'The most important thing [is] to make the benefits of our agricultural [biodynamic] preparations available to the largest possible areas over the entire earth, so that the earth may be healed and the nutritive quality of its produce improved in every respect … This is a problem of nutrition. Nutrition as it is to-day does not supply the strength necessary for manifesting the spirit in physical life. A bridge can no longer be built from thinking to will and action. Food plants no longer contain the forces people need for this.'[5]

The implication was that if we dumb down our farming we dumb down our food, and seeing as we are what we eat we'll risk entering a vicious circle of thinking that there's actually really nothing wrong with dumb, even dangerous, farming – dangerous in the sense it threatens our very existence.

A pertinent example of this very risk is the 'terminator' or 'suicide' seed technology developed in the United States whereby second-generation seeds are either sterile or need to be coated with a commercially patented compound to become capable of reproduction. Farmers must therefore either pay for new seeds each season or pay to activate saved seeds. Farmers who find patented genes have migrated into their own seeds are at risk too of being threatened by the patent holder for theft of patented property. This is like being sued for the theft of paraffin and matches by the stranger who just used them randomly to set fire to your house. So rather than face up to a multinational, farmers find it easier to switch to patented seeds, meaning the seed company has a client for life.

In contrast, biodynamic agriculture aims to make farmers as independent, as self-reliant and as self-sufficient as possible. They are encouraged to save seeds from crops of the same type which have been open-pollinated naturally, by letting plants flower and then become fertilized by wind-borne pollen. In this way plants exchange characteristics from generation to generation but breed true to type, meaning the saved seed will always closely resemble the parent plants and pass on their characteristics whilst maintaining genetic diversity. Thus each new generation of fertile seeds can be sown the following season. Crops from open-pollinated seeds are both sustainable and genetically unique. This contrasts with both genetically modified seeds and F1 hybridized seeds like the ones you find in the supermarket or garden centre. The enforced

5 Steiner, Rudolf, *Spiritual Foundations for the Renewal of Agriculture* (Rudolf Steiner Press, 1958), trans. by G. Adams, p. 70

inbreeding means these seeds will eventually produce unviable crops if left to set seed in future generations, meaning new seeds must be bought.

Seed saving (by open pollination) has been part of farming since people ceased hunter-gathering at the end of the Neolithic, roughly 10,000 years ago. Rudolf Steiner said that 'in the seed we have an image of the whole universe'.[6] As today's seed is tomorrow's food it stands to reason that terminator seed technology implicitly promises humanity a barren future, a world in which nature is selectively patented by the few and ransomed back to the many at our collective expense.

The biodynamic alternative is a free, safe, unpatented and therefore universally available technology reliant on cows, some wild plants and a few handfuls of the world's most abundant mineral. By working with, rather than against, nature to resolve problems, biodynamic farmers see themselves as but one tiny part of a much bigger cycle of life, both guiding nature and being guided by it.

Ecology is rapidly shifting from being a good idea to being a matter of life and death as we face the combined challenges of climate change and the depletion of both biodiversity and basic natural resources like fresh water. Our fellow humans can increasingly be divided up between those who eat way too much and eat the wrong stuff – it takes eight kilos of grain to make a kilo of meat – and those many more who get to eat way too little. Writer Michael Pollan's much quoted dictum that we should 'eat food, not too much, mostly plants', is the perfect starting point for improving the environmental and physical health of our surroundings. The United Nations reports that there is no more potentially farmable land left to develop and that the dramatic yield increases of the type witnessed since the 'green revolution' of the 1960s onwards are essentially over. This means we'll have to make do with what we have already, but without further degrading, eroding or polluting the land. We'll have to become better and more self-sufficient stewards of what land we already farm.

The biodynamic principle of low-input, self-sufficient agriculture revitalizing both for ourselves and our natural surroundings seems useful, necessary and perhaps most conveniently of all, easily achievable.

---

6   Steiner, Rudolf, *Spiritual Foundations for the Renewal of Agriculture* (Bio-Dynamic Farming and Gardening Association, Inc. USA, 1993), trans. by C. Creeger and M. Gardner, p. 35

BULGARIAN WINE'S NEW ERA

Caroline Gilby MW charts the arduous and complex route Bulgarian wine took after the fall of communism, as land was restored to individuals and the state-owned monopoly replaced by private producers. From *The wines of Bulgaria, Romania and Moldova*, published in 2018.

Throughout the 1970s, Bulgaria was still supplying wine largely to the Soviet Union and Comecon countries. The industry structure was set up so that 70 per cent of all grapes were grown by the state-sponsored cooperative farms known as Agro-Industrial Complexes (AICs). Another 20 per cent came from vineyards owned directly by Vinprom (the state wine production monopoly) and the remaining 10 per cent came from privately owned vineyards (individuals in rural populations were allowed to own 0.1 to 0.2 hectares). Vinprom's winemaking facilities were subdivided into groups, each with a central winery and two or three satellite wineries, which often performed only part of the vinification or maturation process. Eighty per cent of wine was produced by the 29 Vinzavod, or state-run processing plants under the Vinprom umbrella, one of which was for bottling only. The other 20 per cent was produced in Perushtitsa, Targovishte and Septemvri, which were set up as a new form of experimental economic organization or 'vine and wine complex'. They had their own vineyards and winemaking facilities, but still functioned under the direction of Vinprom. Christo Boevsky, the retired head of department for Controlled Origin wines, explains, 'Implementing some new technology or equipment was always according to the wish of Vinprom Production Department, so if there was something new on the market we bought one, the Wine Institute in Sofia tested it in some of these wineries and then decided to buy it or not.'

All exports went through the state monopoly Vinimpex. When it decided to expand its export markets to the West, such as in the key market of the UK, it worked initially through an agent (Halewood International, in the 1970s) then, in 1980, Vinimpex set up a subsidiary in London called the Bulgarian Vintners Company. This turned out to be perfect timing, because demand from the vast Soviet market started to decline. This accelerated in the mid-1980s with President Gorbachev's campaign against alcoholism in USSR. This meant that thousands of hectares of Bulgarian vines were uprooted or abandoned, and few were treated to any systematic training or pruning. Dead, dying or diseased vines were not replaced. Some of these were poor quality sites, but better locations were also abandoned. Grape prices were fixed every year, irrespective of quality, which encouraged the state farms to turn their attention away from vines to other crops. Schmitz et al. report that Bulgaria lost 15 per cent of its vines between 1980 and 1990, and that the Soviet Union market demand fell from 1.4 million hectolitres to 0.8 million hectolitres by 1989 approximately (15 to 9 million standard 12-bottle cases).[7] Comecon countries were still taking 84 per cent of Bulgaria's exports in 1985, with the Soviet Union taking nearly two-thirds of this volume, but as this fell, focus on hard currency markets in western Europe became increasingly important for Bulgaria.

The UK started with 95,000 standard cases (8,550 hectolitres) of Bulgarian Cabernet Sauvignon in 1982 and Bulgarian wines quickly built up a reputation for being a good source of cheap, cheerful and easy-to-understand wines. Volumes increased rapidly, reaching 193,000 hectolitres (more than 2 million cases) by 1990, according to Schmitz et al. Bulgaria became the fourth largest red wine supplier to the UK market after France, Italy and Spain, and the UK was by this time one of Bulgaria's most important export markets.

Bulgaria was the first country to market its wines under their varietal names, long before the New World jumped on this bandwagon. There was a rumour that at one time Sainsbury's own-label Bulgarian Cabernet Sauvignon was its single biggest selling wine. Former head of Beers, Wines and Spirits at Sainsbury's, Allan Cheesman, can't confirm this, but does remember in the mid-1980s selling 100,000 cases of Cabernet Sauvignon in just a fortnight on promotion at £1.99. His colleague

---

7   Schmitz, A. et al., *Privatization of Agriculture in New Market Economies: Lessons from Bulgaria*, Springer Science and Business Media, 2012

Howard Wynn, recalls placing an order one Christmas for a million cases of Bulgarian Cabernet Sauvignon, their biggest ever order at that time.

By 1994, 3.3 million standard cases of Bulgarian wine were shipped annually to the UK, while Germany and the Benelux countries also became important customers. As a wine buyer for Augustus Barnett I was also buying significant quantities of Bulgarian wine in this period and a buying file from 1994 shows that I was purchasing a range of six different Bulgarian wines. These included a Riesling at a cost price per dozen bottles of £9.00, Cabernet from Sliven at £11.50 and a Cabernet Reserve at £15.20.

At this time, there were also rumours that embargoed South African wine was making its way to Bulgaria to be relabelled. This seems hard to believe for several reasons: one is that Bulgaria had a scientifically advanced industry with high technical standards and knowhow developed in the 1970s and 1980s; second South African red wines then were very different to the style of wine that Bulgaria was producing, and that could be tasted directly at wineries. At that time, there was a high level of virus infection in South African red grapevines, resulting in wines that were pale, thin and harsh. Third, during visits to Bulgaria at the beginning of the 1990s it was easy to see vineyards that, though large-scale and collectivized, were well-managed and clearly capable of producing substantial volumes of wine. Indeed, it is clear that Bulgaria's climate is more than suitable for producing the kind of soft fruity reds that made it famous. Historical import/export data from this period is limited but Kym Anderson at the University of Adelaide confirms that there were no shipments recorded from South Africa to Bulgaria in the period from 1988 to 1990.

*

The year 1989 saw the beginning of a new era for Bulgaria with the end of one of the Eastern Bloc's most staunch, hard-line communist regimes.

Land reform was critical in shaping the future direction of the wine industry. This started with a 1991 law for agricultural land ownership and use. It aimed to return land to the original owners prior to 1947. Agricultural cooperatives were liquidated, and their assets distributed or sold. One winemaker reported that to make this process easier vines, animals and other assets were often destroyed, or stolen to sell for cash, because few people had money to pay for these assets. In 1989 vineyards covered 3.7 per cent of Bulgaria's cultivated land or about 170,000 hectares. Because of the right to a small patch of family land under the previous regime, individuals actually held 37 per cent of the country's total vineyard, though most of this was for home consumption and fell outside official statistics. This has had far-reaching consequences for the significance of home-made wine in the Bulgarian market.

The details of land restitution laws changed up to twenty times in the first ten years after independence. Land had to be restituted in the same amount and location, and according to old boundaries where possible, and where evidence was available (such as land deeds, photographs, village registers). Poor evidence was often a problem as families had become divided, and in many cases family members had moved abroad. For a very short period at the start of the 1990s land could be returned in consolidated plots, but this did not last long and most land was returned in very small parcels.

Later, the government assigned local committees for land distribution to the previous owners and these worked for many years to assign unique pieces of land to each (that is, exactly those which had been given as in-kind contributions to the cooperatives some 50 years previously). Private companies were commissioned to reorganize the land register (often called a *cadastre*) and to enter each individual land plot on to the digital map of the area and country. Often people got land of the same size and quality as their original holding but in a different location, while one winery owner explained that land commissions sometimes acted for personal benefits or for the benefit of their friends and associates.

Officially the land restitution process ended in 2000, having taken up to five years to complete for individual owners, though in reality it is still not completed in full nor entered on to the digital map and *cadastre* of the country. There were many legal appeals because of poor evidence and this halted any market reallocation of land. In 1999, the government adopted a short-term scheme allowing land transfers based on temporary documents. This was intended to address a problem with co-ownership. Where there were multiple owners (such as descendants of the original owner), documents did not specify ownership shares and this created conflicts. This turned out to be serious in the wine sector where it was estimated that around 40 per cent of the land was held in co-ownership. Small plot sizes and the fact that land had been reallocated to often absentee owners was a problem for viticulture. Such people usually had no interest in wine because they had other careers, so this meant that land fell into disrepair. The small size of plots meant that any sort of professional viticulture was also impossible, so even where vines were managed, it was an occasional evening or weekend hobby. A lack of information in *cadastre* offices about ownership made it difficult to track them down for anyone interested in buying land.

Another problem was that while land ownership was being disputed, there was no incentive for any investments into permanent crops like grapevines. Vineyards are expensive, and no one would risk long-term investments like vines, posts, wires and so on, if they are not certain who actually owns the land. By the year 2000, national statistics showed that 72 per cent of vineyards were older than 21 years, indicating that very little had been replanted during this period. In 1999, data showed that yields had also decreased to 3.1 tonnes per hectare, indicating lack of professional viticulture.

Winery owner Nikola Zikatanov summed it up: 'The results were tragic – for many years the land was in transition and nobody knew who was the owner of any specific land plot. Investments stopped, nobody was taking care of orchards and vineyards, on the contrary – in many cases vineyards were burnt, supporting systems were taken out and sold abroad.'

In 1990, the wine sector was suddenly liberalized, and Vinprom itself was disbanded in 1991 as part of the free-market reforms introduced in the wake of the fall of communism. The wineries themselves were privatized in two stages. First, winery groups were established as separate organizations, each with a foreign currency account, managed separately but still state-owned. Second came privatization, mainly to worker-manager teams, similar in principle to western management buyouts, though as one source points out there was 'only nominal participation of workers and usually one, or two political "paratroopers" as managers. For years, the goal of the leading persons in these teams was milking the companies while making no investments or development.'

Privatization of the wineries was slow but by the end of the 1990s, all major wineries were in private ownership and Vinimpex was sold to the French-based Belvedere group in 2003. The main disadvantages were lack of funds and the ban (since rescinded with EU membership) on foreign investment in land and buildings. This was a marked contrast with the position in Hungary, which benefited greatly from foreign investment in developing its wine industry. As much of the industry was privatized through management buyouts, with little or no external capital, grape purchases were frequently funded using bank loans (at high interest rates). This meant that many wineries found themselves in serious financial trouble and were not able to invest in up-to-date equipment or vineyards.

Bulgarian wine was also hit by the twin scourges of economic problems, with the loss of spending power in the domestic market, and the collapse of export markets in the former Soviet Union. Wine exports fell by 71 per cent between 1985 and 1991 but wine production only decreased by 20 per cent, leaving a considerable amount of unsold stock in a saturated market. This meant that demand for grapes also fell, leaving growers struggling for income and lacking money for plant protection products and fertilizers. The separation of grape-growing and wine production continued very largely unchanged until the early 2000s when statistics show that there were 23,000 growers and 130 wine processors. Vineyards remained the main permanent crop and in 2004 still accounted for 4 per cent of total cultivated land.

The separation of grape production and winemaking under communism left a legacy of poor understanding by winemakers of the issues of fruit quality and control of their raw materials. By 2002, only 4.6 per cent of grapes came from wineries' own production. Even worse, most of the grapes were sourced through intermediaries, so there was very little contact between wineries and growers. In 2005 winemaker Dimitar Panov commented that, 'The gulf of understanding was so huge, growers and wineries hated each other.'

Even in the mid-2000s, very few wineries actually owned vineyards, and winemakers rarely got involved in managing any viticultural issues, believing that their role began when grapes arrived in trucks. Grape growers tended to be focused on harvesting and getting paid as quickly as possible, before bad autumn weather – or indeed theft, of which there was a high risk – lost them their harvest. At the same time, a continuing lack of professional viticulture or vineyard management meant already low yields declined further.

The position was not helped by a series of low-volume vintages and by the end of the 1990s, the Bulgarian wine industry was suffering from a serious shortage of fruit. This led to wineries competing for supplies and they often would take fruit early to secure grapes and pay a premium to do so, and in many cases, growers wouldn't release grapes until they were paid. This led directly to much thinner, under-ripe wines with higher costs at a time when the West had got used to ripe, fruity New World styles, and Bulgaria rapidly lost export market share. This was exacerbated by the arrival of New World countries like Australia, which was not only making varietal wines better, fruitier and more consistently than Bulgaria was now able to

Old and new winemaking methods sit side-by-side inside Better Half winery, Zmeevo, Bulgaria

achieve, but was also creating much more effective marketing to a fellow English-speaking market – the UK – which had been so important to Bulgaria's export success.

In the 2000s, many wineries found themselves in trading difficulties, due to falling sales, reliance on bank loans and lack of investment. A further round of secondary privatization and takeovers then followed, with investment largely from foreign sources or, if Bulgarian, from outside the wine industry (banks, lawyers, industrialists, magazine publishers, vegetable growers and more).

From around 2000 onwards, Bulgaria's state fund for agriculture supported over one hundred projects aimed at creating 2,200 hectares of new vineyards in preparation for accession to the European Union. Undoubtedly, the EU's pre-accession funding programmes such as SAPARD (Special Accession Program for Agricultural and Rural Development) were significant. Subsidies of up to 50 per cent for both winery and vineyard investments brought in substantial foreign investment, described by one high profile investor as a 'massive scale [vine] BOGOF' ('buy one, get one free'). It also enabled the rise of small individual projects and wine estates, which were a novelty in Bulgaria at that time. By the time of EU accession in 2007, the industry had benefited from an estimated €115 million.

The realization that wine quality could only be regained through control of fruit sourcing meant that many wineries took on the huge bureaucratic burden of putting together consolidated landholdings. EU funds were tempting enough to make it worth the legal paperchase of tracking down multiple tiny landowners to put together the sizeable vineyard plots that the industry so desperately needed. Nikola Zikatanov (owner Villa Melnik) summed up: 'In theory, by the year 2000, almost any single piece of land had its owner, boundaries, known neighbours, etc., identified. The problem was that the title was in the name of the owner from 50 years ago, who had most likely died and his heirs were five to ten people, or even 50 individuals, living all around the globe. For a legitimate land sale transaction, it was a requirement to have all of the heirs appear in front of the Notary Public to declare and confirm a sale. But at least by this point, once a land parcel was purchased, it was very clear where is this land and it was possible to start working on it.'

Stephan von Neipperg of Château Canon La Gaffelière (St-Emilion) and German partner Karl Hauptmann invested in one of the first new private wine estates. This project, the Bessa Valley winery at Pazardijk near Plovdiv, reported dealing with 600 landowners to assemble its 200-hectare plot. The team at the new Castra Rubra investment took three years to buy its land in the Harmanli area and had to negotiate with over 1,000 people, some of whom were abroad. Other wineries such as Katarzyna Estate chose to buy up land in the unplanted no man's land border zone to avoid dealing with such paper trails.

One downside of the EU SAPARD programme was that producers had to be able to fund the project upfront and then claim back subsidies later. They also had to be debt-free, which was a problem in an industry where bank loans to fund grape purchases were common, and this limited the possibility of raising further funds against a future SAPARD project. The bureaucratic burden was also huge, requiring hundreds of documents, and a real headache for small producers who simply did not have the skills or people to write funding applications. Additional complications came when Bulgaria was accused of mismanaging funds by the EU, putting a temporary halt on the process. This created an additional delay and headache for wineries who had secured loans which needed to be repaid within a tight timescale and had started projects using these funds. Despite the bureaucracy and political challenges to be overcome, there's no doubt that EU money made a huge difference in kick-starting a new era for Bulgarian wine.

A BRIEF HISTORY OF AUSTRIAN WINE

A short trip through Austria's wine history from *The wines of Austria*, by Stephen Brook (2020), focusing in particular on how the wine adulteration scandal of the 1980s forced the regulation and reinvention that elevated the country's wines into the top tier.

Earlier writers on Austrian wine have had to urge their readers to accept their premise that Austria can make great wines. That is no longer necessary. Austrian wines have for many years been accepted by writers, sommeliers, and even consumers, as world class. The white and nobly sweet wines have attracted the most attention, and rightly so, but there has been great progress in red wine production and quality over the past decade.

It took a while for Austrian wines to make their mark. This is largely because until relatively recently they were mostly sold within the country, with some exports to Germany. Yet its history as a wine-producing nation is ancient. It is known that vines were cultivated in eastern Austria in Celtic times, and there were extensive plantings by the Romans, especially in the Danube valley and Styria. 'Styria' is the English name for the area known in German as Steiermark, just as Wien is often referred to as Vienna. In AD 92, Emperor Domitian ordered existing vineyards to be pulled out for fear of over-production across the empire; to what extent this decree was observed in remote Austria is not known. At any rate, two centuries later Emperor Aurelius Probus reversed the decree.

After the Romans left in the late fifth century many vineyards were abandoned, and Hungarian invasions in the tenth century made matters worse, especially in Pannonia, the region now straddled by the border between Austria and Hungary. Styria too had many masters before the Habsburgs established their hold over the region in 1282. Charlemagne proved a stabilizing influence after he captured what is now Austria in 803 and rules were drawn up for viticulture and winemaking. The next major influence was the arrival of mainly Cistercian monks, who came to found monasteries from the eleventh century onwards, notably Stift Heiligenkreuz near Vienna and its outposts. This gave a boost to local viticulture. Wine was needed for sacramental purposes as well as providing a beverage that was safe to drink at a time when that was rarely true of water. Many of the sites planted by monks, most of whom had come from the wine regions of France, Burgundy in particular, are still in production and still under monastic ownership. In the late twelfth century the Viennese were permitted to plant vineyards, which still exist, within the city limits. As the vineyards developed, so did trade, and many wines were exported to northern Europe.

By the sixteenth century, it's estimated that the area under vine throughout Austria was around 150,000 hectares, thrice its present area. At around the same time the sweet wines from Rust benefited from royal approval. Rust, however, was not the first village within the Burgenland to produce sweet wine of exceptional quality. Donnerskirchen produced a Trockenbeerenauslese-style wine in 1526, and the cask, judiciously tapped over the years, was only exhausted in 1852. The Thirty Years' War had little effect on life in eastern Austria, but on the other hand the area was all but destroyed by invading Turkish armies in the seventeenth century. These vineyard losses as well as the abandonment of sites as a consequence of falling prices meant that the area under vine would continue to diminish.

In the nineteenth century, according to Philipp Blom's book *The Wines of Austria*, the varieties grown in Austria were rather different to those cultivated today. Pinot Gris (Grauburgunder) had been present since medieval times, and St Laurent, Blaufränkisch and Pinot Noir were also planted here and there. Grüner Veltliner was certainly cultivated but far from ubiquitously, and various forms of Muskateller as well as Welschriesling would also have been grown.

In 1860 the country's first wine college and viticultural research centre was established at Klosterneuburg on the outskirts of Vienna and would have a significant influence over the century that followed. But not instantly. Henry Vizetelly, a British visitor to the Universal Exhibition held in Vienna in 1873, was unimpressed by the wines he tasted there, finding the good vastly outnumbered by the bad. It didn't matter all that much, as by this time phylloxera had already been discovered in Austrian vineyards and would prove the same lethal scourge as elsewhere in Europe, with losses of around 25 per cent of all vines. Gradually the vineyards were able to recover, and by 1914 there were almost 50,000 hectares under vine. However, the break-up of the Austro-Hungarian monarchy after the First World War led to the loss within the revised borders of 18,000 hectares. Viticultural research continued. In 1922 the head of the Klosterneuburg college, Friedrich (Fritz) Zweigelt created a crossing of St Laurent and Blaufränkisch that bears his name, and went on to create Goldburger and other new varieties. Zweigelt remains the country's most widely planted red variety, but Zweigelt's contributions to Austrian viticulture were tarnished by his membership of the Nazi Party, which enabled him to remain at the head of the college until 1945. The college's advice was not always sensible. Until the late 1980s, long after the French had realized that it was essential for red wines to go through malolactic fermentation, the Klosterneuburg staff advised against it, a recommendation that set back the progress of Austrian red wine production for many years.

Grüner Veltliner only began to dominate Austrian viticulture after Lenz Moser, the first of many producers of that clan bearing this name, developed a method of high training in the 1950s that was particularly well suited to the variety; it was easy to mechanize, and gave high yields. But the elevated canopy also reduced ripeness levels, and although the system was capable of producing wines of decent quality, it is clear that other systems that are planted to a higher density such as Guyot or cordon give better results. Moser's *Hochkultur* is rarely glimpsed today.

Austria had, and has, a deeply embedded wine culture. This is embodied in the institution known as the Heurige or Buschenschank. It was set on a legal basis by Emperor Joseph II on 17 August 1784. A Heurige is an inn at which the proprietor can only serve wine and food of his own production. Known as Heurigen in Vienna, the same kind of inn is more often known as a Buschenschank in other wine regions. Rules stipulate the opening times for each; they are not year-round establishments. For many Austrians a weekend excursion to a favourite Buschenschank is a popular pastime: a relatively inexpensive way to eat and drink copiously and meet friends.

So the Buschenschank, as well as the country's plethora of other eating and drinking establishments, largely accounted for high levels of

Winelovers drink, eat and relax at a typical Heurige, or wine tavern,
among the vineyards

domestic consumption. Any exported wines were generally dispatched to Germany, and mostly came from the Burgenland. Until 1922 this region, dominated by its lake-shore resorts, was a popular tourist destination, and German visitors in particular got to know and like its wines, especially the sweeter styles. After the Second World War its popularity accelerated, and the 1970s and early 1980s were boom times for the Burgenland. But this would lead to the Austrian wine industry's temporary downfall. It was slowly becoming apparent in the 1980s that more wine was being exported than could be produced, both from the Burgenland and from the prestigious but small wine village of Gumpoldskirchen. Competition to provide wines at the cheapest price meant that while the labelling was alluring, the wine inside the bottle was often dire as well as fraudulent.

Then in 1985 it was revealed that many of those exported wines had been adulterated – dosed with diethylene glycol, an antifreeze agent, to simulate sweetness. Only a few fairly large wine producers were implicated, but it was enough to put the brakes on the whole industry. I recall visiting a small merchant house in the Burgenland in the late 1980s, listening as the tearful owner told me she had been besmirched by the skullduggery of others and was on the brink of bankruptcy; her firm no longer exists. Four producers were tried and imprisoned. In Britain I don't recall seeing a single bottle of Austrian wine for about two years after the scandal broke. In truth, it wasn't much of a scandal. Nobody got ill, let alone died. A year later more than twenty people died in Italy after drinking adulterated wine, and the Italian wine industry sailed on

regardless. So the Austrians felt hard done by, but even innocent producers acknowledge that they knew something fishy had been going on
since the late 1970s.

The Austrian authorities reacted with speed, prosecuting the culprits
and instituting the strictest wine regulations in Europe. It didn't do
much in the short term to restore confidence, but it gradually took effect. The integrity of Austrian wines had been re-established, and the
best wines, as well as some mediocre ones, took their place on export
markets. My own visits to Austrian wine regions and producers began
in the 1970s, when a friend, who lived in Vienna, and I would make
excursions at the weekend. The red wines were mostly terrible, but there
were many attractive white wines, principally Grüner Veltliner but also
from other varieties. Yet this didn't lead me to take Austrian wines ter-
ribly seriously, other than the finest botrytis wines from the Burgenland.
Changes were, however, taking place, especially a move to elegant dry
wines in place of the innocuous lightly sweet wines, red as well as white,
that were so commonly found in Austria at that time.

The scandal re-energized the best producers of Austria, who were dis-
mayed by the damage done to the reputation of their industry. The highly
regarded Austrian Wine Academy, which has links to Britain's Institute of
Masters of Wine, was founded in Rust in 1991 and continued to educate
and inform thousands of wine professionals. In 1993 Alois Kracher, in a
spirit of confrontational defiance, came to London to present a blind tasting of his own wines alongside top Sauternes, Yquem included. It made a
deep impression on those who attended. Austria's top sweet wines, it was
evident, were world class. Willi Opitz, too, travelled the world with his
wines, and became notorious for spotting passing wine writers at trade
fairs and dragging them into his booth to taste his straw wines and TBAs
(Trockenbeerenauslese), which were usually worth the detour.

If in the early 1990s Austria's reputation for great sweet wines was
re-established, another famous blind tasting in Vienna in 1998 did the
same for its dry wines. Here the country's top Grüner Veltliner wines
were pitted against top white Burgundy. To the delight of the Austrians
the Veltliners took the top three places. As one of the tasters, I was baf-
fled by how difficult it was to tell the two varieties apart, even though
the Burgundies, unlike the Veltliners, would all have been aged in barriques. A similar tasting, but with Chardonnays from all over the world,
was held in London in 2002, with a similar outcome. By now Austria's
white wines were established as among the world's finest. Grüner

Veltliners even became fashionable in many restaurants, as sommeliers recognized their versatility with food.

The biennial Austrian wine fair, VieVinum in Vienna, brought visitors from the world over to taste wines from hundreds of producers. The Austrian Wine Marketing Board tacked on tours to various wine regions to better inform visiting wine writers about what they were tasting. In the alternating years when VieVinum was not being held, the same organization held Wine Summits at which groups of writers, sommeliers and importers toured the regions before gathering in Vienna for some grand tastings and events.

In the meantime Austria's red wines were in hot pursuit of the sought-after whites. In the 1990s Austria's red wine producers, principally in the Burgenland, but also in other regions such as Carnuntum and Thermenregion, often aimed for maximum power and extraction. Lavish use of new oak was the norm, and many producers planted French varieties, hoping for more international renown. This was nothing new: a German merchant called Robert Schlumberger had planted the Bordelais varieties in the Thermenregion in the mid-nineteenth century. By the 2000s this would be recognized as a dubious strategy. There are corners of Austria where grapes such as Merlot or Syrah can ripen, but in general Cabernet Sauvignon in particular struggles to ripen and never does so consistently. Many producers opted to express the merits of native varieties such as Blaufränkisch, St Laurent and even Zweigelt. Some Pinot Noir could be grown successfully, but was often picked too late and overoaked. It remains a work in progress, whereas many wineries have mastered Blaufränkisch and St Laurent, producing a range of delicious wines in differing styles.

The tirelessly energetic Austrian Wine Marketing Board, which was founded in 1986 as part of the reaction to the scandal, worked closely with the regional committees representing each wine region to introduce a new appellation system. This was the DAC, or Districtus Austriae Controllatus. The idea behind it was to promote regional typicity, but it was to prove controversial. The Weinviertel was selected as the first region to have its own DAC. In an attempt, which has proved largely successful, to recapture Grüner Veltliner as a quintessentially Austrian variety, the Weinviertel's Veltliners were – subject to some regulations and tasting panels – allowed to carry the name Weinviertel DAC on the label. The downside of the system was that any wines that did not conform to the rules – in practice all other varieties grown in the region

– were only allowed to be labelled as Niederösterreich, which to many seemed in effect a downgrading to a broader appellation regardless of the wine's quality.

In 2005 the first red wine DAC was created for Blaufränkisch from the Mittelburgenland, and as the decade moved on more and more DACs were created. Frequently they came in two or even three guises: Klassik for the more basic wines, and Reserves for the more serious, generally oak-aged, wines. The difficulty is that while domestic consumers may have come to terms with the intricacies of the system, wine lovers outside Austria haven't got a clue. Moreover, there are prestigious growers' associations in Austria – such as Traditionsweingüter in Lower Austria, Pannobile in Burgenland, Eruption in Styria, and the Vinea Wachau group in the Wachau – that operate their own systems of quality control and branding.

Throughout Austria the term 'Klassik' (sometimes spelled 'Classic') is used to denote a basic style of wine, generally aged in stainless steel tanks, with no oak influence. But the word has been adopted by private growers' associations such as Steirische Klassik, which contains within its structure single-vineyard wines that may be aged in oak. In almost all contexts, however, the use of the term Klassik (or Classic) on a label or website refers to a fresh, unwooded style, fruit-forward and intended for relatively swift consumption.

The aim of the DAC appellation is laudable – the designation of Vienna's sole DAC as Gemischter Satz has revived and validated a style of wine for which the city is celebrated – but in practice it can lead to much confusion. And it seems odd that the Neusiedlersee, famous worldwide for its sweet wines, has awarded its DAC to Zweigelt. Even more confusingly, some regional names have been altered to the DAC name: for example, the former Neusiedlersee-Hügelland, admittedly a cumbersome name, is now transformed to Leithaberg, the name of its DAC. But some parts of the former Hügelland are not part of the DAC zone, so the historically celebrated Rust, for example, has to label its wines as mere Burgenland. By 2019 Carnuntum and the Wachau were on the brink of devising a DAC system for those regions, but Wagram and Thermenregion have yet to do so.

The production criteria and the role of tasting panels do help maintain the quality of DAC wines, although the DAC letters on the label are no more a guarantee of high quality than the French AOC system or the Italian DOC. It also tends to refuse DAC status to wines that step out of line. There has been a growth in what one might call atypical wines such as 'orange' wines, in which grapes receive prolonged maceration on the skins, a style that the existing wine or DAC regulations cannot recognize or accept. This does not greatly matter, but these wines often have to be released as Landwein or Weinland or some other lowly tier in the Austrian hierarchy. Austria is also home to many organic or biodynamic estates, a trend encouraged but not imposed by the wine authorities.

Today the quality of Austrian wine, in all its manifestations, has been fully vindicated, and few would deny that average quality is extremely high. There are inevitably some wines that are boring or clumsy or dilute, but overall the quality of winemaking is impeccable. The renown of Austrian wine is constrained only by its limited production. After the Austrians' own thirst has been slaked, there isn't a great deal of wine left over for export, though the best wines are much sought after and appreciated. Nonetheless exports have been rising steadily for nine years in succession, with Germany and Switzerland the most important markets. It has to be remembered that with 46,500 hectares of vineyards, Austria's wine surface is still less than half of that of Bordeaux alone.

Many of those hectares are family owned, and this may be one explanation for the high average quality of the nation's wines. It is a country with very few cooperatives, and those that remain are often as dedicated to high quality as private estates. There has also been a change of generations over the past decade. It often surprises me, when visiting wineries, how often I am greeted by a man or woman under the age of thirty who is in complete control of both the farming and the winemaking. Moreover, these young owners have in most cases travelled the world and gained a truly international perspective that was rarely accessible to their parents and grandparents, who were often tied to their farms by practising polyculture in order to support their families. For the older generation, grapes were a form of nutrition and quantity was more important than quality. The younger generations, often to the dismay of their forebears, sharply reduced yields and sharply increased quality. All this bodes well for the future, though of course Austria is far from unique in this respect.

CHANGES IN BRITISH WINE STYLES

Since the 1990s, changing tastes in wine have led British producers to reconsider the varieties they grow and the wine styles they make. Sparkling wines in particular have revolutionized the country's wine industry, as this extract from Stephen Skelton MW's 2019 book *The wines of Great Britain* shows.

The past 30 years have seen a marked change in wine styles and types sold in Britain. In the late 1960s and 1970s, when English wines started making an impact on consumers, the biggest selling wines in Britain were Liebfraumilch and other German or Germanic styles. While there is no doubt that price played a great part in their popularity, these wines did find favour with a large sector of the wine-buying public who liked this easy, unpretentious style. In many respects the better English wines were similar – light and fruity, with a little residual sugar and not too heavy in alcohol – and they met with the approval of many consumers. In the 1980s, the tastes of wine drinkers in Britain started to change. Consumers seemed to want drier wines, perhaps because wine was appearing more and more at meal times, perhaps because palates were becoming more sophisticated. Wines from Australia, New Zealand and California started making a big impact on consumers and gradually the liking for German style wines reduced so that today's largest selling brands in Britain are the Australian Hardy's range and the Echo Falls and Blossom Hill ranges from California.

English and Welsh wines have reflected these changes in the market, and today no producer would risk bottling their still wines in tall

German-style Hock or Mosel bottles. The preference today is to use the non-country-specific Burgundy (in brown or green) and Bordeaux (in green or clear) bottles. The few growers still using Germanic varieties such as Müller-Thurgau, Reichensteiner, Schönburger, etc., now tend to give their wines non-varietal names believing (correctly in my view) that Germanic varietal names are both confusing and off-putting to the consumer. Those making wines from varieties such as Bacchus, Ortega and Pinot Noir, which appear to be more acceptable names to consumers, continue to do so. Bacchus, which occupies 8.45 per cent of the area under vine, is definitely the best white still wine variety grown and as growers and winemakers gain experience with it, the wines get better and better. Its Sauvignon Blanc-like taste profile and its un-German name (no umlaut) make it attractive to regular wine buyers.

As the climate has warmed, the spectrum of still wine varieties has also widened and now Pinot Blanc and Pinot Gris wines can be found with regularity. Sauvignon Blanc is starting to be used, although results to date show that in most years it's a hard variety to ripen and most growers blend it with Bacchus or Reichensteiner. A very few growers are trying Albariño, with mixed results – again, ripening problems tend to see it blended with other varieties; Riesling, that other cool-climate favourite, resists all attempts to be grown successfully in Britain. Rathfinny bravely planted 1.5 hectares (3.71 acres) of Riesling vines in 2012 and another 0.73 hectares (1.8 acres) in 2013 and the owners, Mark and Sarah Driver, trumpeted that they were 'looking forward to pouring the first glass of Cradle Valley Riesling in 2014', and hoped 'to release a limited quantity of this richly complex, aromatic still white wine next year'. They said, 'the climate and soil in East Sussex are perfect for growing Riesling grapes', but admitted defeat in 2016 and grubbed-up all the vines. This experience is not dissimilar to that of Denbies, which also planted Riesling in the late 1980s, but their only viable crop with the variety in twenty years was in the very warm year of 2003 and they too eventually grubbed it up.

*

The production of sparkling wine in Britain – although not from home-grown grapes – is verifiably over 350 years old, and we know from the two papers read at the newly founded Royal Society in December 1662 that sugar added to a fermented product and sealed in a bottle with a tightly bound stopper produced a 'brisk and sparkling' product. The

Reverend John Beale's 'Aphorisms on Cider', read to the Royal Society on 10 December 1662, says that 'bottling is the next best improver' for cider and that 'two to three raisins into every bottle' plus 'a walnut of sugar' – a recipe guaranteed to produce a secondary fermentation – works wonders on the cider. A week later, on 17 December, it was the turn of the now famous Dr Christopher Merrett to read his paper, 'Some Observations Concerning the Ordering of Wines', and describe how Britain's seven-teenth-century 'wine coopers' were making their wines 'brisk and sparkling' by the addition of sugar. This practice was certainly happening before 1662 and followed the development of the strong *verre Anglais* bottles which Sir Kenelm Digby had been perfecting since the 1630s.

Exactly when the first sparkling wine made from English grapes was produced is open to debate. Certainly wines being made in England in the 1750s were considered comparable to Champagne and the wines produced at Painshill Place between 1741 and 1779 were often de-scribed as such. Of course, Champagne in those days was not always the sparkling wine that we know today. I have a wine list from the *Magasin de Vins Fins Chez Terral* from Pontac, a village just outside Bordeaux, dated 1760, which lists *Champagne mousseux* and *Champagne non-mousseux* both at the same price.

The first recorded production of bottle-fermented sparkling wines – made from British-grown grapes – is probably that carried out by Raymond Barrington Brock at his Oxted Viticultural Research Station in the 1950s. The *Daily Mirror* of 17 August 1950 carried an article en-titled 'A bottle of Maidstone '49' which praised the work of Brock and that other viticultural pioneer, Edward Hyams and ended by saying: 'perhaps ten years hence you'll be raising a glass of sparkling Canterbury in honour of the men who made an English wine industry possible'. In September 1959 Brock welcomed members of the wine trade to a tast-ing and offered a number of different wines, including sparkling wines, to them. I have a letter dated 11 September 1959 sent to Brock by John Clevely, then a young Master of Wine, in which he thanks Brock for the visit and tasting and ends with a postscript saying: 'Moët must look to their laurels if you really start going "commercial" with that sparkling wine. I thought it was wonderful.' Praise indeed. Some of these spark-ling wines survived undisturbed in the Station's cellars until the 1980s.

Sir Guy Salisbury-Jones at Hambledon, whose initial (1953) plantings included 20 Chardonnay vines, experimented with the production of a bottle-fermented sparkling wine, and in 1969 Bill Carcary, his vineyard manager, produced a batch of 60 bottles. Salisbury-Jones expanded the plantings of Chardonnay in 1970 with a further 1,000 vines but whether to make still or sparkling wine is not known. In 1979 his winemaking consultant Anton Massel helped produce a batch with apparently favourable results and as Salisbury-Jones also grew Auxerrois and Meunier, which ripened more easily, these became the basis of their sparkling wine cuvée. However, Sir Guy considered that the production costs were too high and the length of time the wine needed to mature was too long to make the product commercially viable and production ceased.

The first producers to make commercial quantities of bottle-fermented sparkling wines were Nigel (de Marsac) Godden at Pilton Manor in Somerset – first planted in 1966 – and Graham Barrett at Felsted Vineyards in Essex – first planted in 1967. As was quite usual at that time, the main varieties grown were Müller-Thurgau and Seyval Blanc and it is probable that it was these that were used. Their wines – never produced in large volumes – were certainly interesting, maybe even worth drinking and in the 1979 English Wine of the Year Competition (EWOTYC) the 1976 Felstar Méthode Champenoise won a silver medal and the NV Pilton Manor De Marsac Brut Méthode Champenoise won a bronze. These early successes, however, didn't seem to help sales much and their production faded out.

The next appearance of a bottle-fermented sparkling wine in the EWOTYC (ignoring the carbonated 1983 Barton Manor Sparkling Rosé that won a gold medal in the 1984 competition – delicious though it was) was in 1987, when the first Carr Taylor sparkling wine won a medal. David and Linda Carr Taylor first planted vines at their vineyard in Westfield, near Hastings, East Sussex, in 1973 and until 1983 their grapes were sent to Lamberhurst Vineyards for winemaking. From their huge 1983 vintage, however, when Reichensteiner cropped at 15 tonnes per acre and their total output came to 186,000 bottles, they decided to start making bottle-fermented sparkling wines. They engaged Clement Nowak, a Champagne-based Polish-French consultant winemaker, whose name at one stage actually appeared on the neck-label. For a few years Carr Taylor became the major producer – in fact almost the only producer – of bottle-fermented sparkling wines in Britain and achieved considerable success. Their Vintage Sparkling won a gold medal in the 1988 EWOTYC and their Non-Vintage Sparkling won the Jack Ward Trophy (best large volume wine) in the 1989 EWOTYC. In 1993 they won the IWSC English Wine Trophy with their 1987

Vintage Sparkling. They also entered their wines into overseas competitions – a rarity in those days – and did surprisingly well. Their 1988 Vintage Sparkling Wine was awarded a gold medal at the prestigious Concours European des Grands Vins beating 1,800 Champagnes and other bottle-fermented sparkling wines from around the world, and in 1999, in the same competition, their 1996 vintage was awarded a gold medal, this time out of 4,300 entrants. A fact that tends to get forgotten in these days of Britain's mega-vineyards planted with Champagne varieties is that the Carr Taylors were certainly the first to make serious commercial quantities of bottle-fermented sparkling wines. They did, however, only ever use what might be termed 'native' varieties for Britain: Reichensteiner, Schönburger, Kerner and Huxelrebe being the most important ones. This reliance on non-classic varieties, while it gave their wines a point of difference from other Chardonnay- and Pinot-based wines, also gave the wines a character more akin to Sekt or Asti than Champagne, something not all critics and commentators liked.

The next on Britain's sparkling wine scene was David Cowderoy, son of Norman Cowderoy who had established a vineyard at Rock Lodge near Haywards Heath in 1963 (the vineyard is now leased by Plumpton College). David had been to Wye College to study agriculture (and met Jo, now his wife and currently WineGB Operations Manager, who was also studying there) and after getting his degree went to Roseworthy College in Australia to study winemaking. Returning to Britain in 1986, and with the knowledge that marriage to Jo was on the horizon, he made a batch of sparkling wine using Müller-Thurgau and Reichensteiner from that vintage. Thus, when he and Jo got married in 1988, they and their friends and family were able to celebrate with what was to be the first of many batches of English sparkling wine. David continued with his experiments in sparkling wine and, working at his father's winery at Rock Lodge, produced the 1989 Rock Lodge Impresario[1], which won the IWSC English Wine Trophy in 1991.

When David joined forces with others to create Chapel Down Wines (in 1992) one of their first wines, the non-vintage Epoch Brut, made from a blend of Müller-Thurgau, Reichensteiner and Seyval Blanc, was in fact a re-badged Rock Lodge wine. The fact that Chapel Down was not using the classic Champagne varieties (which, with the exception

---

1 It had originally been called 'Rock Lodge Imperial' until Moët & Chandon complained as Impérial is one of its brands.

Nyetimber, the largest vineyard owner in Great Britain and inarguably the producer making the country's best sparkling wines, has vineyards spread across the south of England

of New Hall Vineyards, were not being grown in enough quantity for them to buy) gave them something of a marketing advantage and enabled their prices to remain reasonable – under £10 – although at the time this was at least twice that of still wines. In the end though, once Chardonnay- and Pinot-based wines started to appear in 1997–98, this marketing edge disappeared and their Müller-Thurgau, Reichensteiner and Seyval Blanc based wines, although very good and well-priced, were always playing second fiddle to the Champagne lookalikes in quality (and quality perception) terms. At much the same time, John Worontschak, winemaker at Thames Valley Vineyard (today's Stanlake Park) made a sparkling wine using Pinot Noir from Ascot Vineyard, a 1-hectare (2.47-acre) vineyard planted in 1979 on Crown land near Sunninghill Park and owned by Colonel Robby Robertson. Called Ascot Brut NV, it was released in 1992 and won a silver medal in the 1994 EWOTYC. Worontschak produced a number of Ascot sparkling wines from both Pinot Noir and (unusually) Gamay Noir, winning several silvers and bronzes between 1994 and 2004.

The production of sparkling wines using the three classic varieties – Chardonnay, Pinot Noir and Meunier – started in the mid-1980s when growers such as Piers Greenwood, Martin Oldaker at Surrenden Vineyard, near Ashford (planted between 1984 and 1986) and Karen Ostborn and Alan Smalley at Throwley, near Faversham (planted in

1986),[2] both in Kent, all started growing Chardonnay and Pinot Noir with the encouragement of Christopher (Kit) Lindlar. After leaving the Merrydown Wine Company,[3] based in Horam, East Sussex, where he had been one of the winemakers since 1976, Lindlar set up as a contract winemaker, first at Biddenden Vineyards, and then, in 1986, at his own High Weald Winery at Grafty Green, near Ashford, Kent. Lindlar, who also supplied vines, persuaded the two Kent vineyards above to experiment with these varieties, which had until then been very unsuccessful in Britain. Brock had grown Chardonnay in his collection at Oxted but could never get it to ripen properly. Ian and Andrew Paget at Chilsdown Vineyard planted Chardonnay and also had no luck getting it to ripen. In 1981, a very dismal year for British vinegrowers, the acidity (in grams per litre) in their Chardonnay was higher than the degrees Oechsle. Ouch. Extreme unripeness was a common finding among those early growers who persevered with it, although most decided to give up and removed the offending variety. Only in really hot years would Chardonnay produce anything like ripe grapes and tolerable wine. Pinot Noir, like many of the black varieties then being grown, suffered from terrible botrytis and was very difficult to ripen without huge losses. It is only since the arrival of better anti-botrytis sprays – initially Rovral and Ronilan, but more recently Scala, Switch and Teldor – that growing fungus-sensitive varieties like Pinot Noir has been possible. Meunier, in the guise of Wrotham Pinot, had always been grown in small amounts, but never used for anything other than blending with other, riper, reds. Lindlar's biggest, and subsequently best-known clients, were Stuart and Sandy Moss who decided, in 1988, to plant a vineyard at Nyetimber near Pulborough in West Sussex.

The Mosses had, by all accounts, been looking at various locations to plant a vineyard – California was at one time the front runner – but it was Sandy's love of (and business in) early English oak furniture that persuaded them that England was the place. In 1985 Hambledon Vineyards was up for sale and the Mosses viewed it and made a bid for it, but lost out to another bidder, John Patterson, who owned it until 1994. Bill Carcary, who had been at Hambledon since 1966, got to know the Mosses quite well at

---

2 The 1989 Throwley Chardonnay Sparkling won the IWSC English Wine Trophy in 1992.

3 Merrydown was partially owned by Jack Ward, who was its MD, as well as being Chairman of the English Vineyards Association. Merrydown owned a small vineyard, Horam Manor, but more importantly operated a cooperative winemaking scheme for British vineyards, where in exchange for a percentage of the grapes, they made your wine.

the time and when they then bought the 49-hectare Nyetimber estate in 1986, they asked Carcary to come and work for them as estate manager and eventually as winemaker and got so far with this idea as to refurbish a cottage for him and offer him a contract of employment. In his discussions with them about planting a vineyard on the land at Nyetimber, Carcary remembers it being his idea that they should plant the Champagne varieties for sparkling wine production, something he had long wanted to do at Hambledon but which, as has been stated above, Salisbury-Jones had ruled out on cost grounds. In the end, Carcary decided for family reasons not to leave Hambledon and stayed, working for the new owner. Whoever actually came up with the idea to produce bottle-fermented sparkling wines on this (for the time) very large scale is uncertain, but the Mosses went ahead and planted the classic Champagne varieties, something which at the time was revolutionary – some said bonkers.

The vines for the Nyetimber plantings between 1988 and 1991 were sourced from France and it was to Lindlar's High Weald Winery that the first commercial vintage, the 1992, was taken for processing under the watchful eye of consultant Jean-Manuel Jacquinot. As Lindlar modestly says, 'while they did hire Jacquinot, the winemaking buck stopped with me; that is to say, had those early vintages flopped it would definitely have been down to me.' Given the importance of the Mosses' enterprise, which when all was said and done was still something of an experiment, one has to give praise to Lindlar where it is due. After Nyetimber's first release, the 1992 Blanc de Blancs Première Cuvée, won the English Wine Trophy in 1997, and subsequent releases went on to garner further awards, the English wine world started to take notice.

A few years after the Mosses planted, another Lindlar client, Mike Roberts, also decided to establish a dedicated classic-variety, bottle-fermented sparkling wine business at Ditchling in East Sussex. Ridgeview Winery was established in 1995 with thirteen clones of Chardonnay, Pinot Noir and Meunier and today it covers 6.48 hectares (16 acres), although it has access to grapes from a much larger area. A modern winery, with underground storage cellar, was built and equipped with the contents of the High Weald Winery, which was acquired when Lindlar closed the winery. In order to kick-start Ridgeview's production line, Chardonnay and Pinot Noir grapes were bought from other growers, including Surrenden, and the 1996 Cuveé Merret Bloomsbury was produced. This wine won the 2000 EWOTYC Gore-Browne Trophy, awarded for wine of the year. Since that first release, Ridgeview has produced a range of wines, all named after London squares or areas – Belgravia, Bloomsbury, Cavendish, Fitzrovia, Grosvenor, Knightsbridge and Pimlico – and the tally of awards has been impressive. They won the Gore-Browne Trophy in 2000, 2002, 2009, 2010 and 2011 and regularly win gold and silver medals in the major wine competitions. Their most notable success was probably winning the Decanter World Wine Awards International Sparkling Wine Trophy (beating four very prestigious Champagnes in the process) with their 2006 Grosvenor Blanc de Blancs.

When first Nyetimber and later Ridgeview started selling wines and achieving the sort of prices that many in the wine business in Britain had thought impossible, the way forward for home-grown sparkling wines started to look a lot different. Following their significant commercial and competition success, plantings of the three classic Champagne varieties in Britain increased year on year and since the very warm year of 2003, several significant vineyards have been planted. Nyetimber changed hands twice and under its current ownership has expanded on various sites from its original 15.8 hectares to a whopping 258 hectares (638 acres) and growing. Owner Eric Heerema told me he was looking for another 200 hectares (500 acres). Other large sparkling wine producers include the largest, Chapel Down, who own or lease 220 hectares (544 acres), take grapes under contract from another 101 hectares (250 acres) and have a further 64 hectares 158 acres) of land to plant at Boarley on the North Downs. The third largest by vineyard size, although with only a small percentage of the planted land yet cropping, is Mark Dixon's MDCV Ltd with vineyards in East and West Sussex, Kent and Essex currently totalling 284 hectares (700 acres). The next three largest sparkling wine producers are: Hambledon with 90 hectares; Rathfinny with 93.5 hectares; Gusbourne with 93 hectares; and Ridgeview with 90 hectares (both owned and under contract). Other major sparkling players include Balfour Wine Estate, Bluebell Estates, Bolney, Camel Valley, Coates and Seely, Laithwaites, Langham, Exton Park, Furleigh, Greyfriars, Hundred Hills, Roebuck, Simpson's, Squerryes, Tinwood, and Wiston. Together, there are around 30 British producers who control 50 per cent of Britain's vineyard area and probably nearer 65 per cent of its sparkling wine production. The two French-controlled producers, Domaine Evremond (Taittinger) and what is currently called Pinglestone Estate (Vranken-Pommery) will be added to this list in time.

ADDRESSING SOUTH AFRICA'S APARTHEID LEGACY

After apartheid ended in the early 1990s, embargoes against South African products, including wine, were lifted. But this was just the beginning of the wine industry's rehabilitation. In this piece from 2020's *The wines of South Africa*, Jim Clarke explores how the industry is working to give more power to black and coloured workers.

In terms of employment generated in proportion to capital invested, South Africa's wine industry is one of the most effective job creators in the country. More than 167,000 people work directly in wine production, and the industry supports approximately 300,000 jobs when one takes into account ancillary activities like logistics and tourism. The industry aims to boost that number to 375,000 by 2025. However, more than half of the employment opportunities offered are low-wage, unskilled positions. Coloured and black workers hold the great majority of these posts; farm and winery owners are almost entirely white. While profitability remains an existential threat to the industry, successfully addressing the legacy of apartheid is equally vital. The South African government has named this process, and its goal, 'transformation', and the dominant mechanism for carrying it out, Broad-Based Black Economic Empowerment (BBBEE, or often just BEE).

At the core of BEE is the scorecard, used to evaluate almost every business in South Africa. The scorecard takes into account transformational improvements across five different aspects of each business, including ownership, management control, skills development, enterprise and supplier development, and socio-economic development. The government monitors and assesses progress and goal setting across these different categories, and the resulting scores fall into nine grades. There are no legislated penalties for low scores, but governmental agencies and large companies are incentivized to employ and source from high-scoring businesses.

The Wine Industry Transformation Charter adapted this model into its own BEE scoring system in 2007. Companies with an annual turnover of over 35 million rand are subject to evaluation by the full range of elements, whereas companies with turnover between 5 and 35 million rand are scored on a simplified scale. Companies with turnover below 5 million rand are exempt. This breakdown brings more of the industry into the fold compared to the national model, which set the exemption cap at 10 million rand. Nevertheless, given the typical small size of the Cape's wine farms, 80 per cent of wine farms receive exemptions, though the Charter calls for them to strive to achieve similar goals regardless. Since farming is more capital intensive and less profitable than other parts of the industry, land ownership is weighted more highly in the wine industry scorecard as an added incentive. The wine scorecard also includes an element covering rural development and poverty alleviation which rewards efforts to improve housing, access to medical services, education and similar activities. Overall its categories encompass a broad range of concerns.

Land ownership is a deeply emotional issue in South Africa. It lies at the heart of colonialism, and at the heart of twentieth-century segregationist and apartheid policies. Three years after the formation of the Union of South Africa in 1910, parliament passed the Native Land Act, which dispossessed black South Africans of more than 90 per cent of the country's arable land. Under the National Party, the 1959 Bantu Self-Government Act created the so-called black homelands or bantustans, divided along tribal lines. These laws moved populations out of their homes and into the various townships and similarly designated areas, and progressively denaturalized and further disempowered the non-white population. In principle, land claims could go as far back as the first arrival of the Dutch, but to bring some semblance of manageability to the process, South Africa's land restitution programmes limit themselves to dispossession attributable to racial discrimination dating from 1913 through to 1994.

Nationally, restitution cases have not actually restored much land to the original owners. The vast majority of the almost 80,000 cases filed have been settled via cash compensation instead. Rural claims, how-ever, which make up as much as a quarter of the total, are more likely to result in land restitution than urban ones. Restitution is also just one aspect of government land reform policy, which also prioritizes redistribution and tenure reform. Redistribution is divided into two programmes; the Land Redistribution for Agricultural Development (LRAD) programme concerns itself with farming as opposed to hous-ing. Within LRAD, qualifying recipients can use government land re-distribution grants to purchase property from the state, but this can be challenging in some areas. In the early 1990s in Stellenbosch, for example, the local government granted long-term leases to a number of white-owned wine farms, effectively removing them from the market just as land redistribution programmes came into being. Other govern-ment-owned tracts of land currently used for grazing could be viable for wine grapes if the government provided water rights, but ongoing con-cerns about drought and climate change make that unlikely. As of 2017 blacks owned 1.5 per cent of South Africa's vineyards; the government's stated target at the time was to reach 30 per cent by 2030.

Equity sharing

From many perspectives, today's black entrepreneurs who choose to invest not in wine but in other parts of the South African economy are making sound financial decisions. This is especially true when it comes to owning land; as mentioned, wine farms are the least prof-itable segment of the industry. Wine farming is also long-term and capital-intensive compared to other forms of agriculture. Many new black landowners have found themselves without sufficient capi-tal to run their farm; oftentimes the farm is effectively abandoned. In response, the wine and fruit industries developed Equity Sharing Schemes (ESS). These programmes allow workers to use their govern-ment grants to become partners in new wine companies that own not just land but other assets; they often do so in partnership with estab-lished, white wine farmers, so in these cases they are effectively join-ing an already operating concern rather than starting from scratch. In many regards this model seems to be a way forward in terms of addressing the problem of ownership and working capital, as well as skills transfer. LRAD funding has supported at least half of the land reform projects in the Western Cape, and about one-fifth of those are Equity Sharing Schemes.

Under the ESS model, workers form a trust and use government grants to buy a portion of the farm they work at. Thandi, in Elgin was one of the earliest successful examples. In 1996 the forestry station adjoining Paul Cluver's de Rust farm in Elgin was closing down and laying off workers. Cluver collaborated with the state-owned forestry company to donate 180 hectares towards a joint venture together with workers and members of the local community, creating the country's first BEE company in the agriculture industry. As of 2009 they became fully independent; the local farming communities, mostly workers at Thandi's farms themselves, own two-thirds of the company, and their exporter, The Company of Wine People, owns the remainder. Today Thandi is the biggest black-owned wine exporting company in South Africa.

More recently, in 2006, Bosman, a large grower and nursery in Wellington, renovated its wine cellar and began producing its own wines after a fifty-year hiatus. At the same time, it negotiated with workers to create the Adama Workers Trust. Two years later the Bosman family and the Trust became co-owners of Bosman Family Vineyards. In this arrangement, the Trust is not just a co-owner of the land, but of all the company assets. Beneficiaries own 26 per cent of the company. Bosman was able to pay dividends on that investment from the beginning, and as of 2019 about one billion rand of dividends have been distributed, which amounts to a yield of about 3.5 per cent.

Approximately 90 farms, scattered across every part of the Cape, have embraced the ESS model. In Stellenbosch, the Deelnemings Trust owns 74 per cent of Bouwland; the Trust's members include the farm's own workers as well as workers from nearby Kanonkop and Beyerskloof. The latter assist with winemaking, viticulture and marketing. Riebeek Valley Partners is the largest BEE company in the Swartland, with over 160 workers owning shares. In Robertson, the Retief family, which owns Van Loveren, purchased a 138-hectare farm together with the De Goree Employees Trust and their 116 members as majority owners. Some schemes allow for incremental increases in worker ownership; they also typically include provisions for buying out workers who depart the farm.

Equity Sharing Schemes can be advantageous for businesses operations as well. 'What it's done for absenteeism and productivity is amazing,' says Neil Büchner, at the time the Brand Manager at Bosman. Within the wine industry, the joint venture between the Bosman Family and the trust was already the largest empowerment deal at its formation. Since then the company has expanded its hectarage from 430 to 700, with a new farm in the Upper Hemel-en-Aarde Valley, and they've also purchased the vine improvement facility on Nederburg's Ernita farm in Wellington as a natural complement to their operations as a vine nursery. Their success has also created additional jobs, with the total workforce expanding from 260 to 420.

ESS companies do tend to face some internal problems. Financially, such models have to limit outside investment if workers are to maintain a minimum percentage of ownership, making it hard to raise additional capital. Workers themselves tend to prioritize short-term assets that can provide immediate dividends rather than addressing long-term needs. Ensuring worker members can monitor company decisions is often challenging. Workers can find it hard to diversify their portfolio and control the risk level of their investments; their financial fate is largely tied to the success of the farm. Given the average performance of wine farms in recent years, some have suggested that workers would have done better with their money in a well-chosen mutual fund instead.

While many ESS ventures have been successful, it's definitely a struggle. Often the biggest problem is getting all the parties on the same page. Farmers may wish to avoid the old paternalistic patterns of making decisions on the workers' behalf, but workers often need financial education before they can fairly weigh the risks and alternatives presented, or offer sound input on the running of the joint venture once established. One of the most common criticisms of the ESS model is that the workers are reduced to silent partners with little or no power to influence company decision-making. In some cases workers complain of a lack of dividends or quality-of-life improvements.

Out-of-the-box thinking is sometimes encouraged and sometimes laid low by government regulation or conflicting priorities. In 1997 Charles Back assisted workers on his Fairview wine and cheese farm in establishing the Fairview Trust, and with government assistance they purchased a 16-hectare farm which they named Fairvalley. By 2002 sales of Fairvalley wine had enabled them to build eight small houses on the property, but zoning regulations blocked much more ambitious plans to develop a mixed-use community including 450 residential units as well as shopping and light industrial areas. Fairvalley has continued to succeed as a wine brand, but almost three dozen other Trust members are still waiting for their houses.

More tragically, Solms-Delta, an ambitious estate touted for some time as the face of transformation in the winelands, filed for bankruptcy in 2018. The story of the estate's rise and fall would make a book on its own. Mark Solms, a South African neurosurgeon living in London, had purchased the property in 2000. He undertook huge investments in the property, the workers living on the estate, and the community, eventually bringing in his friend Richard Astor as an additional investor. Housing, education and a host of other post-apartheid issues were addressed, and the project was moving from one-third to one-half worker ownership when it collapsed. Big ambitions, failure to build sufficient export markets, and at the very least confusion about the nature and amount of government support the project would receive all led to liquidation proceedings.

Coming to wine from the outside

While worker-owned models like ESS attempt to rectify the ownership balance among those already in the wine industry, there are also a number of black or coloured businesspeople who have had some success in other fields before entering the wine industry, typically by purchasing a wine farm. In 2002 Malmsey and Diale Rangaka founded M'hudi, the first black-owned and family-operated winery in South Africa. Both were clinical psychologists with no agricultural background when they started the project. Their neighbours at Villiera mentored them, advising on viticulture and urging them to create their own brand rather than selling wine in the bulk market. They also helped them source grapes from farms elsewhere in the Cape so they could diversify their offerings.

Other black-owned brands have eased their entry into the industry by avoiding capital-intensive land purchases, at least at the beginning. Seven Sisters launched in 2007 as a virtual winery, buying and bottling bulk wine to create their own range. Vivian Kleynhans, one of the sisters and a former owner of a recruitment company, leads the project. One of the founding principles of Seven Sisters was to create a network among women from disadvantaged groups in particular. While the initial supply model for Seven Sisters relied on purchased bulk wine, Kleynhans pushed for greater control of production. In 2009 an LRAD grant allowed the company to purchase an 8.7-hectare property in Stellenbosch. They have since planted their own vines and built a tasting room to enable them to tap into direct sales rather than relying on distribution. In 2016 they launched the Brutus Family Reserve line, their first wines to include grapes from their own vineyards.

Wine drinking was not common in black communities during the latter decades of apartheid, especially outside the Western Cape. The resulting lack of a wine culture is another reason potential black investors might look elsewhere. It has also inhibited the development of black winemaking talent. However, a small but increasing number of black and coloured winemaker-owners are appearing, many of them women. Ntsiki Biyela's profile rose dramatically when she launched her own brand, Aslina, in 2013 after several years as winemaker at Stellekaya. Brought up by her grandmother in KwaZulu-Natal, in 1999 she received a South African Airways bursary to study wine at the University of Stellenbosch, despite having never tasted wine. 'It could have been anything,' says Biyela. 'I wanted to study and I wanted to change my life.' In fact, only after she was accepted did she realize what she would be studying. Today Biyela sources from several vineyards around Stellenbosch and other areas and vinifies her wines at a custom crush facility. Whereas many virtual wineries and worker-owned brands focus on lower-priced wines, Aslina operates within the premium tier.

One advantage of that higher price point is a more knowledgeable customer base. Competition is still quite fierce, but drinkers of premium wine are more likely to pay attention to the story behind the wines compared to those who buy budget-tier wines. Domestically and in some export markets consumers seem to view BEE brands with scepticism. Diemersfontein owners David and Sue Sonnenberg returned to South Africa from the UK in 2000 and set up Thokozani as an empowerment company in 2007. In many ways it's a model example of a transformation wine company, but ironically one of their biggest successes to date involved stepping back from overtly black or coloured branding. Managing director Denise Stubbs says that when Woolworths, a dominant South African retailer, came looking for a transformation brand, Thokozani's wines scored highly. But the retailer felt that their customers were skeptical of black-owned brands and asked them to rename the wine. Thokozani changed the brand name to 'Ovation', and turnover tripled in a single year.

Thokozani also diversified successfully. Most of their assets are in the land itself, which has more than doubled in value. Aside from the vineyards they've built on their assets by operating guest houses and a conference centre, giving them an income stream that's unrelated to the state of grape prices. In fact, some of the most successful BEE programmes in the wine industry actually lie outside the production and

Denise Stubbs with some of the Thokozani harvest team

sale of wine. Meerlust started Compagniesdrift as a BEE project for its workers in 2010. The company began as a bottling, storage and logistics provider for four producers; today they have over forty clients. Workers from Meerlust as well as Vriesenhof and Ken Forrester are members – 72 in all. Building on its success as a service provider, Compagniesdrift actually began producing its own line of wines in 2015.

More than fifty transformation brands work in these support areas, which are generally more profitable, especially in the short-term. Michael Fridjhon, among others, has argued that while disparities in land ownership are real, transformation efforts directed into supporting industries as well as distribution and retail can have a more immediate impact on workers' lives given their greater profitability and the increasing urbanization of the workforce.

The skills that pay the bills

For the individual, training and skills can mean a more immediate and dramatic quality of life improvement than shares in a wine brand, especially a struggling one. Research suggests that while migrant labour became more common in the first decade or so of democracy, employers across South Africa (that is, not just in the wine industry) are now opting to employ a smaller number of full-time skilled workers rather than larger numbers of part-time, unskilled workers. Programmes to improve worker skills pre-date the end of apartheid; some students at Elsenburg Viticultural College formed what would become the non-profit organization Wine Training South Africa in 1987. The programme offers accredited training for cellar workers; Elsenburg's alumni association administered it until 2005, when it became a stand-alone programme. Since 2006 the programme has trained more than 6,000 people. VinPro, too, has instituted almost 250 different training programmes, with more than 4,500 workers trained since 2015.

Other programmes help individuals prepare for leading roles in the industry – not necessarily as owners, but as winemakers and viticulturalists. In 2006 the Cape Winemakers Guild, building on their Development Trust, introduced their Protégé programme, which provides internship opportunities for oenology students as they complete their studies. The first Protégé, Howard Booysen, began a three-year internship that year, spending time at several different wineries working with members of the guild. In 2014 the guild added a viticulture programme as well. More than 30 Protégés have completed the internships and gone on to work in the industry.

On top of institutional efforts, it's hard to underestimate the impact individuals have had. Charles Back at Fairview is supportive of institutional efforts like Fairtrade and WIETA, but he changed his own approach after he had a University of Stellenbosch professor survey his workers about what they wanted for themselves. Out of 47, only one said they wanted their own farm; instead, 'They wanted the same things you or I want: better pay, a house, access to medical services, schooling for children and a pension.' With these goals in mind, Back felt he could make immediate, lasting improvements by asking himself how he could use his own farm and assets to create auxiliary opportunities that the people around him could take advantage of. Outsourcing his laundry services led to ex-farmworkers' wives owning and operating a laundry company with an annual turnover of two million rand. He discovered a tasting-room employee was studying human resources; now that former employee is the co-owner of an HR company with sixteen large accounts, including Back's.

Black and coloured people have of course driven change in their own right, too. Jabulani Ntshangase left South Africa in 1979 thanks to a United Nations scholarship. He studied business administration in New York and worked as a stock clerk at Acker Merrall, an Upper West Side wine shop. Despite being warned away from alcohol by his Zulu grandmother, he took an interest in wine, and after a dozen years he returned to South Africa with plans to import wines to the US. Since then he's played many roles in the industry, including being the first black partner-owner of a South African winery when he joined Back, Gyles Webb and John Platter in the founding of Spice Route. In 1995 he approached South African Airways and convinced them to establish the Wine Education Trust, which sponsors bursaries for persons of colour to study winemaking at Stellenbosch University.

In support of the programme he travelled across South Africa, spreading the word and encouraging people to apply. Many of the recipients then stayed at his home in Malmesbury during their studies, and many had their first tastes of wine there. Ntsiki Biyela, owner-winemaker at Aslina; Dumisani Mathonsi, white winemaker at Zonnebloem; and Unathi Mantshongo, former CEO of the VinPro Foundation, all benfited from Ntshangase's support and tutelage.

These winemaking students faced prodigious challenges. In 1995, Carmen Stevens became the first black winemaker to graduate from Elsenburg. With good grades, she had applied multiple times before even being accepted, at one point threatening to go to the newspapers to expose the discrimination against her. At the time there were only five female students, and only two were black. After a year-and-a-half of poor treatment from her fellow students she complained to the agriculture department head and once again threatened to go public with her situation. Only after a group of students apologized to her did things improve.

Later, overt confrontations became less common, but there are still many barriers facing black students. Language was and is a problem. The lectures at Stellenbosch University are in Afrikaans, which most black people don't learn or speak growing up, especially outside the Western Cape. The simple culture shock of moving from an all-black village to a white-dominated setting was troubling for many, even when people were welcoming. Almost every black student seems to have a story about being astonished by their first taste of wine – 'Do people really drink this?' Family and friends back home also struggled to understand what their children were going to Stellenbosch to study. Some students hid the fact that they were learning how to make alcohol. Parents in farming communities were sometimes disappointed to see their children go off to study viticulture – a real step up, in their view, would be to get away from farmwork entirely.

Ntshangase and many others – professors, winemakers, winery owners – have served as a support network. Charles Hopkins, cellarmaster at De Grendel, has made educating young black winemakers a priority, and has mentored more Cape Winemakers Guild Protégés than any other guild member. Confronted with a winemaker dinner where she was both the only black person and the only woman, Biyela says the late Professor Eben Archer pushed her to take her place rather than run away, saying 'If you don't go in, it's not going to change.' On an everyday level, Professor Charl Theron provided her and other students with extra lessons and notes in English rather than Afrikaans. Some students persevered; many dropped out. Nonetheless, industry attitudes overall are encouraging. 'I'm not going to focus on the negative ones,' Biyela says. 'When I encounter someone negative I go on to the next one and then the next one, because I realize there is always someone willing to help. I realized that the wine industry, when you look at it from the outside, is scary; but when you are inside and you are settled you understand that actually, it is not.'

VINEYARDS AND VARIETIES

THE SPARKLING WINE VINEYARD

Anthony Rose questions to what extent sparkling wines express their terroir and asks how changes in climate are affecting the wines produced. In this 2022 piece from *Fizz!* we discover what winemakers are doing to retain flavour and freshness, and the regions where sparkling wines might flourish in the future

Starting out with the givens of location, grape variety, clone and rootstock, the job of the viticulturalist is to manage all the necessary processes required in the vineyard and take account of the variables, not least the weather. In the case of sparkling wine, the potential alcohol at harvest has to be low enough to accommodate the extra 1–2 per cent alcohol created by the second fermentation. Achieving flavour ripeness (with tartaric and malic acid in roughly equal proportions) at relatively low potential alcohol is a difficult balancing act that requires the right grape varieties and can only be achieved with a helping hand from Mother Nature. Only a cool climate with the minimum amount of heat distributed over a sufficiently long growing season (conventionally 100 days) can ripen the grape in such a way that it has accumulated sufficient sugar and yet remains low enough in potential alcohol when picked to be able to accommodate not just one, but two fermentations.

Different soils contain varying amounts of nutrients and many need supplementary nutrients to ensure balanced, healthy vine growth. Chalk for instance, while it has great water absorption and transmission capacity and reflects sunlight efficiently, is a high-alkaline soil that is lacking in organic matter and doesn't hold much iron. Compaction has to be avoided to ensure adequate aeration. Soils need minerals and the capacity to transmit those nutrients to the vine for its development. Among the minerals

Sap rising in the vine, Langham Estate, Dorset, England

required for healthy vine growth are iron, magnesium, boron, zinc, nitrogen, potassium and phosphorus. Soil samples will tell the vineyard manager what nutrients are required and what cover crops should be grown in order to encourage microbial life and add nitrogen. Sheep in winter can provide manure and, as it were, mow the lawn. 'We are worm farmers and sun farmers as much as grape farmers,' says Exton Park's Fred Langdale.

In winter the vineyard manager needs to prune for the balanced growth of the vine to achieve the optimum yield. Cordon spur pruning has one permanent horizontal arm (Cordon de Royat) along which a number of canes are typically pruned back to two buds, or two arms (Cordon double). The Chablis cane pruning system has three to five branches from which a short cane is retained, growing from the central trunk, and generally brings higher yields. Guyot is cane pruning, with one cane and one spur (single guyot) or two canes and two spurs (double guyot). Vallée de la Marne (for Meunier) is cane pruning. Only Cordon de Royat and Chablis can be used in *grand* and *premier cru* vineyards in Champagne.

Climate change is resulting in earlier budbreak in spring, increasing the threat of exposure to spring frosts. Just a short period below 0°C can be devastating, especially if there is more than one frost event. Throughout Europe, 2020 and 2021 were brutal as night-time temperatures fell below zero in the spring. With later budburst than many of Europe's classic wine regions, England got off relatively lightly, but England had severe frost problems of its own in 2016 and 2019. Combating frost is based on displacing cold air with fans, candles or driving frost-busting machines that blow warm air through the vineyard, the latter contributing to the climate

Veraison - Pinot Noir changing colour, Josef Chromy, Tasmania, Australia

change that caused the problem in the first place. Ploughing at this time can encourage the roots to delve deeper into the soil, and a variety of cover crops add nutrients, helping to balance growth, protect against soil erosion and encourage microbial life.

With the trellis adjusted to expose the canopy to sunlight and create ventilation to protect against mildew and rot, good early summer weather at flowering allows for an even fruit set. Leaf removal after flowering is a method of opening up the canopy to sunlight, while bunch-thinning after flowering maximizes the energy in the grape. The summer months are crucial for the ripening of the grapes and the process of *véraison*, the changing of the colour in the grapes. With best practice in mind, vineyard managers are increasingly using organic-based products to feed the leaves for the maintenance of photosynthesis and keeping mildew, both powdery and downy, and botrytis at bay.

As harvest approaches, in Champagne a data summary is notified to technical teams who supply pre-harvest meetings with harvest date estimates. The Comité Champagne sets the harvest dates, whereas elsewhere producers rely on their weather stations and apps. The start date is dictated by technique and measurement, but growers are increasingly tasting before deciding when to analyse for average weight, estimated sugar and total acidity. Grapes are manually picked, by law in most quality-oriented appellations such as Champagne and England PDO, in order to retain whole, undamaged bunches for pressing and, in black grapes, to avoid any colouring of the must. It's also the case that phenolic compounds from the grapeskins can have an adverse effect on foaming properties. Some producers opt to pay by the hour rather than by crate in order to ensure a critical sorting in the vineyard for health and avoiding moisture before the bunches are brought in for pressing.

It may sound like a statement of the obvious to say that sparkling wine begins in the vineyard, but a blinkered focus on the process alone can obscure the simple fact that good sparkling wines are made from the right kind of grapes grown in the most suitable of locations; in a word, terroir. Bubbles may all look identical in the glass but not all bubbles are created equal. The potential for quality and authenticity varies according to the nature of the terroir and human input. That's the inescapable logic behind, for instance, Champagne's Échelle des Crus, in which grape prices were fixed on a sliding scale based on an informal but long-standing hierarchy with the most prized terroirs commanding the highest prices.

At first glance however, the notion of terroir as it relates to sparkling wine is in some respects a paradox. Two major features of sparkling wine threaten to derail the terroir argument. The first is the blend, the second the process itself. Blending is the *sine qua non* of sparkling wine thanks to the vagaries of climate, the multiplicity of vineyard sources and the crafting of a consistent house style year in year out. Rare is the fizz that goes to its second fermentation without some form of blending, whether of permutation of grape variety, vineyard, vintage or reserve wine. In addition, whether native yeasts or commercial yeasts are used, what type of fermenting vessel is deployed and whether or not the wine undergoes malolactic fermentation all play their part in the resulting base wine.

Once the first fermentation has been carried out, does blending automatically obscure the characteristics of vineyard location? Robert Walters, a champion of terroir, argues that blending in Champagne, where the houses dominate the market, has always been a necessary expedient in the face of commercial realities. It's true that blending is a prerequisite for creating large, consistent brand volumes, but there's an element of special pleading in his argument that the region's best wines – 'every bit as great, as complex, as terroir rich, as delicious and moving as the finest Burgundies' – come from growers alone.

The author of *Champagne*, Peter Liem, makes the case for a strong link between blending and terroir, saying: 'terroir is no less important in a blended wine than in a single vineyard wine. What changes is its role.' He points out that vineyard sources are used specifically for their contrasting characteristics and the fine distinctions they can bring to the blend. Far from being a negation of terroir, blending in this way is, rather, an enhancement of it. Nyetimber's Brad Greatrix agrees: 'We like our vineyards to show through in our wines – since we work with 100 per cent estate-owned sites it's a way to ensure inimitable wines. Blending in and of itself needn't overwhelm terroir.'

Whether house or grower, an experienced producer understands the potential of specific sites to bring their varied characteristics to the blend. Discussing his various vineyards, Rodolphe Péters states that Le Mesnil is 'austere', Avize shows 'ripe citrus, candied citrus peel', Oger is 'elegant, white flowers, orange blossom, white pear' and Cramant shows 'creamy vanilla, cinnamon, saffron'. In the knowledge of the relative freshness of Cuis, the structure of Cramant and voluptuousness of Chouilly, the top Côte des Blancs grower, Didier Gimonnet, blends all three. Exton Park in Kent is a single vineyard on chalk, and while each cuvée blends different grape varieties, single parcels and a library of vintage reserves, for winemaker Corinne Seely, 'you always find in Exton Park an iodine taste, a saltiness'.

Recognizing vineyard origin through the prism of the sparkling wine process itself is more of a challenge. Even if we acknowledge that a greater focus on the vineyard is bringing a more precise sense of place to the wine, the question still arises: to what extent does the alchemical process by which base wine is transformed into liquid golden bubbles preserve the expression of terroir, if at all? Put more prosaically, is it possible to reconcile the many steps taken to influence flavour – among them autolysis, long lees-ageing and dosage with oak-aged wines or brandy – with an expression of place? And to what extent does the language of descriptors developed for the perception of bubble-related characteristics intrude on the expression of terroir?

In a world in which intervention in the vineyard and the cellar is increasingly seen as manipulation, it's easy to assume that less intervention leads to wines better placed to express their terroir. But since all wine processes involve an interpretation of the terroir of some sort – without the hand of man or woman there would be no expression of terroir – why should the second fermentation be the pantomime villain? In the view of Exton Park's Corinne Seely, 'I don't think that the second fermentation of sparkling wines in the bottle has any more impact on terroir flavours than the first alcoholic fermentation. It is likely that the terroir is even more pronounced in sparkling wine made from one terroir than in the *vin clair* – the still wine – it is made from.'

The purpose of the second fermentation is not simply to add bubbles for the sake of it but to bring complexity, depth, length and harmony. If it enhances subtlety and transparency in a wine, why should these characteristics not lead to recognition of the wine's origin and enhance the expression of place? Comparing the process with bâtonnage in Burgundy, Corinne Seely believes that autolysis, while bringing aroma, body, richness and texture, doesn't alter the provenance. For Mark Driver at Rathfinny in Sussex, 'the fundamentals of terroir – soil, microclimate and vineyard practices – are the key drivers for us. We try to practice low intervention and add nuances through malolactic fermentation and longer bottle ageing and let the fruit sing.'

So rather than the second fermentation detracting from a wine's terroir expression, the opposite, with the second fermentation helping to create a complete and fully expressive wine, is more likely to be the case. Compare a *vin clair* with the finished article. It's logical then to conclude that given the extent to which the DNA of the wine's origins is preserved in the sparkling wine process, the resulting fizz is indeed no less an authentic product of its terroir than any other wine. However much human input with all its complexities appears to be doing its best to disguise the vineyard location, in working in fact to interpret its identity as faithfully as possible, it allows us, the consumer, to identify and appreciate a good bubble when we taste it.

*

The year 2020 was Europe's warmest on record – and then came 2021. If you blinked, you may have missed Japan's cherry blossom season, the spring awakening, which peaked at its earliest date since records began 1,200 years ago. Perhaps you were not aware of the heat dome in Lytton, British Columbia that broke Canada's temperature record with a brutal high of 49.6°C, Sicily's record 48.8°C, Montoro in Spain's 47.4°C, or the catastrophic July flash floods that killed more than 170 people in western Germany, or the raging wildfires in Siberia, California, Greece, Turkey and Algeria, or that almost a year's worth of rain fell in Zhengzhou, China, in three days, leaving 51 dead. If only there were some sign of a climate crisis.

After an 11,000-year period of climate stability, planet Earth is warming up. Apart from the direct impact on precipitation and rainfall caused by the warming of the earth's atmosphere, climate change is also bringing with it more frequent extreme weather events: heatwaves, drought, wildfires, hurricanes, monsoons, flash floods, frost, hail and a significant rise in sea levels with all the catastrophic damage that such unpredictable extremes entail. It goes without saying that climate change is having knock-on effects for wine producers such as vine shutdown, a growing risk of fungal disease, sunburn and, most significant of all, disparities between the speed of the uptake of sugar and physiological ripeness.

An increase in potential alcohol and a corresponding decrease in acid levels will have long-term consequences for the flavour, freshness and longevity of sparkling wine. The key element of climate for fizz is the link between temperature and the ripening of the grapes used. A cool climate, preferably accompanied by a notable day and night temperature difference, is the prerequisite for encouraging the required development of natural acidity in the grape. In a cool climate, if the growing season between flowering and harvest is long enough, it allows the grapes to ripen to produce a base wine of between around 9.5–11.5 per cent alcohol. This base wine needs to have sufficient flavour and natural acidity to allow retention of freshness and balance following a second fermentation.

A common metric for the growing season temperature (GST) is to take the average temperature for the seven month growing season from spring to harvest. Typically, the average figure to qualify for very cool climate is between 13.5°C and 14.4°C, while between 14.5°C and 15.5°C is cool. The correlation between heat summation and vine development is subject to other influences, however. Frost or winter freezing where there's an average of below 0.5°C may rule out an area that might otherwise have potential. Additional factors include sunlight intensity, rainfall, humidity, soil moisture and, most relevant perhaps in the context of climate change, extremes of temperature. The effects of climate in any given location will vary according to the specifics of the location.

In climatic terms, the sparkling wine benchmark is Champagne, which, at 49°N, is at the margins for grape-growing. Like that of most sparkling wine regions, the climate is mainly maritime, thanks to the influence of the Atlantic, so summers are generally warm and rainfall is steady. At the same time, there is a continental climate influence, manifesting itself mainly in the potential for hard frosts, damaging hail and extreme heat spikes in the summer.

Over 300 years of sparkling wine history and today's multi-billion pound industry is predicated on the assumption that Champagne has the perfect climate for sparkling wine thanks to an average annual temperature of 10°C. Since the 1990s however, changes in the climate have accelerated. Harvests have been getting earlier. Natural alcohol has risen by 0.7 per cent by volume while total acidity has fallen by 1.3 grams per litre. The traditional period of 100 days between flowering and harvesting has reduced substantially over the past 70 years. Beginning around mid-September, the harvest is starting a week to three weeks earlier than at the end of the 1980s. Cyril Brun, Charles Heidsieck's chef de cave, recently warned that finding ways to preserve freshness in Champagne will be one of its biggest challenges. To conclude that climate change is an existential threat to Champagne is no exaggeration.

Due to earlier ripening and higher sugars induced by climate change, there's a growing trend towards the option of only partial malolactic fermentation or blocking malolactic altogether in order to retain the wine's natural backbone and freshness. Clover Hill in Tasmania, Graham Beck in the South African Cape's warm, sunny Robertson region, Colet in Spain, the Loire's Bouvet Ladubay, Ambriel in England and Gancia in Piemonte are among many who avoid malolactic fermentation to retain as much bright acidity in the wines as possible. Louis Roederer Champagne and Chapel Down in Kent are among another expanding group who, with acids in danger of becoming too low in warm years, will do a partial malolactic fermentation, depending on vintage conditions, to maintain freshness.

There is a school of thought too that suggests that a judicious amount of bitterness caused by an increase in tannins may compensate for the lower levels of acidity induced by climate change. In Cyril Brun's view, 'in the light of global warming, a higher level of ripe bitterness in warm vintages like 2005, 2006, 2009 and 2015, provides support to the acidity and helps with the ageing process'. In the case of his 2008 Charles Heidsieck Rosé for instance, he says 'you need a bit of positive bitterness to ensure length and ageing'. Moët & Chandon's Benoît Gouez makes a similar point when he says, in talking about vintages with low acidity like 2003, 'stylistically a winemaker can replace some acidity with bitterness'.

Responding to reduced day to night temperature differences in warmer summers, measures such as the use of new grape varieties and adapting the viticulture and the winemaking are being looked at. One region that has already added a new grape variety to the roster is

Franciacorta in Italy, where the ancient Erbamat grape was added to the Franciacorta Production Code in 2017 (and allowed up to 10 per cent in blends) for its distinct acidity. In Slovenia, the native Rumeni Plavec grape is being harnessed for its notable acidity and local distinction.

If climate change is 'the curse that keeps on taking', as Mark Carney, UN special envoy for climate action, has put it, there is a sense in which the alteration in climate also brings with it clouds with silver linings. As cold regions start to warm up, new regions or pockets of regions are emerging where extreme cold has become just about warm enough to ripen grapes for sparkling wine. Instead of spending sleepless nights worrying about getting enough sugar into the grapes and avoiding excessive acidity, today's vineyard manager is as likely to be having nightmares about the rapid accumulation of sugar at the expense of acidity.

A gradual change in climate has mitigated the strident acidity that once made English wine hard to love. After Peter Hall planted his Breaky Bottom vineyard in East Sussex in 1974, he struggled for years with adverse conditions. He says that the 1970s and 1980s were 'BAW: Bloody Awful Weather, rainy and cold, with difficult vintages producing small yields.' Into the 1990s and the twenty-first century, the climate changed for the better, from a vine growing perspective, and after 20 years of making still wines, in 1995 Peter made the successful leap from still wines to fizz. 'What the change has meant to viticulturalists,' says English wine expert Stephen Skelton MW, 'is that once marginal varieties – Pinot Noir and Chardonnay being the most widely planted – have suddenly started to move into the mainstream. Natural sugars have increased, acids are still high, but nowhere near as high as they were.'

Prosecco DOCG has experienced a similar phenomenon. The harvest has gradually crept forward and now takes place in mid to late September, sometimes earlier. Other Italian regions have looked to the skies. In Piemonte, sparkling wine producers have found a haven, if not heaven, in the high ground of Alta Langa. At altitudes of 250–500 metres or higher, Alta Langa today is recognized as the new *terra cognita* for Italian traditional method sparkling wine. At Soalheiro in Portugal, altitude has been key to coping with the current and future impact of climate change, with recent new plantings at 1,100 metres above sea level. In Spain, Cava producers such as Can Sala, Torres, Loxarel and Juvé & Camps, have found that by ascending to 700–900 metres in the highlands of Mediona and the foothills of the Pyrenees, they experience a longer growing season, which brings more freshness and vitality to their Cavas.

As Australia has found with Tasmania's maritime climate, proximity to the cold influence of the Southern Ocean is a significant factor in the development of vineyards suited to flavour accumulation with the necessary accompanying juicy acidity. Faced with the threat of heatwaves and forest wildfires, California's fizz producers have increasingly inched closer to oceanic influences to meet the challenge of climate change. On Canada's Atlantic seaboard east of Maine, Nova Scotia is one of the new frontiers of Canadian fizz thanks to the moderating influence of Atlantic saltwater breezes. A hot area such as Robertson in South Africa's Cape works for fizz thanks to the cooling breeze that blows up from the Breede River mouth at the Indian Ocean.

'Indicative' maps in Tom Stevenson and Essi Avellan's *World Encyclopedia of Champagne and Sparkling Wine* suggest that, with latitude, altitude and proximity to the oceans in mind, southern Chile and Argentina, parts of Bolivia and Lesotho, north-east Germany and large swaths of New Zealand's South Island could be the new frontiers of sparkling wine. I wouldn't rule out Argentina and Chile's Patagonia, or Ningxia in the central-north of China, or Japan's Yamagata or Hokkaido either. It's no coincidence that these two cold-climate prefectures in Japan's far north are already starting to produce some of the country's finest fizz.

MADEIRA VINEYARDS OLD AND NEW

In this 2022 excerpt from *Madeira: The islands and their wines*, Richard Mayson takes us on a guided tour, discovering the network of small vineyard holdings scattered across a rugged island whose land is increasingly given over to tourism, leisure pursuits and crops such as bananas.

There is, at long last, an official register or *cadastro* of vineyards on Madeira and Porto Santo. This has been a knotty problem ever since the *Instituto do Vinho da Madeira* (IVM now IVBAM) was established in 1979, but a visit to Madeira's vineyards will reveal just how intractable this problem is. IVBAM calculates that there are currently 455 hectares of vineyard on Madeira, of which an estimated 403 hectares are planted with grapes for the production of Madeira wine (2018 figures). This area is split between 1,940 growers taking the average size of a holding to just over 0.2 hectares. Yields are high and are not strictly controlled, the grapes swollen by regular irrigation from the *levadas*. However, the maximum yield permitted under the 2015 law is high at 150 hectolitres per hectare. In practice, yields are often considerably higher with some vineyards attaining yields of 200 hectolitres per hectare. Under the law, IVBAM is permitted to alter the maximum yield according to climatic conditions and the potential quality of the grape musts. In 2020, a year when just 271.39 hectares were declared for the production of Madeira wine (this was the year of the Covid pandemic) the total production was 3,650,510 kilos.

At just under 10 hectares in extent, much the largest vineyard on the island belongs to the shipper Henriques & Henriques. Although many of the shippers owned vineyards in the nineteenth century (for example, Leacock's São João), most subsequently disposed of their holdings and relied increasingly on an army of individual growers. With the grapes pressed in *lagares* on site and transported to Funchal as grape must, the shippers came to exercise very little control over the quality of the fruit. Today Justino's, the largest shipper in terms of volume, buys grapes from over 700 growers. For most of these farmers, grape growing is a secondary occupation. In recent years the shippers have been working much more closely with growers to improve the quality of their grapes. The shippers employ their own agents in the outlying villages to coordinate the harvest and help small farmers during the growing season. A computer system can trace the contents of any one wine back to the individual grower. In 2012 the Madeira Wine Company took another big step forward when they leased two vineyards (together amounting to nearly 7 hectares) on the north side of the island in order to secure more white grapes. They are also managing just under a hectare of vineyard now planted entirely with white grapes belonging to Andrew Blandy at Quinta da Santa Luzia in Funchal.

Vineyards on Madeira have been cultivated in much the same way for hundreds of years. Older vineyards are supported on *latadas*, low pergolas about a metre or so in height, under which other crops such as potatoes, cabbages and beans are frequently grown. Frequent summer irrigation and the application of fertilizers to the horticultural crops below the canopy serves to increase yields and debases the quality of the grapes. Apart from the fact that metal or timber supports have replaced bamboo, the following eighteenth-century description of a typical Madeiran vineyard would apply today: 'one or more walks a yard or two wide, intersect each vineyard ... Along these walks, which are arched over by lathes about seven feet high, they erect wooden pillars at regular distances to support a lattice work of bamboos, which slopes down from both sides of the walk, till it is only a foot and a half or two feet high, in which elevation it extends over the whole vineyard. The vines are in this manner supported from the ground, and the people have room to root out the weeds which spring up between them. In the season of the vintage they creep under this lattice-work, cut off the grapes, and lay them into baskets: some of the bunches of these grapes that I saw weighed six pounds upwards.' On the north side of the island it used to be common to train vines up chestnut trees, just as in the Minho region of northern Portugal. On Madeira this practice died out with oidium in the mid-nineteenth century.

Most of Madeira's vineyards are planted on *poios*, the small terraces with retaining stone walls often constructed centuries ago. When the vines are in leaf, the terracing is hardly visible. Looking upwards at the huge slope of vines at Estreito de Câmara de Lobos, the houses appear to be surrounded by one giant canopy. Although the *latada* system seems to suit some varieties (Malvasia Cândida, for example), many of the vineyards planted since the 1990s are trained on to vertical cordons (referred to locally as *espaldeira*). These vineyards are laid out at a much higher density (typically 4,600–5,200 plants per hectare as opposed to 2,500–3,000 in traditional vineyards), tend to be larger in size and are much easier to cultivate. They also lend themselves to producing riper grapes for unfortified wines. However the *latada* system helps to maximize exposure to the sun on the cooler north side of the island as well as increasing aeration and reducing erosion. On vertiginous slopes, some of which at Seixal (see below) have an inclination of 65 per cent, the *latada* is the only practical way to cultivate. However, some producers feel that *vinha latada* leads to a loss of concentration in the wines.

Where are the vineyards?

This is a question asked by many a visitor to Madeira. The answer is that until as recently as the 1960s, many of the finest wine grapes were grown in the western outskirts of Funchal and in nearby Câmara de Lobos. Pico de São João (St John's Hill), São Martinho, Santo António and São Roque were all important grape producing areas, noted primarily for the quality of their predominantly sweet wines. Vizetelly describes Leacock's São João as being about 13 acres in extent in the late 1870s, and supported like modern vineyards on horizontal wires. He also describes São Martinho as 'an important viticultural district yielding a high class wine with a fine bouquet'. São Martinho frequently appeared on bottles of fine nineteenth-century vintages. One of the island's leading nineteenth-century vineyards was at Quinta Stanford, just above the modern day Pestana Miramar Hotel where the Rua Dr Pitta now runs. At nearby Ribeiro Secco, Vizetelly mentions a vineyard belonging to the sherry shippers Messrs Davies planted with Palomino (Listrão). Richard Davies owned the famous Quinta Vigia most of which was demolished in the early 1970s to build the Casino Park Hotel. As the city of Funchal has grown these vineyards have been taken over piecemeal by modern hotels, housing and warehousing. One of the last historic plots of Terrantez disappeared as recently as 1999 under Madeira

Shopping, the island's largest shopping centre, close to São Martinho. Vizetelly states that the vineyards of Santo António 'usually yield a good wine'. Although a few small plots of vines can still be found cheek by jowl with houses around Santo António and Virtudes, at 0.89 hectares the largest vineyard in Funchal today is surprisingly close to the city centre at Quinta de Santa Luzia. The entire Funchal municipality now has just under 3 hectares of vineyard.

To the west of Funchal, the former fishing village of Câmara de Lobos (or Cama de Lobos as it was once known) is reputed to be the site of Madeira's first vineyards. The Pico de Torre above the town was once the centre of the huge Torre Bella estate, which once extended along the south coast as far as Arco de Calheta. Vizetelly describes the scene as 'a fertile hollow, formerly covered with vines which yielded one of the finest and most robust Madeira growths' and goes on to say how phylloxera destroyed nearly all the vineyards and that they were replaced by sugar cane. The Torre Bella estate was broken up after the 1974 revolution and much of the best vineyard land around Câmara de Lobos has either been built on or given over to bananas. There are still one or two small plots of well-tended vineyard at the top of Pico da Torre (beside the *miradouro*), but banana plantations have largely colonized the agricultural *poios* above Câmara de Lobos up to about 200 metres above sea level.

Most of the island's vineyards (around 180 hectares) are now to be found at higher altitudes around Estreito de Câmara de Lobos. The principal grape variety here is Tinta Negra but there are small plots of Boal and Verdelho in the deep sheltered valleys of Marinheira, Vargem, and Jesus Maria José. Henriques & Henriques have some Terrantez and Malvasia Cândida visible from the *Via Rapida* (expressway) at Ribeira de Caixa below Estreito. Above Estreito, Quinta das Romeiras is one of the larger estates to remain intact, belonging to the Araújo family. Vineyards on the south side of the island are found up to an altitude of 800 metres, some of the highest being at Jardim da Serra above Estreito where some of the best Sercial is still grown.

At the foot of Cabo Girão just to the west of Câmara de Lobos is one of Madeira's most historic vineyards, Fajã dos Padres. The result of a huge rock fall from a 300-metre cliff, the *fajã* was only accessible by sea until a rather precarious lift was built down the cliff side in 1984. It was once the property of the Jesuits and the chapel became the *adega*. The 9 hectare Fajã dos Padres is now a tourist destination in its own right with a beach bar and a cluster of self-catering holiday cottages. Tropical fruit

Picking Malvasia Cândida at the famous Fajã dos Padres vineyard on the south coast of Madeira

is the principal crop but there is still a small vineyard capable of producing some of the best Malvasia Cândida on the island as well as a small quantity of Terrantez, both of which are bought by Barbeito.

Above Cabo Girão, Quinta Grande is one of the most fertile parts of the island, where vines mingle with vegetables and other crops. Above the old main road (EN 229) at Ribeira do Escrivão is Madeira's largest single vineyard with 10 hectares of vines belonging to wine shippers Henriques & Henriques. This looks very different to any other vineyard on the island, having been laid out by Miguel Corte Real, a viticulturalist working for the Port shipper Cockburn on the mainland. The terraces, which have been bulldozed from the hillside, resemble those of the Douro and are known as *patamares*. Rising up to 750 metres above sea level, the vineyard is mostly planted with Verdelho and Sercial, but in cool years even these varieties struggle to ripen. Henriques & Henriques have recently had more success with Terrantez.

Travelling west and staying above the jagged coastline is Campanário, described by Vizetelly as 'not so important as Cama de Lobos' but 'yielding a wine of even higher character – less powerful, but altogether more refined in flavour and bouquet'. He goes on to conclude that in 'our judgement the best Campanário growths surpass the more generally prized Cama de Lobos vintages by reason of their greater delicacy of flavour and more fragrant bouquet'. Despite this, I have come across very few wines with Campanário on the label. Today Campanário is home to a few good Boal vineyards; a plot can be seen below the church and immediately above the road tunnel that now takes the *via rapida* from Funchal to Ribeira Brava. Nearby Caldeira (meaning 'boiler') is, as its name suggests, very warm and productive. These are among the first vineyards to be harvested, usually in late August.

There are few vineyards on the south coast between Ribeira Brava and Ponta do Sol, much of which is too steep for agriculture, and the coastal zone around Lugar de Baixo and Madelena do Mar is mostly given over to bananas which are reputed to be the best on the island. At Arco de Calheta, so called because of the natural amphitheatre facing south-east and out to sea, bananas form the dominant crop with just a few vineyards in between, and some very good Bual is grown here. Sadly, many of the growers around here are getting old and are not being succeeded, leading to a future shortage of Bual with more land being given over to building.

Above Calheta (between Arco de Calheta and Estreito de Calheta) are some of Madeira's best individual vineyards, planted on the well-exposed *lombos* (literally 'loins') or headlands that slope down from the south-easterly flank of the Paúl da Serra. Plots of vines on Lombo do Doutor, Lombo do Salão, Lombo das Laranjeiras, Lombo dos Reis and Lombo dos Serrões produce good grapes, particularly Bual. The narrow Santa Catarina valley nearby produces both grapes and sugar cane. There is a distillery on the coast at Calheta that still produces the *aguadente de cana* (sugar cane brandy) that used to fortify Madeira wine.

One of the five government-run experimental vineyards can be found at the appropriately named Quinta das Vinhas at Estreito de Calheta. Over a hundred grape varieties can be found here, including foreign varietals such as Cabernet Sauvignon, Merlot, Chardonnay and Chenin Blanc as well as indigenous Portuguese grapes and varieties from Madeira and the Canaries.

West of Jardim do Mar, the island is too cool and windswept for bananas but there are plots of cereals, vegetables and vines. Vineyards at Raposeira and Fajã de Ovelha, 400 to 600 metres or so above Paúl do Mar, produce some of the best Verdelho. Sercial used to be grown on Fajã Grande and Fajã Pequena but these narrow coastal platforms have now been abandoned. However, the land around Ponta do Pargo is relatively level compared to the rest of the island and used to be valued

Terraced latada *vineyards at São Vicente in spring time*

for its Sercial. The area is still intensively cultivated, producing apples, sweet potatoes and cereals. There is a relatively new and well-tended vineyard, close to the lighthouse below Ponta do Pargo, that serves as a minor mecca for the tourists who make the two-hour journey from Funchal to visit the most westerly point on the island. Disappointingly, for those like me who enjoy the traditional Madeira countryside, work began in the 2000s on a huge golf course in this area.

With the decline in viticulture on the south of the island, the valley of São Vicente, immediately north of Ribeira Brava, is now second only to Estreito de Câmara de Lobos as the main area for grape growing, with 140 hectares. This whole area has been given new economic impetus by the construction in 2000 of a road tunnel under Encumeada linking the north coast with the south, and putting São Vicente within a forty-minute drive of Funchal. Vineyards on the lava slopes around the communities of Ginjas, Feiteiras, Lameiros and Lanço above the town of São Vicente are extremely productive. Ninety-five per cent of the production is Tinta Negra but there is also a small and increasing quantity of Verdelho (14.57 hectares at the last count). Although sheltered from the northerly wind, the area is considerably cooler than on the south side of the island and there are few vineyards above 350 metres.

The village of Seixal, west of São Vicente on the north coast, has the steepest and most spectacular vineyards on the island, like hanging gardens cascading into the sea. Seixal is known for Sercial (7.03 hectares), whereas the adjacent communities of Ribeira da Janela and Porto Moniz traditionally grew Verdelho (11.1 hectares) although there now are much larger quantities of the direct producers (mostly Jacquet). The vineyards at Porto Moniz, the most north-westerly point on the island, are a patchwork of tiny plots sheltered from the north winds by windbreaks made from *urze* or brushwood. However, one of the best tended vineyards on the island can be found at Lamaceiros; 3 hectares belonging to Manuel Ramos Lucas. Here, direct producers have been replaced by Verdelho.

The villages east of São Vicente towards Santana still produce large quantities of American hybrid grapes (again mostly Jacquet). With the exception of the steep sided and rather dank valley of Boaventura (still mostly planted with direct producers, mostly Herbemont), many of these vineyards have been either abandoned or replaced with European *vinifera* varieties. There is an impressive new 5-hectare vineyard on *patamares* at Ponta Delgada producing Verdelho and Arnsburger, as well as Cabernet Sauvignon and Merlot. At Arco de São Jorge there is an experimental vineyard with a number of different clones of Malvasia and Verdelho. There is also a small wine museum in the centre of the village next to the rose garden. Further west, the towns of São Jorge and Santana are the source of Malvasia de São Jorge (34.17 hectares), the principal variant of Malvasia growing on Madeira. The largest vineyard here is Quinta do Bispo, a property belonging to the church, at São Jorge. This has been leased by the Madeira Wine Company who have planted 4.5 hectares of Malvasia de São Jorge, Verdelho and Sercial, partly on newly constructed *patamares*. At nearby Achada do Gramacha between São Jorge and Santana the MWC have 2 hectares of organically grown Sercial and Verdelho at Quinta do Furão. This relatively flat clifftop vineyard was initially developed by the MWC in the early 1980s but was sold off in 1993. A small hotel was subsequently developed on the site and the vineyard was leased back again in 2012, as the Blandy family took a strategic decision to take greater control from the grape to the bottle.

Historically there have been few vineyards in the east side of the island although Henry Vizetelly describes a visit to a 4-acre vineyard (mostly Verdelho) at Santa Cruz belonging to Messrs Krohn in the 1870s. Today the municipalities of Santa Cruz and Machico claim just 2 and 10 hectares of vineyard respectively. The climate becomes progressively arid as you near Ponta de São Lourenço and historically was considered much less suitable for viticulture which explains Vizetelly's comment about the wines being 'light' and of 'fair quality'. However, with the recent fashion for unfortified wines, a number of new vineyards have been planted here. A 6-hectare vineyard at Caniçal in the Machico municipality (clearly visible from the plane shortly before landing at Santa Catarina airport) has been planted with Touriga Nacional, Touriga Franca, Trincadeira, Merlot and Cabernet Sauvignon, varieties which are better suited to the relatively warm, dry climate.

Grapes from the island of Porto Santo have always been included in Madeira wine and were once favoured by winemakers due to their high natural sugar content. But due to long-term shortage of water, coastal development and the cost of transport, vineyards have been largely abandoned. There are still a few vines growing in the sand at Vila Baleira and in the centre of the island where there is a government-funded experimental vineyard. A large area of vineyard was lost with the construction of the airport runway in 1960 which, having subsequently been extended, covers much of the central part of the island. Porto Santo is known for the white Listrão grape, the same variety as Palomino.

THE *CRUS* OF CHABLIS

This chapter, from *The wines of Chablis and the Grand Auxerrois*, by Rosemary George MW (2019), offers a detailed description of all the *crus* of Chablis, explaining how minute differences in soil and geography can lead to notable variations in the way the Chardonnay grape expresses itself in the region's wines.

The vineyards of Burgundy are based on terroir, on the minute differences between one plot of land and the adjoining plot. The aspect, the altitude, gradient or soil composition may be slightly different, offering an explanation as to why, for example, in Chablis, Blanchots will never taste like Les Clos, or Vaillons resemble Mont de Milieu. The permutations are infinite, and it has to be said that the differences can be blurred by the wine grower's own individual talent and preferences in vineyard and cellar, where considerations such as *élevage*, yields and age of the vines come into play. Younger vines tend to produce softer wines as the root system is not so well developed, whereas wine from old vines will have more concentration. I must admit that I am more able to distinguish between the wine style of Domaine Raveneau and Domaine des Malandes than between a Vaillons and a Montmains, or a Vaudésir and a Preuses. However, those who have lived and breathed Chablis all their lives can see the parameters that define and separate the various *crus*. For the less initiated, a comprehensive tasting with one of the growers or *négociants* whose portfolio contains a full range of Chablis, such as Louis Michel or William Fèvre, also offers some guidelines.

The *grands crus*
The seven *grands crus* of Chablis are grouped together on one slope just

outside the town, totalling about 100 hectares in total. The river Serein runs along the foot of the hill and in broad terms the aspect of the vineyards is south-west. The altitude varies from 130 metres for the vineyards at the bottom of the slope, rising to about 220–230 metres at the top, below the trees. The *grands crus* are the wines with most concentration, the firmest structure and the greatest potential for longevity. The difference between a *grand cru* and a *premier cru* should be immediately apparent in the mouth.

Les Clos, with 26 hectares, and some twenty owners, is the largest of the *grands crus* and is generally considered to be the most long-lasting, with the firmest structure, a steely backbone and a fine concentration of fruit – in other words, as more than one grower said, a more masculine wine. A firm backbone of structure is essential and that also allows the wines to respond well to an *élevage* in oak. Not surprisingly, there are soil variations within the 26 hectares. Chez Drouhin has two plots of Les Clos, one with stony soil at the top of the slope and one with a high clay content at the bottom of the hill. For Benoît Droin, Les Clos is 'le plus grand, le plus puissant, le plus minéral', in short, 'un grand vin'.

The smallest domaine *grand cru* is Grenouilles, which consists of 9 hectares. La Chablisienne controls the lion's share, with just over 7 hectares, including the 2-hectare plot of Vieilles Vignes attached to the Château de Grenouilles. The other owners include Jean-Paul and Benoît Droin, Daniel Defaix, Raoul Gautherin, A. Régnard and Domaine Testut. Cyril Testut's 32 ares give him just 2,000 bottles in a good year. The vineyards face south, but are not especially steep, and it is the vineyard closest to the Serein. Indeed, the name may well originate from the noisy frogs in the river. As for taste, in comparison with Les Clos, it is easier and more accessible, with an underlying charm. Benoît Droin described it as rich and *gourmand*, not especially mineral, but ripe, 'un grand aimable'.

Valmur, with 13 hectares, tends to be fuller and more concentrated. It is situated next to Les Clos, with the Kimmeridgian soil giving density and freshness. Samuel Billaud talked about the *droiture* of Valmur, while Benoît Droin described it as masculine and more closed.

Vaudésir, in contrast, is more elegant, more aromatic than Les Clos. It comprises 14 hectares, on the higher part of the slope of the *grands crus*, between Valmur and Preuses and is situated in quite an enclosed valley, with vineyards facing both north and south. For Benoît, it is the

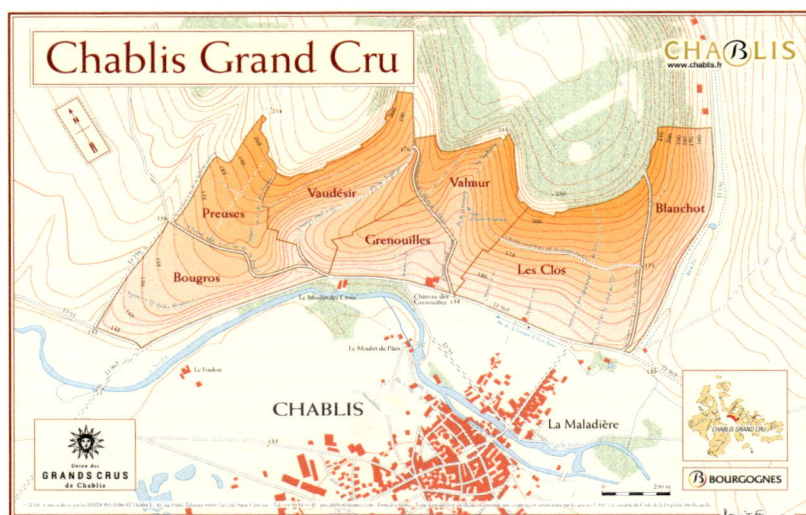

quintessence of a warm valley, that accentuates its amiability. At Domaine William Fèvre they have 1.20 hectares just next to La Moutonne, in the heart of the amphitheatre, facing south. The grapes ripen early but the wine ages well, becoming more expressive with age. At Domaine Louis Michel they have two plots, one on each side of the valley and Guillaume Michel can observe the differences, with the south-facing slope making for riper wines, but always retaining freshness.

Preuses is the epitome of elegance, with 11 hectares. Domaine William Fèvre is the largest owner, with 2.5 hectares, in two plots, one on a steep slope that faces south-east, which gives minerality to the wine, while the other, in a flatter area, with deeper clay soil, provides the richness to complement the minerality. Preuses should be *fin, elegant, aérien*. Vincent Dauvissat talked about sucking the pebbles of Preuses, not any old pebbles, but *des cailloux soyeux*, silky pebbles, that give a sensation of minerality.

Logically La Moutonne, the 2.35-hectare plot that includes land in both Preuses and Vaudésir, combines the qualities of both, with an underlying elegance.

Bougros, the *grand cru* nearest to the village of Fontenay-près-Chablis, is a 12-hectare vineyard, with steep slopes facing west, so that it can be quite frost prone. Half of Bougros is cultivated by Domaine William Fèvre, with two separate plots. They have 4 hectares on the plateau, with deep soil, which makes for richness as well as freshness in the wine, and 2 hectares that face due south on a very steep slope by the river, that they call the Côte de Bouguerots. For Didier Seguier, this is one of the great terroirs of Chablis. Here the grapes ripen later, and again the two plots complement each other, so that the underlying style is quite rich and rounded. Plain Bougros seems softer in comparison. Didier Defaix contrasts the more powerful Bougros with the elegance of Vaudésir.

At the other end of the slope, next to Les Clos, the 12 hectares of Blanchots (of which Domaine Laroche owns four) with soil consisting mainly of clay and marl, make more feminine and elegant wines, yet with a firm backbone. The clay soil retains water, so the vines here fare better than most in a hot summer.

The *premiers crus*

In broad terms the *premiers crus* can be distinguished as to whether they are on the right bank, and adjacent to the slope of the *grands crus*, or on the left bank and facing the *grands crus* across the valley. For Edouard Vocoret the wines of the right bank, even the village Chablis, are fatter and more rounded, whereas the Chablis of the left bank are more citrus, sharper, *ciselé*.

Then there are the newer, outlying *premiers crus*, that are further from the heart of the vineyards. Another generalization came from Jérôme Garnier that the wines in the northern part of the appellation are softer, with more clay, whereas the vineyards of the south with more limestone, make for more incisive wines. He thinks it is easier to obtain riper grapes in the north, making for more *gourmand* wine, but that is all relative. Chablis will never ever be as *gourmand* as the wines of the Côte d'Or and it will always retain a memory of the sea with saline, iodine notes.

The right-bank vineyards are Montée de Tonnerre and Mont de Milieu, to the east of the *grands crus*, with Vaucoupin closer to the village of Chichée, and Fourchaume to the north-west of the *grands crus*, stretching towards Maligny.

Separated from the *grands crus* by the narrow road leading to Fyé, Montée de Tonnerre includes the rarely seen Pied d'Aloup and Côte de Bréchain, as well as Chapelot, which is at its most expressive in the hands of Isabelle Raveneau. It has a very similar aspect to the *grands crus*, with more weight, depth and power than the *premiers crus* on the opposite side of the valley. It can be quite austere in its youth, but essentially it is considered to represent elegance and minerality. Samuel Billaud called it *le petit grand cru*, or *le grand premier cru*, with its southeast aspect, just like Les Clos.

Mont de Milieu is inevitably compared with Montée de Tonnerre. Lilian Duplessis has just taken over a plot of Mont de Milieu, which he thought would have the depth of Montée de Tonnerre, but in fact he finds it more *aérien* and floral, and more akin to Vaillons than to Montée de Tonnerre. Philippe Rossignol from Régnard considers Mont de Milieu to be more masculine, whereas Fourchaume has elegance. For Hervé Tucki of La Chablisienne, with a south-facing plot with one of the best aspects of Chablis, Mont de Milieu is steely and incisive, with energy. Samuel Billaud has three different plots of Mont de Milieu, two that are 70 years old, at the top and the bottom of the slope, and in the middle, a plot of 35-year-old vines. They are picked at different times, and although there are nuances of difference, the wines are blended into one cuvée.

Fourchaume is the very largest of the *premiers crus*, significantly bigger than the whole slope of the *grands crus*, totalling at least 130 hectares, with more than thirty producers. Exact figures of ownership are difficult, as more than one member of the same family may own the vines of a particular estate. Fourchaume extends from the road to Fontenay along the valley slope towards Maligny. The soil is deeper than in some vineyards, and the wines may have less ageing potential. There are several other names that come under the all-encompassing umbrella name of Fourchaume, namely Vaupulent, Côte de Fontenay and L'Homme Mort. Vaulorent too, on the other side of the road to Fontenay, is grouped under Fourchaume. Fourchaume tends to be quite supple; Gérard Tremblay talked of white flowers, while for Hervé Tucki it is the epitome of finesse.

Adhémar Boudin was the first to separate his L'Homme Mort from his Fourchaume. L'Homme Mort is close to Maligny, whereas the heart of Fourchaume is near Fontenay, and the soil is different; L'Homme Mort is very stony, and the vines are at a slightly higher altitude, and on steeper slopes whereas there is more clay in Fourchaume. Others have since followed Adhémar's example, with L'Homme Mort now produced by Jean Durup, La Chablisienne and Yvon Vocoret, among others. Francis Boudin, Adhémar's son, explained the difference that he sees between the two wines: Fourchaume is more supple and feminine, while L'Homme Mort is more mineral, with more *pierre à fusil*, and requires bottle age.

For Didier Seguier, the best part of Fourchaume is Vaulorent, as it touches Preuses and has the same aspect as Vaudésir, and consequently more power than most Fourchaume. The soil is different, with Fourchaume and Vaulorent looking at each other from opposite sides of the road to Fontenay, and they get the sun at different times. Hervé Tucki would agree, as would Guillaume Michel, for whom Vaulorent has more weight and concentration. Vaulorent and Montée de Tonnerre would be the two *premiers crus* that most resemble a *grand cru*, with concentration and structure, whereas Fourchaume has a 'côté charmeur' for Thomas Ventoura.

In Fourchaume particularly there is an infinite variation in winemaking styles. In the autumn of 2005, in an attempt to see whether I could discern a common thread between the wines, I blind tasted 27 examples of Fourchaume from the 2002 vintage. I have to say that I failed dismally. The variations were infinite: some were oaky to a lesser or greater degree; some were beginning to develop mature notes of gunflint, with varying amounts of minerality and acidity; some were more developed than others and the best were taut and finely crafted. As Claude Roy observed, some people throw themselves on Fourchaume, because it is called Fourchaume, but there is no single style of Fourchaume; it is simply too big. In contrast, some of the smaller *crus* are much more homogeneous in character and taste.

On the opposite bank Vaillons and Montmains are the two most important *crus*, situated on adjoining slopes, with Côte de Léchet towering above the village of Milly. Montmains stretches from Chablis to Courgis and also includes Forêt and Butteaux. With stonier soil, it tends to be more powerful and complex than Vaillons, certainly in the hands of Guillaume Michel, who is particularly enthusiastic about Butteaux. There is more clay in the soil, which gives balance and power. Laurent Pinson observed that although his Forêt vineyard is only 100 metres from his Montmains vines, the soil is quite different, with white chalky marl. Chez Pinson they always separate Forêt from Montmains – Forêt has more limestone, and Montmains more clay, and in the glass Montmains is firm and mineral while Forêt is richer and more rounded. Vincent Dauvissat is also one of the principal exponents of Forêt, seeing it as more introverted and more discreet on the nose than Montmains, with minerality and length.

Didier Seguier contrasted Butteaux with Montmains, observing that Montmains has elegance while Butteaux has power and structure.

At William Fèvre they have 3.5 hectares of Montmains, in all three *climats*, and Didier can see the differences – Forêt gives elegance, Montmains richness and Butteaux, which is later ripening, freshness and minerality. A blend of the three makes for a wine that is nicely rounded, with good structure from Butteaux. Originally at Louis Michel they did not separate the various *climats* of Montmains, but Guillaume finds them very different, so they now make Butteaux and Forêt as well as Montmains. The 2016 Montmains has an underlying richness, the character of the vintage, while Forêt is firmer and more intense and Butteaux quite austere, with considerable ageing potential. Forêt has a lot of limestone, while Butteaux has more clay, so is more *costaud*. 'Pour les amateurs de Chablis' (for those who really love Chablis), suggested Guillaume.

Vaillons is inevitably compared with its neighbour, Montmains, and can also be compared with Fourchaume, with Olivier Savary observing that Fourchaume, is 'la danseuse avec elegance, qui arrive en finesse', the elegant dancer, whereas fuller-bodied Vaillons with matière, is 'le paysan avec sabots', the peasant in clogs. The vineyards are stony, with clay, making for the minerality and elegance that are its hallmark. For Samuel Billaud, Montmains is more austere, whereas Vaillons is more flattering. Vaillons includes other vineyards, Les Lys, Sécher, Les Epinottes, Roncières, Châtains, Beugnons and Mélinots. For Samuel, Sécher is the most *tendu* or taut part of Vaillons, the Montée de Tonnerre of the left bank.

Chez Louis Michel, Guillaume has separated Sécher from Vaillons since 2010, finding Vaillons more *solaire*, while Sécher has more finesse, with more Kimmeridgian. At Vincent Dauvissat you can also compare Sécher with Vaillons itself. For Vincent, his Sécher is simpler, and characterized by its *nervosité*, while his Vaillons comes from deeper clay soil and is less nervous, and more demonstrative. Others say that Vaillons is more floral and Montmains more mineral, for the white clay gives acidity, length and minerality. However, for Benoît Droin, Vaillons can be either mineral or floral. For Romain Collet, Montmains is always more *vif*, coming from cooler vineyards, whereas Vaillons is warmer and the soil has more clay. Vaillons is their largest *cru* and they make all the *climats* except Les Lys. Domaine Daniel Dampt cultivates 5 of the 16 hectares of Les Lys, and other owners include Long Depaquit and William Fèvre. Daniel Defaix is the most enthusiastic exponent of Les Lys, considering it the best of the *premiers crus*. The kings of France drank Les Lys, hence its name, and Daniel observed that 'the *grands crus* may earn you money, but are not necessarily the best', adding that his grandfather always said that *premier cru* Chablis aged better than *grand cru* Chablis.

Vaillons is also compared with Côte de Léchet, the steep vineyard which dominates the village of Milly. It is a challenging slope to climb, as

I found when I walked up it one sunny June day, for a picnic at the top, with the roofs of Milly at my feet. There are differences in the soil; on the Côte de Léchet it is very poor limestone and you can see nothing but pebbles. Côte de Léchet once belonged to the monks of Pontigny and has more weight, so that it ages well. It tends to be warmer than Vaillons. Fabien Dauvissat talked of the weight and balance of Côte de Léchet, with the hallmark of elegance, whereas Vaillons is tighter and firmer.

Fourneaux, a relatively recent *premier cru* which was planted in the 1980s, on a very steep south-facing slope, above Mont de Milieu, is the *premier cru* of Fleys. For Lucie Thiéblemont at Domaine Charly Nicolle, the effects of the warm microclimate come out in the wine. The name Fourneaux derives from *four* or oven and the soil is mainly clay, so that the wines are richer, with less tension, than neighbouring Mont de Milieu. Samuel Billaud described it as more *gourmand*, the most flattering. For Eve Grossot it comes between Mont de Milieu and Vaucoupin in style. It is richer and more expressive, with less acidity than some, and ready earlier than Mont de Milieu. Vaucoupin too, is on a steep (55 per cent) south-west facing slope, between Fleys and Chichée, where mechanization is well-nigh impossible. The site has very stony soil, with clay and limestone, and a sunny aspect, and the wine is generally elegant, with a fresh acidity, and good ageing potential.

Vosgros and Vaugiraut are adjoining *premiers crus* outside Chichée. Vosgros comprises 15 hectares in a semicircle with an aspect varying between full south and due west; the soil is rich with oyster shells and the wine has a mineral elegance and good structure, while Vaugiraut is broader and richer. Cécile Gueguen observed that the subsoil of Chichée can make you think of wood, when none has been used. That was certainly the case with her Vaucoupin, which was more restrained than the concentrated Vosgros. Vosgros is very saline and needs time.

Beauroy, which also encompasses Côte de Savant and Troême, is a 40-hectare *cru* in the valley between Poinchy and Beine. It is generally considered to be softer and lower in acidity than the other *premiers crus*, and needs to be picked at the beginning of the vintage or it becomes too heavy. For Denis Pommier there is more clay in the soil, and consequently it is less elegant than Côte de Léchet. Margaux Laroche of Domaine d'Henri considers Troême the best part of Beauroy, which they share with Laurent Tribut, Domaine Grossot and Denis Pommier. It is tiny, just 1.32 hectares of south-facing vines, on white marl, giving floral, sunny wines, which are ready to drink relatively early.

Vau, which features as part of the name of several of the newer *premiers crus*, means a valley. So there is Vaudevey, in a valley outside Beine, along with Vau Ragons and adjoining Vauligneau, which is a long, south-east facing valley owned principally by the wine growers of Beine, namely the Michaut family, Louis Moreau, Alain Geoffroy and members of La Chablisienne. Thierry Hamelin made a colourful comparison between Vauligneau and Beauroy: Vauligneau is a lady dressed in silk, while Beauroy is much more 'sportif, un rugbyman'!

Vaudevey, which is in quite a cold, narrow valley, was abandoned after phylloxera struck as the slopes were so steep and difficult to work. Planting began again in 1978 and Jean Durup, who had 15 hectares, the largest holding, has recently sold 7 hectares, which have been divided among ten younger growers, in most cases allowing them to make their first ever *premier cru*. The wine is generally quite floral in character and considered to be one of the lighter of the *premiers crus*.

Beauregards, with white clay, situated between the villages of Courgis and Chitry, and Côte de Cuissy, a steep slope at 300 metres above the village of Courgis, are also recent additions to the list of *premiers crus*. Both are quite floral in style, and Beauregards has good acidity. Côte de Jouan, near Préhy, was a vineyard before the Second World War, and was planted again in the 1970s. The soil is predominantly clay and the wine more floral and feminine than some of the more established *crus*.

There is no doubt that there are discernible differences between the various *crus*, but those differences can be distinctly blurred by the individual wine growers' practices and preferences. Maybe the last word should go to Vincent Dauvissat who observed, 'il faut savoir qu'on a des terroirs grandioses et de les mettre en valeur' – we have to realize that we have the most wonderful terroirs and know how to make the very best of them.

PRINCIPAL CÔTE D'OR VINEYARDS

The vineyards of the Côte d'Or stretch for little more than 30 miles, from the outskirts of Dijon in the north to just south of Santenay, but the area is complex and heterogenous. In 2017's *Côte D'Or*, Raymond Blake provided this demystification and assessment of the most important vineyards of the region

For many people, their mind's eye picture of the Côte d'Or stretches from Gevrey-Chambertin, the first commune that is home to *grand cru* vineyards, to the last, Chassagne-Montrachet. Until recently this was a safe mental attenuation, lopping off the northern and southern country cousins and not paying much heed either to some others in between, such as Prémeaux-Prissey or Saint-Romain. Not a lot was lost in the process and memory space could be reserved for the wines that really mattered. Such an exercise today would be ludicrous, ruling out a host of yet to be celebrated vineyards at the northern and southern extremities of the côte as well as others in between.

A brief overview of the vineyards, running from north to south, begins in the outskirts of Dijon, whose urban sprawl has engulfed land that was previously home to the vine. The first vineyards are in Chenôve, though it is at Marsannay-la-Côte that the shopping centres and light-industrial zones segue into unbroken vineyard. The slopes are gentle here and, as yet, there are no *premiers crus*, a situation that may change in the future if current efforts to get a proportion of vineyards upgraded are successful. Some producers already use *lieu-dit* names such as Longeroies, probably Marsannay's best site,

Clos du Roy, which lies in the Chenôve commune, and Es Chézots, which is noted as much for how it should be spelt (Les Echézeaux, Echézots) as for the quality of its wine. Other communes seeking to have vineyards upgraded include Nuits-Saint-Georges, Pommard and Saint-Romain, but however strong their claims I believe Marsannay's is strongest.

Continuing south through Couchey, which is included in the Marsannay appellation, we come to Fixin, whose handful of *premiers crus* are the highest in the commune, all lying above 300 metres and abutting the forest. In total they amount to about 20 hectares and the remaining 100-plus hectares qualify for the Fixin or Côte de Nuits-Villages appellations. The best known of the *premiers crus* is Les Hervelets, a *climat* that includes the *lieux-dits* of Le Meix-Bas and, confusingly, Les Arvelets. The latter may be made as a separate wine but this is seldom done; Hervelets is the name to look for.

Sandwiched between Fixin and Gevrey-Chambertin is Brochon, whose band of southerly vineyards is included in the Gevrey appellation. The best known are Les Evocelles and Les Jeunes Rois, the former high on the slope and easily spotted thanks to the Domaine de la Vougeraie section being planted *en foule*, meaning in a crowd, at a density of 30,000 vines per hectare. Students of orthography will note that the corner of Evocelles that crosses the commune boundary into Gevrey changes its spelling to Evosselles; others will scratch their heads in bafflement.

The paucity of highly ranked vineyards encountered thus far is amply rectified in Gevrey-Chambertin, home to nine *grands crus* and a slew of *premiers crus*. In each category there are vineyards that fully justify their status, none more so than Chambertin and Chambertin-Clos de Bèze, a pair of the Côte d'Or's most esteemed vineyards. The latter may be labelled simply as 'Chambertin' but the reverse is not allowed. At their best these neighbours yield wines of majesty and substance, capable of long ageing, the Chambertin perhaps sturdier and stronger than the slightly lighter footed Clos de Bèze. Together they form an oblong block of some 28 hectares, about 300 metres wide and less than a kilometre long. The *Route des Grands Crus* forms their eastern boundary and travelling along its north–south axis the slope is barely perceptible; a walk up towards the forest and back is needed to notice the roughly 25-metre rise from bottom to top.

The seven other *grands crus* are Chambertin satellites and all appropriate its exalted name to gain recognition by way of reflected glory, as with

Montrachet in the Côte de Beaune, though the Chambertin 'clan' is more scattered and numerous. They claim 'Chambertin' by virtue of being contiguous with it or Clos de Bèze, though Ruchottes' connection is fingertip slim and calls to mind Michelangelo's *Creation of Adam*. The seven are Chapelle-Chambertin, Charmes-Chambertin, Griotte-Chambertin, Latricières-Chambertin, Mazis-Chambertin, Mazoyères-Chambertin (usually labelled as Charmes) and Ruchottes-Chambertin. Mazis borders Clos de Bèze to the north with Ruchottes above it, reaching up to the tree line above 300 metres, while Latricières is Chambertin's southern neighbour. The western flank of all these vineyards, with the exception of Mazis and part of Clos de Bèze, is cheek by jowl with the forest, meaning that the vines there go into the shade of the trees much earlier in the day than those to the east. As such, the siting of these *grands crus* doesn't accord with the oft-repeated tenet that they lie in mid-slope, cushioned above and below by lesser *crus*. The remaining quartet – Chapelle, Charmes, Griotte and Mazoyères – lie on the other side of the *route* and in the case of the latter reach right down to the D974 main road, where there is virtually no slope, a hardly ideal situation that risks devaluing the Chambertin name. The wines from the satellite seven can be excellent even if they never surpass the heights achieved by the first pair.

Some two-dozen *premiers crus* cover over 80 hectares and include at least one – Clos Saint-Jacques – that is worthy of *grand cru* status. It sits above the village with a perfect south-east exposure, plumb in the centre of a crescent of *premiers crus* that girds the hillside. So obvious is its *de facto grand cru* standing that nobody bothers to agitate for its elevation. Supposedly, it was overlooked when the *grand cru* gongs were being handed out because it was not contiguous with Chambertin, though a more colourful suggestion blames a cussed previous owner who so irritated the authorities that they were never going to confer top-rank status on his vineyard. The Côte de Nuits stretches to its widest at Gevrey. From its western extreme at the pinpoint of La Bossière it is over 4 kilometres across to the 18-hectare La Justice vineyard which is located on the 'wrong' side of the D974. Though flat, it can produce vigorous wines well worthy of their appellation.

After the glamour of the Chambertin name it is understandable that Morey-Saint-Denis carries less cachet, less immediate recognition. It is a compact commune, not 2 kilometres from north to south, and is home to four-and-a-sliver *grands crus*, the sliver being Bonnes Mares, which is generally treated as if it resided wholly in next-door Chambolle-Musigny.

The four divide easily into two pairs: Clos de la Roche and Clos Saint Denis to the north, and Clos des Lambrays and Clos de Tart to the south.

Unlike Gevrey's *grands crus* these do sit at mid-slope and straddle the commune in linear succession. Though all four are 'clos', it is Clos de Tart that does justice to that designation, being enclosed by walls in a fashion that is largely absent in, for instance, Clos de la Roche where you can park your car besides the *Route des Grands Crus* and stroll into the vineyard. The northern pair are Morey's standard bearers, with Roche generally regarded as the better of the two, though its greater consumer visibility is down to its size – at a shade under 17 hectares it is nearly three times the size of Clos Saint-Denis. Between them they encompass a dozen *lieux-dits*, including the evocatively named Maison Brûlée that abuts the village dwellings. The name probably derives from the sacking of the region in 1636 by Austrian troops of the Emperor Ferdinand II, with whom France was at war.

While Clos des Lambrays and Clos de Tart are roughly equal in size (8.8 and 7.5 hectares respectively) their shapes differ markedly, the latter's neat rectangle making the former's boundaries look ragged by comparison. In the past it didn't help Morey's standing that this pair seldom lived up to their potential, and despite significant improvements in recent years it could still be argued that their reputations are not as high Clos de la Roche and Clos Saint-Denis. Morey's *premiers crus* cluster mainly downslope of the *grands crus* though some of the best such as Monts Luisants lie above, between 300 and 350 metres. It is best known as a *premier cru* for red wine and also for Domaine Ponsot's famed Aligoté, proof that marvellous wine can be made from this over-looked grape. At *village* level Clos Solon, adjacent to the D974, yields a memorable wine in the hands of Jean-Marie Fourrier.

Chambolle-Musigny is noted for wines of grace and elegance yet its pair of *grands crus* can hardly be considered as two sides of the same coin; they are more differentiated than that. Bonnes Mares and Musigny are the opposite poles of Chambolle, separated by the village itself and a swathe of *premiers crus* that runs between them. Travelling from Morey, Bonnes Mares is the first vineyard you encounter, a substantial rectangle of 15 hectares that crosses the commune boundary, with about 90 per cent of it in Chambolle. It is difficult to generalize about Bonnes Mares because there is a radical difference between the soils in the upper and lower sections of the vineyard. What can be asserted is that by comparison with Musigny it produces a heartier wine, with more spice and something of a *sauvage* character. If it lacks something of the perfumed grace of Musigny its impact is more immediate; visceral to Musigny's sensual.

Musigny overlaps the top corner of Clos de Vougeot and comprises three *lieux-dits*: Les Musigny, Les Petits Musigny and La Combe d'Orveau. Its eastern boundary is completely formed by the *Route des Grands Crus* – or so it appears until a close examination of the map reveals a shred of vineyard that lies across the road from the main body of the vineyard. It sits on a step of ground at the top of Bertagna's *monopole* Clos de la Perrière and is home to a couple of hundred individually staked vines. It is so small that it is hardly worthy of mention but because it belongs to one of the côte's most celebrated of all *grands crus* it is worth cultivating. A final quirk that distinguishes Musigny from all other Côte de Nuits *grands crus* is that it is permitted to plant Chardonnay there, though de Vogüé is the only producer to make a Musigny *blanc*.

It's a hackneyed assertion that Musigny is the Côte d'Or's queen while Chambertin is the king, a memorable, if hardly profound, observation that can be dismissed as an old nugget of *faux* wisdom. Yet it stands up to scrutiny. The power and concentration of Chambertin is absent in Musigny, replaced by more moderate qualities of elegance and poise. There is strength, but it is the finessed strength of the ballet dancer not the overt weightlifter's version. Its qualities have been the cause of much superlative frenzy over the centuries thanks to the extraordinary intensity of complex scents and unfolding, layered fruit flavours.

Of Chambolle's *premiers crus* Les Amoureuses, downslope from Musigny, stands apart and is accorded putative *grand cru* status, much like Clos Saint-Jacques in Gevrey. Thanks to quarrying in previous times, Amoureuses presents a more jumbled appearance than its neighbours and the derivation of its name is fertile ground for speculation. Perhaps it was a venue for torrid trysts; more prosaically it is suggested that the soil when wet clings to footwear with a lover's grip.

Though Musigny and Clos de Vougeot share the same vineyard classification and indeed share a boundary for a couple of hundred metres, along which they are separated by a literal stone's throw, a huge gulf in renown divides them. Where superlatives rule the roost with Musigny it is hard to write about Clos de Vougeot without slipping into cliché, trotting out the rote statistics used for generations to illustrate its shortcomings. It is a roughly square, 50-hectare block of vineyard, a little longer on the diagonal that runs from the south-east corner up past the château to Musigny. The Côte d'Or's usual clutter of tiny, variously shaped vineyards, threaded with roads, tracks and dry stone walls, is absent here, where the vines seem to stretch to the horizon. If it was in Bordeaux it would have one owner and produce two, perhaps three wines; here it has more than eighty, many of whom lay claim to slivers of land so thin that in places the ownership map looks like a barcode. It did once have a single owner – the Cistercian order – but the Revolution saw them dispossessed and their flagship vineyard sold off as a *bien national*. Fragmentation was slow at first but accelerated through the twentieth century to the point where today's ownership mosaic is a cartographer's delight, or not. The best wines rank with the best of the Côte d'Or, carrying the conviction and energy that should be present in a *grand cru*, but they also serve to highlight the deficiencies of the others. In some respects the clos is the Côte d'Or in microcosm; knowing where the vines lie is useful but who farms them and makes the wine is critical, here more so than in any other *grand cru*, save for Vougeot's southern twin, Corton, another behemoth that would be improved by some trimming.

Clos de Vougeot contains sixteen *lieux-dits* that are not officially recognized and so are seldom seen, apart from Le Grand Maupertuis, used by Anne Gros, and the clever use of Musigni by Gros Frère et Soeur. It seems surprising that almost no other producers use them to create a semi-separate identity although it is doubtful if adding names such as Quartier des Marei Haut or Montiotes Basses would add lustre to the Vougeot name – probably the reverse. At *premier cru* level Vougeot continues to confound, for the most prestigious, in this red-wine heartland, is the white Le Clos Blanc, a *monopole* of Domaine de la Vougeraie.

An oft-cited criticism of Clos de Vougeot is that it runs right down to the main road, with a negligible slope in its lower section, while above it and better sited lie the two *grands crus* of Flagey-Echézeaux: Les Grands Echézeaux and Echézeaux. To all intents and purposes they are considered part of the next commune, Vosne-Romanée, home to the most celebrated vineyards in the world: La Romanée-Conti, La Tâche, Richebourg, La Romanée, Romanée Saint-Vivant and La Grande Rue. Taken together this half-dozen amount to about 28 hectares, not much more than half the area of Clos de Vougeot

It is not possible to overstate the renown in which these *grands crus* are held, particularly the two *monopoles* owned by the Domaine de la Romanée-Conti. The eponymous vineyard is a rough square of 1.8 hectares and is marked by a gaunt cross, making it easy to find as you travel up from the village on the small road that runs through Romanée

Saint-Vivant. It is hardly an exaggeration to say that it is a place of pilgrimage for wine lovers from across the globe and, conveniently, there is space for a few cars to park next to the vineyard, with clear sight of the sign on the low surrounding wall asking visitors not to walk through it, a request heeded by some: 'Many people come to visit this site and we understand. We ask you nevertheless to remain on the road and request that under no condition you enter the vineyard.' La Tâche is separated from it by the *monopole* sliver that is La Grande Rue and a fourth *monopole*, La Romanée, is contiguous on the west side and there has been speculation that it was once part of Romanée-Conti.

Of the remaining *grands crus*, Richebourg is the star, yielding a wine of flesh and substance, structure and depth, variously described as 'sumptuous', 'opulent' and 'voluptuous', qualities reflected in the plangent ring of its name. There's ballast in Richebourg. It neighbours Romanée-Conti to the north, and the *lieu-dit* at its northern end, Les Verroilles, turns slightly north of east, causing the grapes to ripen a little later than the rest of the vineyard. Romanée Saint-Vivant lies below Richebourg, close to the village, and takes its name from the nearby abbey of Saint-Vivant at Curtil-Vergy, the remains of which have recently been secured against further decline. The wine is scented, graceful and elegant, a violin to Richebourg's cello.

Les Grands Echézeaux and Echézeaux don't enjoy the same renown, which is hardly surprising in the case of the latter, given that it includes eleven *lieux-dits* comprising a cumbersome 38 hectares. Much the same criticisms that are levelled at Clos de Vougeot apply here – the paramount consideration when searching for quality must be the name of the producer. It is a dictum that applies everywhere in the Côte d'Or, but with heavy emphasis in places like this. Grands Echézeaux, on a barely perceptible slope, is separated from Clos de Vougeot by a narrow road and, with deeper soil delivering more weight in the wine, is generally considered superior to Echézeaux.

After the surfeit of *grands crus* in Vosne-Romanée the next commune south, Nuits-Saint-Georges, is home to none and must settle for the distinction of lending its name to the Côte de Nuits. Because of its size and memorable name it is probably as well known as Vosne, if not nearly as highly regarded. The town in turn takes its name from its most prestigious vineyard Les Saints-Georges, at the southern limit of the commune and reputedly the first plot to be planted in Nuits, in 1000. Efforts to get it upgraded to *grand cru* are ongoing. It is probably the only one of

Nuits' *premiers* to warrant promotion, though a case could be made for Aux Boudots right at the other end of the commune, abutting Vosne. The Nuits appellation continues south into Prémeaux-Prissey, home to the large *monopoles* Clos de l'Arlot and Clos de la Maréchale.

Thereafter the côte is pinched narrow by rock at Comblanchien and Corgoloin, where vineyards give way to the quarries that form the stony sinew connecting the Côte de Nuits with the Côte de Beaune. The final vineyard contains a little flourish in the shape of Domaine d'Ardhuy, whose impressive building is set back from the road and surrounded by the vines of its *monopole* Clos des Langres.

*

Travelling south, the unmissable bulk of the hill of Corton announces the beginning of the Côte de Beaune. The hill is home to an absurdly large band of *grands crus* spread across three communes: Ladoix-Serrigny, Aloxe-Corton and Pernand-Vergelesses. It wraps around the hill, facing east-south-east in Ladoix, continuing to south-east in Aloxe before turning fully south and then west in Pernand. In all there are 160 hectares of *grand cru* vineyard, yet only two appellations: Corton and Corton-Charlemagne. (A third, Charlemagne, is rarely used.) As a rule of thumb, when considering the wines, it is reasonably safe to assume that Corton is red and Corton-Charlemagne is white, save for a tiny amount of Corton *blanc*. Considering the vineyards is another matter, for the appellations overlap – if Pinot Noir is planted in the *lieu-dit* En Charlemagne, for example, the resultant wine is Corton.

With regard to planting, Pinot Noir finds favour on the mid and lower slopes that face south-east and south, with Chardonnay prospering higher up, close to the tree line and in the vineyards that turn from south to west into Pernand-Vergelesses. There's a bewildering number of *lieux-dits* – over two dozen – and it would surely make sense to split the behemoth *grands crus* into these constituent parts and then rank them as appropriate. An obvious trio for designation as *grands crus* in their own right would be Les Renardes, Les Bressandes and Le Clos du Roi, superbly sited as they are on the mid slope with a south-east exposure. Above them lies Le Corton, another candidate for top rank, and not to be confused with plain Corton, which cannot be labelled as Le Corton: the definite article may only be used for wines that come from that *lieu-dit*. As it is, most of the wines are labelled with reference to their specific *lieux-dits*, Corton Clos du Roi, Corton Bressandes and so forth, unless they are blended across several, a reversal of the practice in Clos de Vougeot where the *lieux-dits* names are hardly ever used.

It is hard to generalize about the wines but too many reds hint at greatness by way of fleeting flavours without delivering: artists' sketches, not finished works. A good Corton-Charlemagne is a different matter. In youth it is tight-coiled and unyielding, steely not flashy, seldom lavish or lush, and only with age does it fill out and unfold to reveal a broad panoply of flavours.

South of the hill of Corton the communes of Savigny-lès-Beaune and Chorey-lès-Beaune face each other across the D974, Savigny to the west and Chorey on flat ground to the east, with a toehold on the 'right' side of the road. Savigny's *premiers crus* lie on slopes either side of the valley through which the little river Rhoin flows. Les Lavières and Aux Vergelesses are the best, well sited on the northern hillside, Lavières facing south, Vergelesses more easterly. Chorey possesses no *premiers crus*, a circumstance that works in favour of savvy consumers in search of good wines at reasonable prices.

The A6 motorway forms a rigid border between these two and Beaune itself, and it is hard not to feel that the Côte de Beaune proper only begins once you have crossed the main road. Beaune was dealt a generous *premiers crus* hand, as perusal of any vineyard map shows – their darker colour dominates, with attendant blobs of *village* above and below on the slope. The broad sweep is bounded by Beaune's suburbs to the east and hilltop forest to the west. At its heart lies Les Grèves, a roughly square block of 30-plus hectares that climbs the hillside from 225 metres at its base to 300 at its upper limit. To the north lie Les Toussaints and Les Bressandes and to the south Les Teurons and Aux Cras. Les Grèves, named for its stony soil, is the clear leader in potential – delivered on by the likes of Tollot-Beaut and Domaine Lafarge.

A number of the large *négociants* have flagship Beaune wines upon which they lavish 'spoilt child' care and attention: Drouhin's Clos des Mouches, Bouchard Père et Fils' L'Enfant Jesus and Jadot's Clos des Ursules are examples. These wines stand on their own reputations while some of the lesser *premiers crus* are barely known outside the region.

The Pommard commune begins at the roundabout as you drive south out of Beaune on the D974 – fork right off the main road here to climb the gentle slope to the village itself. Then wriggle through the village to get to its most prestigious vineyard, Les Rugiens, divided by a small road into upper and lower sections – *haut* and *bas* – so much easier for English speakers than *dessus* and *dessous*. The name Rugiens derives from *rouge* and references the reddish soils caused by iron oxide, and it is the lower section that is most prized and frequently mentioned as a candidate for elevation to *grand cru*. Clos des Epeneaux is also mentioned whenever this long-running debate gains new legs but it is unlikely that anything will change in the near future. Of the other *premiers crus* Les Jarolières, adjacent to Rugiens-Bas, produces wine with a finesse not normally associated with Pommard.

As with Pommard, Volnay is solely a red-wine commune and is home to no *grands crus* either. There the similarities end. Pommard has considerably more appellation land, yet curiously the vineyards feel more expansive in Volnay, especially at the southern end, abutting Monthélie and Meursault. Being further up the slope no doubt contributes to this illusion. It is at this end also that the acknowledged top rank *premiers* are found, Clos des Chênes, Les Caillerets and Taille Pieds. All three are evocatively named, none more so than the latter, a steep vineyard, the incline of which forced the *vignerons* to stoop low to prune the vines (*tailler* means to prune), so low that they risked cutting their feet.

Clos des Chênes and Taille Pieds are beautifully situated, straddling the 300-metre contour line on the map, yet it is Caillerets a little lower down that commands the greatest respect, where the stony soil yields the quintessence of Volnay. Other vineyards of note include Clos des Ducs and Les Santenots du Milieu, the chameleon vineyard that lies across the boundary in Meursault but which is labelled Volnay if the wine is red, Meursault if white.

The Côte d'Or stretches to its widest south of Volnay, spanning over 6 kilometres across from Saint-Romain to Meursault. The contrast between the two could hardly be greater, both in situation and renown. Saint-Romain is home to some of the côte's highest vineyards, some of which touch 400 metres in places and, if driving, first gear needs to be utilized as you pull up the hills and used again as you descend. As yet none of the vineyards are ranked *premier cru* though moves are afoot to change this. Next door, Auxey-Duresses' vineyards are strung along the course of the Ruisseau des Cloux, a small watercourse, with a handful of *premiers* at the eastern limit of the commune adjoining Monthélie. Here, the best vineyards face each other from opposite hillsides with the village between.

Opposite: A map of Domaine Roulot's vineyard holdings, highlighted in lime green, illustrates the fragmentation typical in the Côte d'Or

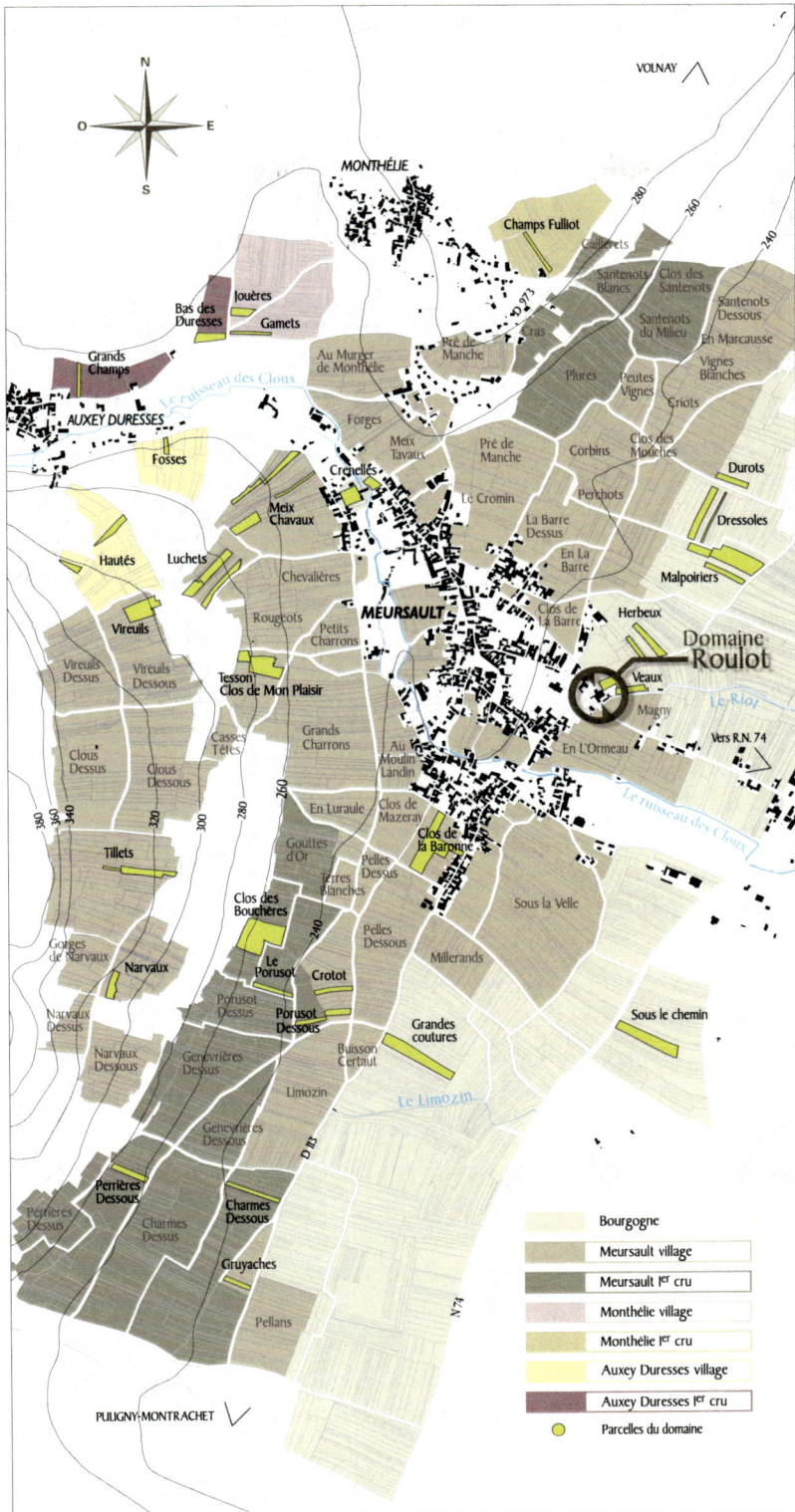

MONTHÉLIE

VOLNAY

N
O E
S

Champs Fulliot

Caillerets

Bas des Duresses
Jouères
Gamets

Santenots Blancs
Clos des Santenots
Santenots Dessous

Grands Champs

Au Murger de Monthélie
Pré de Manche

Plures
Peutes Vignes
Vignes Blanches

En Marcausse

AUXEY DURESSES

Le ruisseau des Cloux

Fosses

Forges

Criots

Meix Tavaux

Pré de Manche

Corbins

Clos des Mouches

Crenellés

Meix Chavaux

Le Cromin

Perchots

Durots

Hautés
Luchets

Chevalières

La Barre Dessus

Dressoles

Vireuils

Rougeots

En La Barre

Malpoiriers

Vireuils Dessus
Vireuils Dessous

Petits Charrons

MEURSAULT

Clos de La Barre

Herbeux

Domaine Roulot

Tesson
Clos de Mon Plaisir

Grands Charrons

Veaux

Magny

Vers R.N. 74

Casses Tétes

Au Moulin Landin

En L'Ormeau

Le Riot

Clous Dessus
Clous Dessous

En Luraule

Clos de Mazeray

Le ruisseau des Cloux

Tillets

Gouttes d'Or

Terres Blanches

Pelles Dessus

Clos de la Baronne

Sous la Velle

380 360 340 320 300 280 260 240

Gorges de Narvaux

Narvaux

Clos des Bouchères

Le Porusot
Crotot

Pelles Dessous

Millerands

Sous le chemin

Narvaux Dessus

Porusot Dessus

Porusot Dessous

Grandes coutures

Narvaux Dessous

Genevrières Dessus

Buisson Certaut

Limozin

Le Limozin

Genevrières Dessous

Perrières Dessous

Charmes Dessous

Perrières Dessous

Charmes Dessous

Gruyaches

Pellans

N 74

PULIGNY-MONTRACHET

Bourgogne

Meursault village

Meursault 1er cru

Monthélie village

Monthélie 1er cru

Auxey Duresses village

Auxey Duresses 1er cru

Parcelles du domaine

Corton-Charlemagne excepted, the Côte d'Or's finest white wine country starts at Meursault, the curiosity being that the commune is book-ended to north and south by anomalous vineyards that, if they produce red wine, are not Meursault but Santenots and Blagny. Only when planted with Chardonnay do they qualify for the Meursault appellation. Meursault is a big commune with a clutch of storied *premiers crus* such as Les Perrières, Les Genevrières and Les Charmes, though no *grands crus*. As if to compensate for that deficit it boasts a superior collection of *village lieux-dits* that in the hands of the best producers are regarded as *de facto premiers crus* and which are easily the equal of lacklustre *premiers* from elsewhere. A quartet – Les Narvaux, Les Tillets, Le Tesson and Les Vireuils – occupy favoured sites to the west of the village at about 300 metres altitude. The bulk of the *premiers crus* lie to the east and south of these, reaching as far as the boundary with Puligny-Montrachet. Named for old quarries, Les Perrières is the star, a fragmented vineyard of some 14 hectares that sits upslope of the smooth sweep of Charmes and Genevrières. In the right hands those two produce superlative wines, but Perrières can top them both by way of greater depth and insistence without losing its elegance.

Elegance is a hallmark often cited for the wines of the next commune, Puligny-Montrachet, along with refinement, breed and poise. These are qualities seen to ultimate advantage in a great Montrachet, though its next-door neighbour a little higher on the slope, Chevalier-Montrachet, is not far behind when comparisons of outright quality are being made. Montrachet's situation is textbook perfect, a mid-slope slice of vineyard on a gentle incline facing south-east. Its 8 hectares divide almost 50:50 between Puligny and Chassagne, hence the appropriation of its name by both villages and, strictly speaking, the Chassagne section is Le Montrachet while the Puligny section does without the definite article, though this distinction is not rigidly applied. It hardly needs stating that the first 't' is silent, thanks to the conflation of two words, 'Mont' and 'Rachet', after which the pronunciation remained as if they were still two. Roughly speaking it means bare hill. Montrachet is the most celebrated white-wine vineyard on earth and when on song the wine is indubitably magnificent but it can also leave expectations unfulfilled, especially when the price is considered.

In the same way that Chambertin has its satellites so too does Montrachet; in addition to Chevalier there's Bâtard-Montrachet, Bienvenues-Bâtard-Montrachet and Criots-Bâtard-Montrachet. Chevalier is slightly smaller than Montrachet and the slope is slightly steeper, with leaner soil that gives racier, less substantial wine. Bâtard's dozen hectares are shared almost equally between Puligny and Chassagne and it borders Montrachet on its western side, separated from it by a narrow road. Compared to Chevalier the soil is heavier, a distinction reflected in the wines: Bâtard plush and plump, Chevalier more clearly etched. Bienvenues lies wholly within Puligny and Criots wholly within Chassagne; separated by about 500 metres, there's a yawning gulf between them in renown. Bienvenues comprises a block on the north-east corner of Bâtard with little to distinguish between them, and the wines are barely distinguishable also, while Criots slopes away from Bâtard on its southern side and is less favourably sited. Criots is the awkward child of the quintet and, for a *grand cru*, too often comes up short where it counts — on the palate.

Puligny is also home to some outstanding *premiers crus*, including Le Cailleret and Les Pucelles, both of which are contiguous with the block of *grands crus* and, in the right hands, capable of rivalling them for quality. A curiosity is the tiny amount of Puligny *rouge* that is produced, a distant echo from a time when Pinot Noir was widely planted in the commune. Indeed, with the exception of the *grands crus*, almost every *premier cru* and all but one of the officially recognized *lieux-dits* (over two dozen) are permitted to make red wine. If the *vignerons* chose to, they could convert nearly all of their vineyards to red and still call it Puligny.

Chassagne-Montrachet's vineyards form a reasonably cohesive rectangle with the *grands crus* at the top, abutting Puligny. These and a few others stand apart, split from the bulk of Chassagne by the D906 road along which the Tour de France rolled in 2007. This road feels like the Chassagne-Puligny boundary but nobody in Chassagne is complaining that it is not, for there would be no *grands crus* in the commune if it were. As a consequence they are part of the commune but stand separate, like a choir balcony in a church. Save for the *grands crus,* every scrap of *village* and *premiers crus* vineyard may produce red or white wine. Some, such as Clos Saint-Jean and La Boudriotte, produce both side by side, which makes for interesting comparative tasting and discussion as to whether this or that vineyard is better suited to Chardonnay or Pinot Noir.

The stony Cailleret vineyard, beside the upper part of the village and facing south-east, is the leading *premier*, though Les Chaumées (not to be confused with Les Chaumes) on the boundary with Saint-Aubin can challenge it. To the south of the commune, Morgeot is a

54-hectare vineyard hold-all that contains well known *lieux-dits* such as La Boudriotte and Clos Pitois and others such as Guerchère and Ez Crottes, whose names only ever appear on detailed vineyard maps.

Saint-Aubin sits west of Puligny and Chassagne, and lacks their compactness, projecting away from the Côte de Beaune in a dog-leg as the vineyards follow the varied slopes. Thanks to the jumble of those slopes the vineyards face in numerous directions, from north-east to south-west. Perhaps unsurprisingly, the two best *premiers crus* are found just around a turn in the hillside from the Montrachet *grands crus*. These are En Remilly and, above it at 350 metres, Les Murgers des Dents de Chien, the latter named for the *murgers* or heaps of stones piled at the edge of a vineyard, created by *vignerons'* clearance work. Some are massive and prompt wonder at the toil that led to their creation.

South of Chassagne the Côte d'Or begins its long sweep westwards through Santenay to finish with a rustic flourish in Maranges. The first vineyard you meet – Clos de Tavannes – vies for top spot with its neighbour Les Gravières and perhaps Beaurepaire, which sits above the village, rising steeply from 250 to 350 metres. All three wines can age well, especially Tavannes. One of Santenay's biggest *premiers crus*, Clos Rousseau, sits on the commune's southern boundary and changes its spelling to 'Roussots' in Maranges. This, along with other Maranges *premiers crus* such as Le Croix Moines and La Fussière, are vineyards with little recognition outside their immediate locality but, as with the best of Marsannay right at the other end of the Côte d'Or, they are likely to become better known in the future.

AUSTRALIA'S OLD VINES

It may come as a suprise to learn that the vineyards of this New World producer are home to an outstanding collection of old vines. In this chapter from 2023's *The wines of Australia*, Mark Davidson explains why this is the case, and asks whether old vines make better wines.

Grape vines are not native to Australia. Early European settlers brought the original cuttings on the First Fleet in 1788. The cuttings were collected in Rio de Janeiro and the Cape of Good Hope. There are limited records of viticulture and winemaking in these early years. In *Riesling in Australia*, Ken Helm and Trish Burgess note that in a dispatch dated 16 October 1791 the then Governor stated that 'he had 3 acres of vineyard in the Government House grounds at Paramatta and that Phillip Schaffer, a German from Hessen had planted one acre of vines on his property on the North Bank of Paramatta River thus entitling him to be recorded as the first vigneron of Australia.'

Some historians have suggested that the vines were also brought in to make wine for practical reasons. Early settlers did not know what to expect so vines were likely planted to make wine for the eventual journey back to Britain. Water on long ship journeys needed to be stabilized and wine served that purpose. One bottle of wine mixed with six bottles of water achieved the necessary stability. There was no understanding of the complexities of chemistry in those days but the vinous addition would have lowered the pH, making the water safe to drink.

Vines were haphazardly brought to Australia throughout the next 40 years but the most significant year for vine importation was 1832. Botanist James Busby travelled to Europe in 1831 and collected vine cuttings from southern Spain and France. From what he had witnessed so far, he was convinced that vine growing and winemaking would be very successful in the new colony.

The following excerpt from his journal, dated 6 January 1832, highlights his systematic and impressive work.

> *I had the good fortune to find in the Botanic Garden at Montpellier a collection of most of the vine varieties cultivated in France, and in other parts of Europe, to the number of 437, and, on application to the professor of Botany, he, (with the greatest liberality) permitted me to take cuttings from the whole. I afterwards, added to this collection 133 from the Royal Nursery of the Luxembourg at Paris, making in this whole 570 varieties of vines, of all of which, with two or three exceptions, I obtained two cuttings.*
>
> *It is my wish to place this collection at the disposal of His Majesty's Government, for the purpose, should it be deemed expedient, of forming an experimental garden at Sydney, to prove their different qualities, and propagate, for general distribution, those which may appear suitable to the climate.*

Busby's request was granted, and his collection was shipped to Sydney. In total, 363 vines survived the journey and were planted in the Botanical Gardens in Sydney. A duplicate collection was planted at his property in the Hunter Valley and subsequent cuttings made their way to various parts of New South Wales, Victoria and South Australia, as well as to New Zealand, where Busby later moved. This distribution marked the start of a more systematic and detailed approach to vine growing in Australia. As a result, many of Australia's old vines can be traced back to the original Busby collection. The timing of his trip was additionally fortuitous as it preceded the outbreak of phylloxera in Europe by 30 years.

Phylloxera has a history in Australia with outbreaks in the early 1900s in parts of Victoria – notably Geelong and Rutherglen. Current issues exist in the Yarra Valley but many regions in Australia remain unaffected. Phylloxera has never been detected in the state of South Australia. This, combined with distribution of vines from Busby's collection, means that Australia is home to the largest repository of ungrafted, pre-phylloxera vines anywhere on the planet.

What constitutes old vines is vague as there is no universal definition. As such, the term is used liberally in many countries and regions. The Barossa is home to the largest acreage of old vine sites in the world and is the only region in Australia that has codified the use of the term old vines. The Old Vine Charter was originally conceived at Yalumba winery but quickly snapped up by the region as a way of classifying and honouring these old vine sites. The Old Vine Charter has four classifications, all based on minimum age.

- Old Vines: 35 years or older
- Survivor Vines: 70 years or older
- Centenarian Vines: 100 years or older
- Ancestor Vines: 125 years or older

While this is a Barossa only classification it serves as a useful benchmark for other regions across the country. Perhaps we may see an Australian Old Vine Charter in the future? There is nothing in the works at present, but it would be helpful as there are many old vine sites spread across the country.

Thirty-five years old is a useful minimum standard for defining old vines but virtually all of Australia's wine producing regions would qualify on some level! The following is a snapshot of regions that have either extensive old vine plantings or historically significant old vine sites.

The Barossa, which encompasses both the Barossa and Eden Valleys, is one of the most historic wine-producing regions in Australia and has vineyard sites that date back to 1843. Barossa is the queen bee when it comes to old vine vineyard sites. A separate chapter could be written on the subject, hence the disproportionate ink space dedicated to them here. There are sixth- and seventh-generation grape-growing families who have served as custodians to these beautiful old-vine vineyard sites. Within a 5-kilometre radius you can visit the oldest vineyards of Shiraz, Grenache and Mourvèdre anywhere on the planet: Langmeil Freedom Shiraz vineyard, Cirillo 1848 Grenache vineyard and a Mourvèdre vineyard planted in 1853 by Freiderich Koch, the fruit of which is used to produce Hewitson's Old Garden Mourvèdre. The Cabernet Sauvignon vines at Penfolds Kalimna Block 42 were planted in 1885, making it one of the oldest Cabernet vineyards in the world.

Shiraz, Mourvedre, Grenache, Cabernet Sauvignon, Riesling and Semillon make up the bulk of varieties that qualify. Below is the full list, taken from Barossa Grape and Wine, of old vine plantings still in production today. Even if you take out the Old Vine level (minimum age 35 years) you are still left with 410 hectares (1,013 acres) of vineyard sites that are at least 70 years old.

Old-Vine Shiraz
• Barossa Ancestor Vine: 12.54 hectares/30.99 acres
• Barossa Centenarian Vine: 100.62 hectares/248.64 acres
• Barossa Survivor Vine: 88.48 hectares/218.64acres
• Barossa Old Vine: 589.06 hectares/1,455.60 acres

Old-Vine Mourvèdre
• Barossa Ancestor Vine: 2.63 hectares/6.5 acres
• Barossa Centenarian Vine: 5.39 hectares/13.32 acres
• Barossa Survivor Vine: 12.2 hectares/30.14 acres
• Barossa Old Vine: 45.5 hectares/112.43 acres

Old-Vine Grenache
• Barossa Ancestor Vine: 7.55 hectares/18.66 acres
• Barossa Centenarian Vine: 23.49 hectares/58.05 acres
• Barossa Survivor Vine: 93.51 hectares/231.07 acres
• Barossa Old Vine: 302.98 hectares/748.67 acres

Old-Vine Cabernet Sauvignon
• Barossa Ancestor Vine: 4.44 hectares/10.97 acres
• Barossa Centenarian Vine: 4.65 hectares/11.49 acres
• Barossa Old Vine: 121.1 hectares/299.24 acres

Old-Vine Riesling
• Barossa Centenarian Vine: 6 hectares/14.83 acres
• Barossa Survivor Vine: 16.24 hectares/40.13 acres
• Barossa Old Vine: 321.47 hectares/794.37 acres

Old-Vine Semillon
• Barossa Ancestor Vine: 3.75 hectares/9.27 acres
• Barossa Centenarian Vine: 1.98 hectares/4.89 acres
• Barossa Survivor Vine: 26.4 hectares/65.24 acres
• Barossa Old Vine: 84.65 hectares/209.17 acres

In McLaren Vale, Shiraz and Grenache are the main old vines. The region has set up an old vine register. Whereas the Barossa Old Vine Charter extends to what terms can be used on labels, this merely serves as a list of varieties that qualify as old vines, categorized in brackets of 35 or more years old, 50 or more years old, 75 or more years old and

100 or more years old. The extent of plantings is not quite the same as Barossa but impressive, nonetheless.

As of December 2021, there were 37 hectares of vines aged 100 years or more, mostly Shiraz and Grenache and 53 hectares of vines of 75 years old or more. These are also mostly Shiraz and Grenache but there are a few surprises such as Chenin Blanc, Sangiovese and Sagarantino.[1]

The Hunter Valley is Australia's oldest producing wine region, with vineyards dating back to the 1860s, and home to some of the oldest vine stock. While it doesn't have as broad a collection of old vine vineyards as Barossa, there are some historically significant vineyards.

There is a notable amount of ungrafted, old-vine Shiraz in the region. Tyrrell's 4 Acre was planted in 1879 and the Stevens Shiraz was planted in 1867. Mount Pleasant Old Hill was planted in 1880. Semillon was part of the Busby collection and found a comfortable home in the Hunter. There are several old vine sites of significance, including Tyrrell's Johnno's Vineyard and Tyrrell's HVD Vineyard, both 1908. There are not a lot of old vine Chardonnay sites in Australia, however Tyrrell's owns the oldest. Chardonnay was planted in the HVD vineyard in 1908 making it one of the oldest Chardonnay vineyards in the world.

Grape growing and winemaking in the Clare Valley dates back to 1852, when Austrian Jesuits established the Sevenhill winery. There are many old-vine sites scattered across the valley but the most significant is the iconoclastic Wendouree. I am not a fan of the term 'unicorn' wine but in the true sense of rare and hard to find, Wendouree qualifies. The dry-grown Shiraz vines were planted in 1893 and there is an old block of Malbec planted in 1898.

Langhorne Creek is also home to sixth-generation grape-growing families and several significant sites. Brothers in Arms winery is custodian of the world's oldest family-owned Cabernet Sauvignon vines, planted in 1891 in the Matala Vineyard.

Nagambie Lakes is a Geographical Indication (GI) that sits within the Goulburn Valley region and the old-vine story here is all about Tahbilk. This is one of the oldest wineries in Australia and has the oldest Shiraz vineyard in Victoria – planted in 1860. Tahbilk is also the custodian of Australia's oldest plantings of Marsanne. The original vines were planted in 1927 and the site has expanded to be the largest single vineyard of Marsanne in the world, at just under 41 hectares (100 acres).

---

1   The full list can be accessed at www.mclarenvalewine.au/wine/old-vine-register

Old vine Malbec in Wendouree, dating from 1898

Great Western is a subsection within the Grampians GI. There are a few old vine sites scattered across the region but the story at Best's is remarkable. In 1866, Henry Best planted what would become some of the oldest vines in Australia. He planted whatever he could get at the time and this original site, now known as the nursery block, is believed to have the greatest variety of pre-phylloxera plantings in Australia – and possibly the world. Recent work has shown that there are 32 different grape varieties in the block. The Pinot vineyards were first planted in 1868, comprising about 85 per cent Pinot Meunier and 15 per cent Pinot Noir. The original Shiraz vines were planted in 1868 and there's a block of Dolcetto reputedly planted in 1889.

*

There is something special about tasting a wine made from vines planted over 100 years ago. Apart from contemplating a vine that has continuously produced for that length of time we just don't regularly consume agricultural products with lengthy history. While I believe strongly that preserving and honouring these special sites is important, the obvious question is: so what? Do old vines matter? Do they make better wine?

A common refrain in the Barossa is that 'old vines don't make great wines, great wines make old vines', the implication being that those old vines produced good wines right from the start. If they didn't, they were pulled out. There is truth to this. Vines planted in good sites typically make better wines but I can't help thinking that this is a bit simplistic and undermines the story of old vines. The discussion around the character and quality of wines made from old vines has, until recently, been mostly anecdotal save for a few practical and physiological realities.

Sarah Ahmed wrote an excellent article on this subject after an old vine tasting and panel discussion in London in 2016.[2] On the subject of old vine versus young vine physiology the panel noted that research has shown that older plants are more efficient than younger ones. As for whether better efficiency translates into better wines? This could be extrapolated to suggest that given the same amount of energy, older vines can go further through their biochemical pathways, producing the flavours and riper tannins that we associate with quality.

With trunk girths and root systems that are both larger, old vines have more carbohydrate reserves, giving the vine a jump start to the season. And it has been observed that vines can draw upon these reserves during times of stress later in the growing season too. The more developed root system of an older vine allows for better access to potential water and nutrients that exist in the different subsoil stratas. In Dean Hewitson's Old Garden Mourvèdre site, vine roots go down 10 metres, which he believes helps them to deal with extremes of weather, whether it's cool and wet or hot. He sees an evenness in ripening year on year.

Naturally balanced canopies could be an explanation for better fruit quality in older vines. Panellist Jamie Goode, who has a PhD in plant biology, speculated that during a vine's first year or two of fruiting, the ratio between vegetative growth and fruit growth is in balance – but only briefly. For a period after this it appears that, in his words, 'adolescent vines push towards growing more shooting tips rather than fruit, canopies grow larger so fruit to canopy growth is out of whack.' His comparison to an energetic, awkward, gangly, growing teen seemed appropriate. Old vine canopies come back into a natural balance of fruit and vegetative growth. The balance of the very young vines Goode mentions does explain the anomaly of some historically famous wines that were produced

---

2   The full article can be found here: https://thewinedetective.co.uk/blog/do-old-vines-make-better-wines-australia-under-the-microscope

from young vines. Quinta do Noval Nacional Vintage Port 1931, Stags Leap S.L.V. Cabernet 1973 and many 1961 Bordeaux (arguably one of the greatest vintages ever) were all produced from 3 to 4 year old vines.

When Australian Dylan Grigg wrote his PhD on old vines, a key element of his investigation focused on epigenetic modification.[3] What is epigenetics? It is the study of stable phenotypic changes (known as *marks*) that do not involve alterations in the DNA sequence. Epigenetics most often involves changes that affect the regulation of gene expression. The term can also be used to describe any heritable phenotypic change. Such effects on cellular and physiological phenotypic traits may result from external or environmental factors or be part of normal development.

Grigg aimed to assess scientifically the the influence of vine age on grape and wine production to find out if the quality of fruit and wine produced went beyond the perception of the wine industry and media. He found that old vines (with a minimum age of around 50–60 years) use epigenetic modification to learn from stress, essentially bookmarking weather events. Over time there's an accumulation of markers, preconditioning the vine to adjust quickly in the event of similar conditions arising. These characteristics are also heritable, meaning that they can be passed on, but this is where it gets tricky. Experiments taking cuttings from old vines and replanting them showed that the new vines did not in fact retain the traits. The heritable characteristics were, however, evident in vines that were established by layering from the parent vine, leaving it connected for five to six years before separating – basically giving the new vine an umbilical cord until it was established. Grigg was quick to point out that this is an area where more research is needed, and as detailed as his work was, it is just the tip of the iceberg. The study also noted that large differences in vine age did not produce differences in basic grape composition, however, the older vines consistently produced grapes with lower pH at similar Brix levels to grapes from younger vines.

So we now have something beyond anecdotal evidence that old vines do matter. With this information we can say with a modicum of confidence that they produce more consistent and potentially better quality fruit than younger vines. Does this mean they make better wine? Theoretically the fruit sourced from the older vines should produce better wines, but much lies in the skill of the winemaker.

---

3 His thesis can be found here: https://digital.library.adelaide.edu.au/dspace/handle/2440/113314

PINOT NOIR

In this extract from *The wines of New Zealand* (2018), Rebecca Gibb MW gives Pinot Noir the full biography treatment, tracing its planting history in the country, exploring the different styles of wine it produces, breaking down the different clones and offering up some ideas on must-try wines.

The early history of the country's most-planted red variety is wonderfully hazy. Pinot Noir may have first graced New Zealand soils as early as 1819 when missionary Samuel Marsden planted grapevines in Northland. Marsden shipped his vines from Sydney, Australia, and at that time Pinot Noir was one of the more common varieties so it is possible that Pinot Noir was among the cuttings. It is also possible that it was not. Similarly, when James Busby planted his vineyard at Waitangi in the early 1830s, it is not unlikely that Pinot Noir was among his selection. What is certain is that in 1883, William Beetham and his French wife Marie Zelie Hermance Frere planted Pinot Noir on their Wairarapa property along with Pinot Meunier, Hermitage and several other varieties. Over lunch with Henry Tiffen, a surveyor and landowner in Hawke's Bay, a taste of Beetham's wine convinced him to take cuttings and plant his own vineyard – Greenmeadows – with Pinot Noir, Pinot Blanc, Pinot Meunier and Black Hermitage (Syrah). Bernard Chambers also planted Pinot varieties on Te Mata Station. There is mention of Pinot Noir being planted by French missionaries in its earliest days and there were clearly a few vines in the ground, as Chambers took cuttings from the Mission Vineyards in 1892 to start his vineyard.

By the time viticulture expert Romeo Bragato conducted his tour of New Zealand, Pinot Noir and Pinot Meunier were thriving in Hawke's

Bay. Bragato's report to the New Zealand government on the 'Prospects of Viticulture' stated that Pinot Noir was one of the most suitable red varieties for the country as well as Black Hermitage, Cabernet Sauvignon, Cabernet Franc, Dolcetto and 'Mueller Burgundy'.

The modern history of Pinot Noir begins in the mid 1970s in what now seems like an unlikely place for the variety: Auckland. The grape has since moved southward to the cooler climes of Wairarapa and the South Island but west Auckland was the early setting for its success. Nobilo's Huapai Pinot Noir 1976 has been singled out as the first quality Pinot Noir of the modern era while Babich's Henderson Valley Pinot Noir 1981 won the variety its first gold medal in a wine competition. Meanwhile, on the South Island, St Helena planted the first Pinot vines in the frosty Canterbury region: planting in this cool climate raised a few eyebrows but they were soon lowered when the 1982 vintage won a gold medal at the Air New Zealand Wine Awards, suggesting that both Pinot Noir and the soils of Canterbury might be a combination worth exploring.

Vineyards were also appearing in Martinborough in the early 1980s following the publication of a report by soil scientist Derek Milne which concluded that Martinborough, Marlborough and Waipara were well suited to viticulture. Dr Neil McCallum first took the plunge in 1979, planting grapes on Puruatanga Road, an avenue that is now lined with some of New Zealand's finest Pinot Noir vineyards. In Central Otago, home to more than 1,500 hectares of Pinot Noir (2017) or a quarter of New Zealand's Pinot vineyards, the variety was just one of many at that time, as its pioneers tried to figure out what would grow best in this arid, rocky land inhabited by sheep and rabbits.

Despite its fragility and fickle nature, Pinot Noir has thus far proven to be a winning variety for New Zealand's cool climate. From less than 500 hectares planted in 1997, that figure has increased eleven fold to more than 5,500 hectares two decades later. This early ripening variety needs a cool climate to slow its race to ripeness, allowing it to develop complexity and finesse while preserving its acidity. Its early budding nature means it can be susceptible to spring frosts, which are common on the South Island, and its thin skin means it is prone to fungal disease, which can cause difficulties in wet vintages.

In the early days, the wines lacked some colour and heft, as the Pinot Noir clones available were destined for sparkling rather than red wine. With the arrival of the Abel clone, a greater availability of improved plant material, increased vine age and a better understanding of the vines and the wines they produce, New Zealand Pinot Noir is becoming increasingly complex. There is also a growing confidence in the New Zealand Pinot Noir-growing community; a sense of self and an attitude that says 'this is who we are, this is what we do, and if you don't like it, plenty of other people do'. This confidence and pride wasn't in evidence in 2010, when I first attended the country's Pinot Noir NZ conference. Held every three years, there were frequent comparisons to Burgundy, the historic homeland of Pinot Noir, at the event. It was put on a pedestal. Yes, the French region makes the world's finest examples that most of us can't afford unless we forgo several mortgage payments, and it is inevitable that any Pinot Noir producer would like to achieve the heady heights of Domaine de la Romanée-Conti or Henri Jayer. But, let's face it, Burgundy also makes a lot of crap wine: opt for the *prix fixe* lunch at a bistro in Beaune and you'll be able to taste wines that aren't worthy of salad dressing.

Today, the pendulum has swung: there appears to be an aversion to comparing New Zealand to Burgundy because the only thing they have in common when it comes to Pinot Noir is the grape. Ted Lemon of Littorai Wines in Sonoma and Burn Cottage Vineyard in Central Otago made it clear that he thought comparisons to Burgundy were unhealthy for New World producers in a speech at the Mornington Peninsula International Pinot Noir conference in 2013. 'Look inward,' he implored. 'Do not measure all things against the Old World. And above all do not see Burgundy as a measuring stick. We must be like Odysseus, lashing ourselves to the mast of the ship in order to resist the siren song of the maidens of Burgundy.' Benchmarking against other Pinot Noir regions is hardly the root of all evil, but when trying to communicate wine styles in New Zealand comparisons with Burgundy are occurring less and less frequently.

Regionality

New Zealand Pinot Noir made from young vines is fruity, fresh and fun. It would be impossible to find a reasonably priced Pinot Noir from Burgundy that offered such attractive juicy fruit. However, there are growing numbers of New Zealand Pinot Noir producers making increasingly serious wines from Martinborough at the bottom of the North Island (latitude 40° S) to Central Otago (45° S), the world's most southerly wine region.

The styles of wine produced across New Zealand's regions are varied and distinctive. In very simple terms, Martinborough Pinot Noir is often described as savoury while Marlborough's Wairau Valley offers joyful fruitiness; Central Otago is naturally bold and black cherry-filled while Waipara's best can be brooding. The existence of regionality in New Zealand Pinot Noir had been discussed anecdotally but there was little research in comparison to the swathe of studies of New Zealand Sauvignon Blanc. In an attempt to remedy the lack of scientific evidence, Elizabeth Tomasino, a former PhD student at Lincoln University, set out to determine whether or not the Pinot Noir styles from the regions of Martinborough, Marlborough, Waipara and Central Otago were distinctive. Her results showed that there were clear and consistent differences. The Pinot Noirs from Marlborough were characterized by 'red cherry and raspberry aromas, greater red fruit in-mouth flavour, and greater balance' while Waipara's wines offered 'greater intensity of barnyard, herbal, and violet aromas and greater fruit density/concentration in-mouth flavour'. Martinborough's wines are typically described as savoury but Tomasino's research panels found 'greater intensity of black cherry, oak, and spice aromas' and Central Otago wines had 'fuller body'.

Tomasino's work seemed to demonstrate that regionality did exist in New Zealand. Since she completed her thesis in 2011, New Zealand has rapidly evolved. Marlborough's reputation as a producer of simple red-fruited Pinot Noir needs to be revised. Yes, it still produces high volumes of juicy, fruity Pinot Noir for entry-level price points but, with an irrigation scheme opening up the clay-loam hillsides of Southern Valleys in the early 2000s, there is a band of producers making increasingly serious wines with depth and richness. Better sites, better plant material and rising vine age means Marlborough's image as a producer of fruity Pinot Noir is outdated. Producers report that they are reducing their use of new French oak as older vines are producing grapes with tannins that ooze and resolve with extended post-fermentation maceration providing natural structure.

Martinborough has a longer track record of making Pinot Noir than Marlborough and serious drinkers have looked to producers like Ata Rangi and Dry River for complex, nuanced examples. The frost-prone, windy region typically produces small bunches with small berries (producers also report thicker skins), and these factors imbue the wines with rich colour, fruit concentration and naturally abundant tannins. Typical aromas include damson, violets and spice as well as a savoury character. Naturally low yields and quality-oriented producers mean that the general standard of wine in Martinborough is high.

In the Omihi area of Waipara Valley, North Canterbury, Greystone makes acclaimed aromatic whites, Chardonnay and Pinot Noir on hillside sites

The Pinot Noirs of Nelson differ in style depending on their site: the alluvial Waimea Plains typically offer light-bodied, finely fruited examples for early drinking, while the clays of the Moutere Hills provide fuller, weightier expressions with cocoa-powder tannins. The Nelson region's gentle maritime climate is expressed in the glass: the bright fruit reflects the area's high sunlight hours and yet the wines retain a gentleness, which might be related to a narrower diurnal temperature range than other South Island Pinot Noir-producing regions.

The Pinot Noirs of North Canterbury are site dependent. In the Waipara area, those on the Awapuni clay loams and Omihi offer a seriousness, broody character and often display a chalky sinew in their tannin structure. The Pinot Noirs sourced from the Glasnevin Gravels are lighter in body, juicy and full of bright red fruit. The two isolated producers on limestone further inland at Waikari – Bell Hill and Pyramid Valley – have shown glimmers of greatness, with the Pinot Noirs going beyond fruit, offering a rare transparency and other-worldly sensation. It is mind blowing to think that North Canterbury's finest Pinot Noir producers did not exist at the turn of the century, and its continued evolution will be one to watch with great expectations.

Between Canterbury and Central Otago, there's a five-hour drive almost devoid of vineyards. That is, except for Waitaki. Centred around the tiny town of Kurow, there is a handful of producers defying the marginal climate to produce aromatic whites and Pinot Noir. Yields are low, in part due to hostile weather: frost, wind and rain make ripening grapes here a risky business. The wines – particularly those grown on limestone

– are elegant with a line of acid that provides dart-like precision and chalky tannins. Beyond Waitaki, most Kiwis south of Christchurch realize that growing grapes at the bottom of the earth is a recipe for high blood pressure. It is only in the semi-continental climate of Central Otago, surrounded by mountains, that Pinot Noir can flourish. The variety accounts for around 70 per cent of the region's plantings and, since making a big impression on the world stage with its bold, big and ballsy 2002 vintage, it is now trying to convince the world that it does finesse. The region's dry, sunny climate with huge fluctuations between day and night-time temperatures and high levels of UV light imbues the Pinot Noirs of Central Otago with deep colour, a wealth of fruit, rich tannins and potentially high alcohol levels (14–14.5% abv is common). There are moves to pick a little earlier to retain greater freshness and rein in the region's natural flamboyance: winemaking has evolved with much gentler extraction, experimentation with whole bunches, longer post-fermentation macerations and more judicious use of new French oak.

The willingness to evolve winemaking processes and trial techniques is not just occurring in Central Otago. It is a countrywide phenomenon with the use of cold soak – which extracts both colour and perfume – common. The use of whole bunches and stems in the fermentation vat is a winery-by-winery decision: some wineries destem all the fruit and there are no stems in sight whereas Nelson-based Michael Glover produces his Mammoth Pinot Noir with 100 per cent whole-bunch fermentation. There once used to be a fear that the technique would make the wines tannic and green but even some of the biggest wine producers in the country have experimented with it and use a small proportion today in their blends. It brings spice and drive, plus the berries aren't crushed pre-fermentation. This means you get a lovely lifted perfume from a little bit of carbonic maceration but it should not dominate the wine, overpowering the sense of place with a winemaking decision. There is a greater willingness to extend post-fermentation maceration time as the vines become older, producing wines that are less fruity and allowing the tannins to resolve.

The objective of New Zealand's finest Pinot Noir makers is to make the truest expression of their place and the season. Each winemaker chooses to guide the grapes to the glass in their own way but maturity has brought greater knowledge, skills and humility: winemakers are increasingly hands off, aiming to guide the wines rather than shape them. That is why it is increasingly difficult to say what New Zealand or Central

Otago or Bendigo Pinot Noir is. Individual sites, individual producers and unique seasons make it wonderfully difficult to generalize.

The clone zone

There are forty-three clones of Pinot Noir according to the Catalogue of Grapevine Varieties and Clones and experts believe that as many as 1,000 genetic variants might exist. In the early 1960s, according to Riversun, Pinot Noir clones first began to be imported. It started with a clone from Switzerland called AM 10/5 (Ten Bar Five) and became the source of Central Otago, Martinborough and Canterbury's first vineyards. Somewhere along the line, however, 10/5 got a little confused, and what producers in Central Otago call 10/5 is very different to the 10/5 in Martinborough. What they do share in common is medium to high vigour, medium to large bunches and a tendency to produce inconsistent yields. It was widely used as a sparkling wine base and has fallen out of favour but there are growers who have a soft spot for it: Dry River's success has been based on 10/5 and clone 5. 'I think a lot of people walked away from 10/5,' says Dry River wine-maker Wilco Lam. 'Early producers put it in their vineyards but people are not keen on it because it ripens late – but that's vineyard management. We are able to harvest it pretty early.' Similarly, Clive Dougall, a Marlborough-based consultant who was winemaker at Seresin Estate for twelve years says, 'I'm actually starting to like 10/5. You used to be a bit embarrassed to say that your Pinot was made from 10/5 when everyone was jumping on the Burgundy clone bandwagon. It retains acidity, has a little bit of green character, it is gently tannic.'

In the 1970s the University of California, Davis (UCD) clones were imported into New Zealand, and the most popular became Clone 5. Riversun explains that the yields are 'typically on the medium to high end of the scale and they're regular – Clone 5 normally sets well. The bunches are medium to large, and often tight, which makes it a bit more suscepti-ble to botrytis than either 10/5 or the Dijon clones. Fruit thinning is re-quired to achieve top-tier wines.' In the late 1980s, the first Dijon clones were imported, eventually being released from quarantine in 1992. There were hiccups early on with some proving to be virused but the clones that are sexily entitled 667, 777, 114 and 115 have become an important part of the Pinot Noir landscape of New Zealand. Each clone has its own personality and each viticulturist has their personal preferences. The most common approach is to plant several – or many – clones in the vineyard. There are some single clone Pinot Noirs produced but each clone brings its own shade to draw a multicoloured artwork. For example, Felton Road has eleven clones planted, and at its Cornish Point vineyard there are twenty-five different clone and rootstock combinations.

In search of quantity and quality

After years of funding for Sauvignon Blanc research, it is time for New Zealand to better understand Pinot Noir. In 2017, the New Zealand government agreed to grant the wine industry more than $9 million to research different aspects of Pinot Noir production and marketing, but the theme which embraces the project is how to increase production of Pinot Noir while retaining quality. It is hoped that researchers will be able to find a way to produce 10 tonnes of grapes to the hectare (around 70 hl/ha) while maintaining the quality currently achieved with 6 tonnes to the hectare (42 hl/ha). Inevitably, industry insiders have been quick to dismiss this ambition: you can't make high quality Pinot Noir with high yields; why would we want to make cheap Pinot Noir? But Damian Martin, science group leader, viticulture and oenology for Plant and Food Research explains: 'Why is it that there is a glass ceiling on yield in relation to quality perception? There's no particular reason for it from a scientific perspective.' In a bid to unravel the relationship between yield and wine quality, chemists will be hard at work in the laboratory deconstructing the components of Pinot Noir from colour to aroma compounds and phenolics while sensory experts will be working alongside them to understand what quality actually means. 'The market for $50 Pinot Noir is pretty small so if New Zealand wants to be a force we have to make the economics of Pinot Noir a little more favourable,' adds Martin.

10 must-try New Zealand Pinot Noirs

- Ata Rangi Pinot Noir, Martinborough
- Bell Hill Vineyard Pinot Noir, North Canterbury
- Burn Cottage Vineyard Pinot Noir, Central Otago
- Craggy Range Aroha Pinot Noir, Martinborough
- Escarpment Vineyard Kupe Pinot Noir, Martinborough
- Felton Road Block 3 Pinot Noir, Central Otago
- Fromm Clayvin Vineyard Pinot Noir, Marlborough
- Kusuda Wines Pinot Noir, Martinborough
- Pyramid Valley Vineyards Earth Smoke Pinot Noir, North Canterbury
- Rippon Tinker's Field Pinot Noir, Central Otago

RIESLING – 'LIFE IS HARD ENOUGH, LET US DRINK LIGHT WINE'

In this profile from her Louis Roederer-award-winning *The wines of Germany* (2019), Anne Krebiehl MW traces the life and times of one of Germany's signature grape varieties and explains in detail its complex and nuanced flavour profile – there's far more to it than petrol aromas.

Nobody knows exactly when or where Riesling originated. We do know that Riesling is ancient, that it has a parent–offspring relationship with Gouais Blanc, this most promiscuous of European grapes, and a possible sibling relationship with Savagnin Blanc. There are numerous theories but historian John Winthrop Haeger has done thorough detective work.[1] He concludes that, 'it is in north-eastern France and astride the linguistic divide [between France and Germany] that both Gouais and Savagnin show the greatest genetic diversity and the most numerous surviving progeny, which makes that area the most likely candidate for Riesling's birthplace.' Haeger also cautions against pouncing on the first documented mention of Riesling in 1435, or later mentions in 1464 and 1490; simply because neither spelling nor ampelography were reliable then. Notwithstanding all these valid question marks, Riesling emerged as a quality variety in Germany over the course of a few centuries. Much is made of two key dates: the Prince-Abbot of Fulda's order

---

1 Haeger, John Winthrop, *Riesling Rediscovered*, University of California Press, Oakland, 2016

in 1720/21 to plant Schloss Johannisberg's vineyards in the Rheingau to Riesling, and Clemens Wenceslaus Elector of Trier's 1787 edict to replace the lesser varieties of the Mosel vineyards with Riesling and other quality varieties. Whether all of Schloss Johannisberg was planted exclusively to Riesling is doubtful and we know that the 1787 edict was never fully implemented – but these dates set important markers in Germany's Riesling history. Riesling was also favoured in earlier instances: in 1669 Freiherr von Leyen ordered the planting of 200 Riesling vines per annum in his Nahe vineyards; in 1688 the clearing of a hillside in Langenlonsheim (Nahe) was permitted on the condition that only Riesling be planted; a 1697 ordinance restricts plantings in the Bingener Scharlachberg to Riesling. In 1780 new plantings in Bechtheim (Rheinhessen) are restricted to Riesling and Traminer. Thus, by the late eighteenth century, Riesling clearly had a reputation for quality. By the late nineteenth century it had reached glory: the world's most expensive white wines were Rhine and Mosel Rieslings. Elsewhere monovarietal plantings were rare, as was quality viticulture. Riesling's attributes, as we know them today, made it eminently suitable for Germany. Riesling can thrive in cool climates and requires minimum growing season temperatures of 13–15°C. Its hard wood makes it particularly hardy in cold winters while its late-budding habit helps it to avoid spring frosts. It requires good exposure to ripen fully but prefers poor soils. It is more drought resistant than other varieties – in short, it thrives where others struggle. This is the case especially on steep slopes. Riesling's mid- to late-ripening habit takes advantage of the longer autumn day-length in higher latitudes. Northerly Riesling is proof that it is light, not heat, that ripens grapes. Light enables photosynthesis while raised temperature increases the metabolic rate of vines. When summer heat has passed and autumns are sunny but cooler, the long ripening with slow sugar accumulation and acid retention enables the synthesis of aromatic compounds and their precursors. These processes are heightened in Germany's cool but sunny Saar, Ruwer, Mosel and Nahe valleys, where Germany's most distinctive Rieslings grow. It is this combination of inherent lightness and aromatic depth that has always marked Riesling out. Its aromatic spectrum is wide and changes with the degree of ripeness. As regards climate, Riesling can thrive in cool climates but has proved itself adaptable to higher average temperatures, both in Germany and in warmer Riesling regions of the world, albeit expressing a different wine style.

*Riesling at every stage of ripeness: all were picked on the same day, 18
October 2018, in a parcel of Clemens Busch's Pündericher Marienberg
vineyard in the Mosel. This explains why selective harvesting, in vineyards
where such conditions can occur, is key. Photo courtesy of Ralf Kaiser*

Flavour and acid

Two groups of organic compounds are greatly responsible for Riesling's
varietal aromas: terpenes and norisoprenoids. Both are bound by sugars
in grape juice but set free during fermentation. Norisoprenoids like
β-damascenone and β-ionone are key to varietal character. Terpenes,
amply present in nature, like citronellol, geraniol, nerol, hotrienol and
linalool, variously give citrus, fruit, floral and spice notes to Riesling.
Terpenes are also responsible for the headiness of Muscat and Gewürztraminer, but Riesling has them in lesser concentrations. As Haeger puts
it, 'Riesling occupies a sweet spot in this complex aromatic space. It is
blessed with enough terpenes and norisoprenoids to be both interesting
and distinctive, and enough variety of terpenes to display a wide range
of aromatic personalities.' The fact that terpenes can be both free and
bound explains the wide aromatic spectrum, depending on the individual aroma composition of a wine. It may also explain the changing aromas
of Riesling as it ages. However, where Riesling really stands apart is in
its acidity. Where other white grape varieties can have total acidity levels
(measured in tartaric acid) of between 4 and 6 grams per litre, Riesling
regularly clocks up 7–9 grams per litre and can even go beyond 10 grams
per litre and still make a balanced wine. It is likely that our personal
predilections for acidity determine whether we become Riesling fans or

not. To me, acidity in wine acts like bright light: it pulls everything into sharp focus and illuminates every nuance of flavour, creating precision and clarity. Or as Egon Müller puts it, 'Acidity is what turns Riesling into Riesling. You have to have acidity, otherwise the wine is not good.'

That Rieslings taste so different even when harvested from adjoining plots is down to a complex matrix of viticultural and oenological conditions. Soil composition, water availability, planting density, rootstock and scion, training, canopy management and harvest point already offer vast permutations of flavour. Oenological practices add another layer of possibility: destemming, crushing fruit or not, skin contact, pressing regimen, settling and clarification of must, yeast, fermentation vessel, temperature as well as cellar temperature all have bearings on how aromas express themselves. Yet Riesling is often described as 'mineral', a semantically treacherous term that implies a direct link between stony soils and perceived flavours. Rieslings from limestone or sandstone, slate or basalt, granite or rhyolite express very different aromas while still preserving the varietal signature of Riesling. But it is simplistic to think that these are the aromas of the soils themselves – plant metabolism is too complex. That different soils, together with numerous other variables – notably water availability – result in different flavours is not in doubt. Even soil colour reflecting sunlight radiation into the canopy affects enzymatic processes within the grape which in turn affect flavour. 'There is however no direct proven link between the soil composition and the taste of a wine although there are some correlations,' notes Geisenheim's president Professor Dr Hans Schultz, drawing on recent research.

Acid and sugar

Whether bone-dry, lusciously sweet or anywhere in between, Riesling can make balanced and compelling wines. This is not down to sugar alone but to acidity, which balances the sweetness. It is wrong to look at sugar levels in isolation when both acidity *and* sugar levels are significant. A Pinot Gris at 4.5 grams per litre acidity and 4.5 grams per litre residual sugar is starting to cloy. A Riesling at 7.5 grams per litre acidity and 4.5 grams per litre sugar comes across as dry. The same Riesling at 7.5 grams per litre sugar would still taste almost dry. Residual sugar occurs mostly as fructose, because yeasts prefer to metabolize glucose. When exploring perceived sweetness–sourness interactions, Zamora et al. found that 'the suppressive effect of tartaric acid on fructose sweetness is stronger than the suppressive effect of fructose on tartaric acid sourness.'[2] It must also be noted that in very small quantities, sugar does not act as a sweetener but as a flavour enhancer of fruit – a fact also evident in side-by-side comparisons of dosaged and non-dosaged Champagnes. This explains why Riesling can take a certain amount of residual sugar and still taste dry. The sensory perception of sweetness and acidity in wine is very complex and not fully understood. Alcohol as well as acid-buffering potassium have an effect. This is indirectly linked to the pH of wines, which in cool-climate Rieslings can be very low. Some winemakers insist that low pH changes the perception of acidity, others refute that pH affects the perception of sweetness or acidity. Context is everything: 'Sugar is a substance you can measure, but sweetness is a human sensation – they are just not entirely related,' another scientist, Clark Smith, says. Whatever your flavour preference is, inherent acidity means that Riesling can be made successfully in a wide spectrum of wine styles. Working towards a desired wine style starts in the vineyard. While certain sites will, for example, favour the development of botrytis, other factors like ventilation and soil moisture also play a role, as does planting density, yield, training, sun exposure, canopy height and management. These are decisive factors. Aiming for *Kabinett* as opposed to *Grosses Gewächs*, encouraging botrytis infection or not, demands different viticultural approaches.

TDN – the famous petrol aroma

Riesling is often associated with one particularly pungent aroma compound: TDN or 1,1,6-trimethyl-1,2-dihydronaphthaline. The perception threshold for this norisoprenoid is just 2 micrograms per litre. High temperatures, berry exposure to sun and vine stress from drought, heat and nutrient deficiency during the growing season will increase the production of non-volatile TDN precursors. These form both free and bound TDN in the finished wine. TDN is more common in Rieslings from riper years or warm climates. Synthesis of TDN is also influenced by Riesling genetics and pressing regimen. Winemakers are wise to this and protect their grapes from sunlight with shaded canopies. Professor Dr Ulrich Fischer of Weincampus Neustadt explains the TDN life cycle in Riesling thus: bound aroma compounds are released during

2 Zamora, M.C., Goldner, M.C. and Galmarini, M.V., 'Sourness-Sweetness Interactions in Different Media: White Wine, Ethanol', *Journal of Sensory Studies*, November 2006

fermentation and ageing. If TDN is present, it will become more intense with time, as bound TDN is released. At the same time free TDN dissipates, so wine is in a constant state of flux. Over time, most wines reach a peak and stay stable for years, until TDN levels recede again as free TDN is dissipated and the reserves of bound TDN are used up. The storage temperature of bottled wine also has an influence on the release of bound TDN: at 7°C less than 2 micrograms per litre is converted; at 15°C less than 8 micrograms per litre, at 25°C less than 30 micrograms per litre. Fischer also compared TDN in Australian and German Rieslings. While some Australian Rieslings show very low TDN readings of as little as 2 micrograms per litre, the lowest median values of 36 micrograms per litre were observed in Adelaide Hills Riesling. Notably, this rather low reading for Australia is still higher than any TDN level measured in 27 vintages ranging from 1959 to 2010 in aged Riesling wines from the Staatsweingut mit Johannitergut in the Pfalz. Here the highest reading was 19 micrograms per litre for the warm 2005 vintage. This may well be down to the fact that solar radiation is weaker in autumn, when Riesling ripens. It is my experience that many people misidentify mature Riesling aromas – often heady like chamomile tincture – as TDN. Not every mature Riesling has that petrol smell.

WINEMAKING

QVEVRI: THE VESSEL OF DREAMS

The Georgian qvevri is rooted deep in the history of wine production but has in recent years captured the imagination of 'natural' winemakers around the world. Here, in an excerpt from her 2020 book *The wines of Georgia*, Lisa Granik MW explains how these traditional clay vessels are made and used by today's winemakers.

Qvevri are the clay vessels used for making wines according to the traditional Georgian winemaking method. (In western Georgia they are called churi.) They are found in the marani, more wine storage shed than cellar in some cases, but it can be a perfectly designed cellar. Whether attached to the house or nearby in the yard, the marani is akin to a sacred temple; indeed, it was often the site of surreptitious baptisms and other Christian rites during Georgia's tumultuous history.

What are qvevri about, how are they made, and what makes them so special? For an object with a history that goes back thousands of years, the literature is remarkably sparse. For generations, qvevri-making and qvevri wine production were oral traditions handed down from father to son. It was only under Georgia's 'Golden Age' in the eleventh to thirteenth centuries, and again under Soviet rule, that the empirical, technical and scientific aspects of the 'Kakhetian Technique' began to be broken down, analysed and taught. While they might have been in the library, these materials were made available primarily to wine science students and professional winemakers who already had learned the fundamentals of conventional winemaking. Home winemakers would not have sought out this information; their winemaking was based entirely on tradition.

At the same time, many nuances and personal experiences were never recorded. Even today, too few producers keep daily logs or detailed journals as to production procedures, treatments, rackings and so forth to inform future decisions and identify long-term trends.[1] Only in recent years have researchers embarked on scientific study of qvevri and qvevri wines; much more needs to be learned. Here, I explore the qvevri's origins, method of production, use and maintenance, along with variations among Georgia's provinces.

The exact origin of the qvevri/churi is unknown, but it is the centrepiece to all of Georgian winemaking historically. The earliest qvevri most similar in shape to those used in Georgia today were found in an Iron Age settlement near the town of Rustavi in eastern Georgia. This qvevri had a flat bottom, a stone lid, and was not buried.

It took some time for the qvevri to reach their current standard shape, as initially they were wide in the middle and tapered at the base and not buried. The shape of the 'modern' vessel continued to evolve from the third millennium BCE, as the bottom became increasingly pinched; it is theorized that this is when producers began to bury them in the earth, first to their 'shoulders' and, by the fourth century CE, up to the neck. The word 'qvevri' is thought to be derived from 'kveuri', meaning 'something dug deep in the ground'[2]. At some point before the Common Era, beeswax began to be applied to the interior. At a later date, a cement lining was added to protect the qvevri when they were delivered to their marani or as added protection in case of earthquakes or tremors.

Until very recently, what has been 'known' about qvevri was based on empirical evidence, although some preferred to invoke myths, legends and romantic stories. Two recent studies have endeavoured to develop a scientific understanding of qvevri production and use. The first was sponsored by Deutsche Gesellschaft für Internationale Zusammenarbeit (GIZ), evaluating the practices of a group of small producers; the second, a doctoral dissertation to examine the clay minerals and their effect on wine.[3] This section will describe the traditional method of building qvevri and the implications of specific practices and choices.

1　This failure to log or chart daily growing conditions, timing of treatments, and practices applies equally to vineyard activities.

2　Gorgiladze, R. *Savoring Georgia*. Tbilisi: Cezanne Printing House, 2013.

3　Giorgi Barisashvili set forth tales about qvevri as well as a trove of empirical evidence and practical recommendations (Barisashvili, G. 'Making wine in qvevri – a unique Georgian tradition'. *Biological Farming Association*. Tbilisi: Elkana, 2011). Glonti and Glonti detail qvevri history and present chemical analyses of distinct characteristics of qvevri wines (Glonti, T. and Glonti, Z. *The qvevri and the Kakhetian wine*. Tbilisi: Georgian Traditional Wine Fund, 2018).

Different qvevri styles

The mineral content of the clay used for qvevri varies among the different quarries from which it is mined. This includes carbon and any organic matter, which must be burnt out;[4] aluminium, silicon, quartz and feldspar are present in various proportions. Variations among qvevri may include:

- Variation among clays from a single quarry (clay granulation and mineral structures vary). For example, the GIZ study concluded that the clay from Tkemlovana quarry is coarse, leading to porous qvevri that tend to leak.
- Variations among the two components mixed with the clay (limestone, clay or river sand)
- The temperature when the clay dries and sets
- The temperature at which it bakes in the kiln
- Beeswax lining (or not)
- Lime/cement exterior
- Style of the individual qvevri master

In the past, qvevri were produced all over Georgia, but today they primarily are made in Kakheti (Vardisubani and Shilda), Imereti

---

4 The GIZ study recommends an extended preliminary phase (to burn out the carbon in the clay) before the actual firing of the qvevri. The temperature of the 'pre-phase' may be anywhere from 250°C to 700°C depending on the clay source.

(Tkemlovana, Makatubani (Satsable), Shrosha) and Guria (Aketi and Atsana). They differ in shape depending on the origin. In Kakheti, they have a bigger middle bulge; in Imereti, they are narrower; in Guria, the exterior is ribbed.

The quarried clay is moistened and allowed to rest for one day to absorb the water, and only clean water from a running source, not spring or still water, is used. The moistened clay is uneven, so it is put into a large grinder to grind, mix and homogenize the particles. Then the clay is shaped into logs.

Qvevris are 'built up' from the bottom nipple. There is no potter's wheel; the tapered base is shaped and set on a wooden tripod. The clay logs (each about 10 centimetres in diameter) are layered, shaped and smoothed to build the sides. After each log is shaped and smoothed, it must dry for two days before the next is placed on top and smoothed into place. In inclement weather, it may be a three to four day wait for each new log. While each layer sets, the top is covered with paper to keep it moist while it waits for the next layer to be fixed. Several qvevri are built simultaneously. The qvevri maker has no measuring instruments, he simply eyeballs the growing vessel as he shapes it. 'It's a sensual, mystical, meditative experience,' says Zaza Kbilashvili, a fourth-generation qvevri 'master' (his son will be the fifth). 'You have a relationship with each one.' Once shaped, the qvevri sits for three to four weeks to set before it is fired. It takes about two weeks to build up a 1,000-litre qvevri. This is seasonal work, lasting only from March to November.

The kiln in which the qvevri is fired is a three-sided brick structure with openings about three-quarters up the back wall. The largest qvevri are inserted into the kiln in rows, with smaller ones fitted in between to fill the space. The fourth brick wall is then constructed; an opening at the bottom is left to insert the firewood. The fire burns around the clock and the temperature is judged by experience – Kbilashvili's father knew it was time to take down the wall by the colour and nature of the emerging smoke. Kbilashvili peers in and judges by the change in qvevri colour – there is an evolution of four shades from brown to the final orange terracotta. The firing process lasts five or six days.

One of the challenges in qvevri production is that they were made according to tradition – without temperature gauges. The lower the temperature, the more porous the vessel and the greater likelihood of leakage. The Gamtkitsulashvili study found that vessels that are baked at 800 to 850°C impart a salty, wet clay flavour to the wine, negatively affecting wine quality (Gamtkitsulashvili 2018). The rate at which the kiln heats up is significant; the GIZ study suggests first heating the kiln to 700°C, maintaining this temperature for at least one day to avoid cracks and fissures.

Over the next several days the temperature should increase to a minimum of 1,000 to 1,100°C and be maintained for at least six hours. If a qvevri cracks during the firing process, some masters may patch the crack. This may mask it, but it is not a permanent fix. In time (one to three years) the crack will reappear, the qvevri will leak, and the crack become a home for nesting bacteria and spoilage organisms, which negatively affects the wine for the unsuspecting winemaker. The qvevri is then useless for winemaking. Thus, producers are increasingly requiring contracts from qvevri masters guaranteeing replacement qvevri should problems arise after three years' use.

Analysing the clay from three quarries, the GIZ study noted that the sintering process starts at around 820°C for the clay, and above 1,100°C or 1,150°C for the quartz and feldspar components, depending on the quarry. Thus, to obtain a homogeneously constructed vessel, the burning temperature must exceed 1,100°C (or 1,150°C for Tkemlovana qvevri).[5] GIZ also recommends using natural gas to heat the oven as it can reach and maintain the high temperatures reliably. After cooling for three days, the kiln can be opened.

After the qvevri is removed from the kiln, beeswax is brushed on if the customer wishes; 1.5 to 2.0 kilos of wax is needed for a 1,000 to 1,500-litre qvevri. The main advantage of the beeswax is to smooth out the interior, making it easier for the skins, stems and juice to circulate during fermentation. Properly maintained qvevri need not be re-waxed. Problem qvevri may have their wax melted off and removed before the vessel is heat-treated to destroy harmful micro-organisms; the qvevri is then re-waxed. The wax penetrates the vessel walls, filling the pores, thereby minimizing the vessel's porosity and preventing leaks.

---

5   Alternative research found that optimal kiln temperature for baking the qvevri is between 950° and 1,050°C (Gamtkitsulashvili, G. 'The research of constituent clay-minerals of qvevri and its influence on wine' (Doctoral dissertation), Telavi State University, Telavi, Georgia, 2018). The GIZ project was based on clay samples from Vardisubani, Tkemlovana, and Satsable; Gamtkitsulashvili's, the same three plus Atsana. Clay vessels made elsewhere in the world are baked at higher temperatures to ensure a complete seal and prevent loss of wine. European ceramicists, for example, fire at high, measured temperatures (1,200°C) and allow customers to set permeability levels according to their specific needs.

The wax-filled pores may cause a hermetic closure of the qvevri and prevent the ingress of oxygen into the wine (to the degree it happens at all). It also forges a barrier between the clay and wine, thereby inhibiting mineral leaching. The wax arguably also is more hygienic: the smoother walls are easier to clean, and the wax-filled pores are not available as nesting places for harmful bacteria.

Opponents of waxing contend that the beeswax has the potential for trapping and disguising bacteria within the qvevri pores; in time these bacteria may multiply and infect the wine.

Research in this area continues.

*

In eastern Georgia, the qvevri are housed inside a stone structure. In the west, the qvevri (churi) traditionally were out in the open, surrounded by tall broadleaf trees for shade; though in Imereti, the churi were outside but often sheltered by a wooden structure such as a small shed or a roof held up by posts. Hygiene is more difficult when the qvevri are outside, as is temperature control. Hence, some western producers recently have moved their qvevri inside or are building structures enclosing them.

Qvevri are 'planted' into the ground in a marani or wine cellar. The wine cellar is dug out, the qvevri manoeuvred in, and the earth filled in around them. How they are planted is crucial as it is difficult to change or extract them afterwards. Some winemakers put approximately 1 metre of gravel as a top layer. This will prevent dirt from getting into the qvevri or, if cold water is poured around the outside of the qvevri walls, prevent overheating. Many, however, tile or cement the marani floor so that it can be washed. Bastien Warskotte has the necks of his qvevri several centimetres above the floor surface so that when he washes the floors of his marani, no dirty water or cleaning fluid can drip into them. Not all are so fastidious.

Modern qvevri range from 100 to 3,500 litres. As with any sort of fermentation vessel, smaller qvevri can be used for experimentation or when there is insufficient fruit available to fill a larger one. It is believed that 1,000 to 1,200 litres is the sweet spot for fermentation: smaller sizes may have difficulty maintaining the proper temperatures for fermentation; in the larger qvevri, there is a greater danger of the fermentation becoming too hot too quickly, thereby burning off some delicate aromatic qualities, perhaps shocking or killing the natural yeasts. Most producers will have qvevri in a range of sizes.

Peak fermentation for white wines is typically at 28°C in the larger qvevris; in 500-litre vessels, it often remains below 20°C. In classic Kakhetian white winemaking – with skins and some percentage of stems, depending on ripeness[6] – the grapes and skins float to the surface of the qvevri due to the captured carbon dioxide; a few producers use a variation of a submerged cap but most punch down.[7] Some may leave all of the solids in contact with the wine for as long as seven months. The fermentation typically lasts a week to twelve days.

While the malolactic conversion may occur simultaneously with the alcoholic fermentation, this is not encouraged for Kakhetian amber wines, which already have lower acidity levels. In Imereti, the lower pH levels and cooler temperatures naturally inhibit the malolactic fermentation. If the malolactic conversion is desired (as with red wines), some producers, before racking the wine off skins, may warm the receiving qvevri with a heating element.

Many small winemakers judge that the alcoholic fermentation is complete when the wine is no longer bubbling (there are both visible and audible cues); larger, professional producers perform laboratory analyses. Once fermentation has completed, the qvevris are then sealed.

In eastern Georgia, traditionally the qvevri were sealed by covering them with slate or other types of rock. Clay, mixed with a small amount of dry sulphur, is prepared to seal the lid. A sulphur wick would be lit just inside the neck, the lid affixed and weighted down; the sulphur smoke inside cools and forms a vacuum – the clay dries to form a hermetic seal. The stone is then covered with earth and dampened periodically to maintain the seal.

In western Georgia, the lid (called by a variety of names, including *orgo*, *badimi*, *lagvinari*) was wooden, made from chestnut, linden or oak trees. The lids would be soaked in water to remove bitter and coarse substances. A hole in the centre allowed carbon dioxide to escape during fermentation. The lids were placed directly on the qvevri, then covered with a thick covering of a yellow soil, packed down and moistened to

---

6   Some use only Rkatsiteli stems as they tend to be the ripest. Some also may lay stems out in the sun to burn off any green character before adding them to the qvevri.

7   The submerged cap generally is not recommended as it prevents punching down, which is the primary form of temperature control.

create a thick clay. A tight complete seal is imperative to prevent oxygen ingress.

Just as producers differ as to their fermentation practices, so do they differ (sometimes vehemently!) as to their qvevri cleaning practices. There is no established cleaning protocol. Hygiene continues to be one of the greatest challenges in Georgia, not least because qvevri are notoriously hard to clean, given the porous nature of the clay construction and the qvevri's immovable underground location. New producers may make an acceptable (or better) wine their first time, but are insufficiently vigilant about cleaning their qvevri, equipment and marani; later vintages show problems that accelerate over time. Part of the challenge is that cleaning is hard physical labour and also requires hypervigilant attention to detail.[8]

Traditionally, first all solids would be removed, whether scooped out or vacuumed. Then a cleaner climbs into the qvevri and scrubs the walls to scrape off any particles that might be stuck. Various brushes, made from natural substances with antiseptic qualities, would facilitate the scraping. Hot water washing (without a person jumping into the qvevri) was also the practice in some areas and in big wineries during the twentieth century.

After scrubbing, the qvevri is rinsed several times with an alkaline solution. Producers vary as to whether they prefer the traditional 'ashwash' (wood ashes mixed with water) or slaked lime (CaOH) solution. Caustic soda and sodium bicarbonate also may be used. Some might burn elemental sulphur to eliminate microbial activity, but producers differ as to whether this is 'traditional', even though it was available and used in Georgia before 1900. The next step is to neutralize the surface with acidified water, usually a citric acid solution.

It was long thought that empty qvevris were best stored clean and dry in a well-ventilated area to prevent mould. If this is not possible (especially as much of Georgia is humid), a soda ash or lime coating may be painted on the walls and neck of the vessel. Some producers are vehemently opposed to this practice, as the lime has the potential of raising the pH of wines that already have relatively lower acidities. Two modern alternatives include filling the qvevri with a sulphur/citric acid solution, checking it biweekly to ensure its condition and/or refresh it, or filling

---

8   This is one reason it is impossible to judge a winemaker after a single vintage. If the ardour for winemaking exceeds that of hygiene, successive vintages can become increasingly problematic.

the qvevri with inert gas, then sealing it hermetically until it needs to be prepared for the new vintage.

Before the harvest, water is sprayed into the qvevri and the lime or ash coating is scraped out (this usually takes several hours for each one). The qvevri is then rinsed multiple times until the coating is removed and the rinsing water is fully clear, and then the next year's grapes can be loaded in. And those grapes must be sorted, eliminating damaged or rotten grapes and any extraneous material, before being put into the qvevri.

Even trained winemakers admit that every year they may have fermentations that go awry: 'You can think a qvevri is clean, but it's not, and the next thing you know, the wine is ruined and you've lost [literally] a ton of fruit.'

Winemaking in qvevri is challenging and laborious – all the more so when one is committed to minimal intervention. The challenges often converge and cascade to produce wine that is muddled and not reflective of terroir. First, the fruit must be pristine, sorting out any damaged, rotten grapes and extraneous material; too many producers say they have no control over their fruit or say they do not have time to sort their fruit. Second, Georgia's warm climate and the lack of temperature control in many wineries, plus the comparatively lower acidities, make the grapes and wines more prone to oxidation. While some oxidation may be a deliberate stylistic choice, oxidation nonetheless can abet microbial contamination and spoilage when winery conditions are more rudimentary. Third, the equipment necessary to facilitate cleaning and to ensure that the qvevri are perfectly clean is another capital expenditure that can be difficult for small producers without economies of scale. Nevertheless, it is crucial that the winemaker be hyper-vigilant about winery and equipment hygiene to ensure that the native yeasts drive the fermentations and spoilage bacteria remain at bay.[9]

*

The first qvevri made by 3D printing technology appeared in 2018, but they are not yet in widespread use. Producers are experimenting with newer methods to improve hygiene and to make certain processes easier.

---

9 Westerners will be familiar with the phenomenon of 'cellar palate', where the winemaker is so immersed in his own work that he is inured to problems that lurk in the cellar. Similarly, those who grew up drinking wines intended only for family and friends might not recognize flaws (e.g. secondary fermentation in red wines; mould and microbiological instability) in the wine.

Many now use mechanical crusher/destemmers (that have the added benefit of being easier to clean). One oenologist has isolated a Georgian fermentation yeast that he is cultivating to allow inoculation with an indigenous product. Beka Gotsadze and Nukri Kurdadze have piping around their qvevri to circulate water and act as a form of temperature control (Gotsadze's allows both warming and cooling). Glass or metal lids are often used instead of stone, as the former allows for some visual inspection to ensure that there is no oxygen ingress. Some producers have adopted stainless steel rods for punching down, which are easier to keep sanitary, instead of wooden sticks and rods. And, in between punchdown, the rods are fully submerged in a sulphur dioxide solution. Similarly, lids often are outfitted with airlocks so that carbon dioxide can escape but air cannot enter. An increasing number of producers are regularly (monthly) checking the condition of the lees during the months of ageing to ensure that no mercaptans or other problems are developing. Other producers are experimenting with microx diffusers to facilitate tannin polymerization without barrels. Food-grade silicon sealant is increasingly used instead of clay to affix the lid. Power washers and washers with rotating heads are used to clean the qvevri more thoroughly. Even 'natural' producers are applying a potassium metabisulphite solution to the qvevri walls and sterilizing the qvevri walls with UV lamps (such as used in hospitals) to prevent harmful microorganisms from reproducing. Careful, judicious use of sulphur dioxide is reappearing. And people are experimenting with cleaning with ozone.

THE APPASSIMENTO PROCESS

Both Valpolicella and Soave produce notable wines from dried grapes. In this extract from *Amarone and the fine wines of Verona*, from 2018, Michael Garner discusses the fine points of the process; should grapes be dried on racks or in nets, how much should a winemaker assist in the drying process and does noble rot have a place in these wines?

While some form of dessert wine is made in most wine-producing areas, the method of production will differ radically from region to region as well as from country to country. Where a reliably warm and dry climate extends through into the early autumn (typical of southern Mediterranean countries), the harvested fruit is left on straw mats to dry in the sun – for example, the French *vin de paille* or, closer to home, the Passito wines from the island of Pantelleria, to name but two. Towards the northern edges of the European vine-growing belt, for instance in parts of the Mosel and Rhine valleys, selected grapes will even be exposed to mid autumn's sub-zero temperatures and left to partially freeze on the plant before being made into Eiswein. Clearly the climate of an area will determine what can or cannot be done to concentrate the sugar content of the crop. For centuries the drying of grapes was a way of preserving the fresh fruit and the means whereby stronger and more stable wines could be produced. They became known as Passito wines (from the verb *appassire*, to wither or shrivel) and they were able to be kept for longer thanks to higher sugar and alcohol levels. Throughout Italy, when macerated together with herbs and other aromatic substances, wines of this style were thought to have medicinal properties and would serve as palliative roborants at a time when no other form of medication was available. They were the original tonic wines which subsequently evolved into the 'digestivo-style' products such as Amaro which still have a massive following in the south of the country. Gradually, though, the focus changed, with the aim of capitalizing on the extra richness and intensity of both aroma and flavour which the process delivers, to produce a more highly prized wine which could typically accompany the sweet course or indeed act as a 'meditation' wine. In central and more northern parts of Italy an 'indoor' method of production was necessary owing to the drop in temperatures and rise in humidity levels that accompany the increased risk of inclement weather in the period following on from the harvest. Nowhere, however, is the practice of drying grapes to be processed into wine so widespread as it is in Soave and, in particular, Valpolicella. While originally the fruit was – as elsewhere – processed for the production of sweet or dessert wines, over the last century a much drier style has steadily evolved to meet more modern tastes and has proven to be a resounding success. As a result the operation has become big business during the last two or three months of the calendar year throughout the many villages of the Valpolicella area. Huge industrial-sized warehouses are crammed from floor to ceiling with layers of plastic crates filled with grapes. The drying process is fully automated, with giant fans to keep the air moving and the extra insurance of dehumidifying machines to protect against rot. This is the modern face of *appassimento*: it is of course a far cry from the traditional method which remained by and large unaltered for centuries.

As we have seen, the art of grape drying in the Veronese has been practised since Roman times, when fruit was left to shrivel on fibre matting. By the sixth century the process had become more sophisticated; Cassiodorus described the painstaking operation of suspending each individual grape cluster from strings or threads hung vertically from the ceiling, a procedure which anticipates the modern obsession with avoiding the onset of rot. Whether the two systems continued side by side is not recorded, nor when, potentially to save space and to some extent labour, the Veronesi reverted back to the original method of laying the grapes out horizontally. This development may well have occurred as a result of the arrival of the silkworm-farming industry during the latter half of the sixteenth century and was certainly common practice by the eighteenth. Racks known as *arele* were used to bring on the silkworm larvae when they became active in the spring. The larvae would feed on their staple diet of mulberry leaves spread out over the *arele*, making the later operation of 'harvesting' the cocoons of silk spun as the

Grapes drying on the traditional arele

animal entered its pupal phase more practical. Over the winter months, before the eggs had hatched, it is logical to assume that the *arele* may well have been put to another use: it is entirely consistent with the resilient and resourceful character of Veronese farmers that the few tools of the trade they possessed would have been used in as many ways as possible. Stacking the racks one on top of another would have been a simple and straightforward way of optimizing storage space. Drying the grapes by laying them out is, in a way, less efficient than suspending the grapes from netting where the laborious task of frequently turning the fruit over to expose each side of the bunch to the passage of air is bypassed and a quick visual check is sufficient. However, turning the bunches regularly these days is not always a practical reality and perhaps not even strictly necessary given the almost industrial scale of the operation where 'controlled' *appassimento* is employed. Where plastic crates are used, and they are by far the most common container, the bottom is usually a perforated diagonal lattice which will therefore permit some air to circulate.

Nowadays bunches are once more laid out to dry, though racks or more commonly wooden or plastic crates are used instead of mats. Those wineries which stick with the traditional system of using the *arele* champion bamboo as the best material for its construction. The canes are lashed together and the gaps between them allow for some passage of air to help maintain the fruit in a healthy state. The hard, round surface of bamboo means that any leakage from the grapes therefore runs off the material rather than being absorbed, thus minimizing the subsequent risk of spoilage. In addition, bamboo is an extremely durable wood and will not need to be renewed with any great frequency. Some however argue that wooden crates are useful precisely because they absorb humidity and thus reduce the risk of infection by grey rot. Meanwhile other wineries prefer plastic to the flimsier wooden crates as not only are they more durable but, crucially, much easier to sterilize and keep clean. Whichever material has been chosen, these plateaux – as they are also known – are stacked together sometimes within an open framework, stretching almost from floor to ceiling in a designated *fruttaio* or drying room often situated on the top floor of the winery building. The time-honoured preference for siting the *fruttaio* in small buildings adjacent to hillside vineyards is still widely in evidence: producers point to the fact that these are ideal locations in order to benefit from the drier and windier positions higher up the slopes. During the initial phases of *appassimento,* when the fruit is most at risk from infection, the simple expedient of opening windows during drier spells and then closing them again when humidity levels threaten to rise maximizes the chances of maintaining the integrity of the crop throughout the process. The fruit is considered to be at its most vulnerable in terms of infection by grey rot during the first fifteen days. Often the *fruttaio* will be equipped with fans, and sometimes with dehumidifiers as well, as growers look to safeguard the health of the harvest they have spent the previous eight months or so working hard to realize.

Many producers rely on a very practical combination of the two approaches: the 'natural' or traditional, artisan way and 'assisted' *appassimento* which incorporates the use of machines to control the drying conditions. A classic example of this pragmatic modus operandi would be Masi's so-called NASA method (Natural *Appassimento* Super Assisted). Having collected and studied the effects of data relating to temperature, humidity, weight variations and ventilation over a number of favourable vintages, Masi looked to reproduce the conditions which can ensure an ideal environment for the drying grapes. Basically the idea is to measure and monitor ambient conditions and then modify them when necessary through the use of fans and dehumidifiers which kick in automatically when required. Masi developed this computer-operated system at their drying room at Garganago and the firm has a further twelve drying lofts at different locations. At the same time, Masi are adamant that the best conditions for the process include the storage of fruit on the classic *arele,* and furthermore are strong advocates for the influence of another 'natural' phenomenon which also continues to divide opinion.

The movement towards 'mechanically assisted' *appassimento* can, in real terms, be traced back to the early 1990s and in particular to the mercurial Franco Allegrini, owner and oenologist at the eponymous Fumane-based wine house. Franco identifies 1990 as the first great modern vintage for Amarone: 'In terms of climate, 1990 was an extraordinarily good vintage with no rain during the harvest and a dry autumn too. As a result, we had a crop of perfectly healthy grapes and we were able to maintain their integrity through to the finished product. That's the sort of wine I was looking for! But how could I continue to work at that level even in less favourable years? High humidity is almost standard in our area in the autumn months. The only solution was to try and control the drying process. That's where the idea of constructing a dedicated *fruttaio* came from. No more leaving things to chance! We could take charge of the whole process and get rid of rot.'

Having lost the entire *appassimento* crop of the 1987 vintage owing to an outbreak of grey rot, Franco was determined not to let that happen again. Roberto Ferrarini had completed his doctorate thesis at the University of Bologna at the end of the 1970s on the very topic of a new system of *appassimento* designed to protect the integrity of the raw materials. He built upon the pioneering studies into the subject in the 1970s of Professor Luciano Usseglio Tommaset, director of the oenological research centre at Asti in Piedmont. Under Ferrarini's guidance, Franco and a group of like-minded producers set about creating the first controlled *appassimento* warehouse close to the centre of the village of Fumane.

However, the presence of that same mould which destroyed Franco's crop can, in certain very particular conditions, have a potentially positive effect on the drying fruit according to a number of die-hard producers, Masi foremost among them. In its fully developed form as grey rot, the fungus can only have negative implications and any grapes showing telltale signs must be discarded immediately to stop the infection spreading. However, if the pathogenesis is limited it may take the form of so-called noble rot or *muffa nobile*, famous for its role in the creation of dessert wines like Sauternes and Tokaji Aszù. According to wine writer and researcher Dr Ronald S. Jackson, latent infections of the pathogen occur predominantly during the spring but may remain inactive. Under cool and dry storage conditions such as *appassimento*, the infection in its so-called 'larval' form is slowly rekindled. With the nascent infection there is little visible surface sporulation (unlike in the vineyard environment) and as well as further shrivelling, the colour of the infected fruit gradually becomes paler, changing from a deep, dark red and taking on more of a translucent lilac hue. In Soave, the colour of Garganega also modifies and the distinctly pink tinge typical of the ripe fruit will intensify. This 'larval' stage of *Botrytis cinerea* is kept in check by cool temperatures but, above all, by low humidity with the risk of the infection reaching its fully 'efflorescent' form more likely to occur under milder and rainier conditions.

One of the main effects of *muffa nobile* on the composition of the fruit will be the formation of higher than average levels of glycerol, evident in the finished wine as a luscious mouthfeel and an illusory sense of sweetness as many of the bitter and astringent qualities will seem softer accordingly. Modification of the aromatic components will also occur with the development of dried fruit notes and the classic 'honeyed' quality associated with botrytis, though this will be accompanied by a certain loss of freshness owing to a negative effect on monoterpenoids, esters and thiols. There are numerous other potential drawbacks including the formation of acetic acid, acetaldehyde and ethyl acetate, all of which are potentially damaging, as well as the production of laccase by the botrytis, one of the principal factors behind colour change and aroma loss. This oxidative enzyme acts on both anthocyanins, causing a certain browning of colour, and phenols, leading to the development of oxidative style aromas. *Muffa nobile* can then be a double-edged sword and its presence must be carefully limited to restrict the effect of its negative features. Overall, an Amarone which has experienced the effect of *muffa nobile* will display the round and luscious mouthfeel referred to above, along with sensations of extreme ripeness and preserved or macerated fruits; those wines without and which depend on maintaining the integrity of the grape skins, will typically have a deeper colour and a more structured and austere style with greater freshness of fruit characters. The production of the natural phenol resveratrol by the fruit as a form of protection against the pathogen is often talked up, though whether this stilbenoid has the health-sustaining properties some claim is open to debate.

It is of course tempting to buy into the somewhat romantic notion of a fine red wine which derives some of its character from partially botrytized fruit. 'Extremists' who defend the old ways argue that modern *appassimento* results merely in a concentration of aroma and flavour, and the nuances associated with the 'natural' method and *muffa nobile* are lacking in the final wine. There is some body of evidence to support such claims. Various experiments have seen grapes inoculated with botrytis and then stored under humidity- and temperature-controlled conditions before going on to produce creditable botrytized wines (see Batt et al.'s *Encyclopedia of Food Microbiology*, 2014); this would seem to demonstrate that the precarious task of managing botrytized fruit successfully is more than just a fantasy. However, many Amarone producers prefer not to expose their fruit to the risk of spoilage, embracing instead the security of controlled *appassimento* and the elimination of rot.

In some ways it's a similar story in Soave, though on a much reduced scale, of course; the two issues of how the grapes are stored and whether or not any presence at all of botrytis should be tolerated remain of critical importance. However, while the tradition of working with semi-dried grapes in Soave has roots that are as deep as those in neighbouring Valpolicella, the focus is more on keeping the tradition alive. While most of the major wineries in Soave continue to produce Recioto, it is usually in tiny quantities (currently around 0.25 per cent of the total of the various different Soave DOC and DOCG wines produced). The wine remains very much a niche product even though it deserves far greater recognition. Recioto di Soave and Recioto della Valpolicella share that common lineage which can be traced back at least as far as the sixth century AD and the Roman statesman Cassiodorus, though a parallel tradition, recently undergoing what might be termed a micro-revival, evolved in the small *frazione* of Brognoligo, part of the township of Monteforte d'Alpone. According to author and painter Massimiliano Bertolazzi, who hails from Monteforte, references to a local wine known as Vin Santo may be traced back to the early eighteenth century. The production of Vin Santo di Brognoligo has been maintained at very much a local family level with 'recipes' handed down from generation to generation. Gelmino Dal Bosco, owner and winemaker of Le Battistelle, explained his family's approach: 'The best grapes we would leave to dry and make Vin Santo. Every family would make some and save it for important occasions such as a marriage or the birth of a child. So we'd choose the best fruit from the oldest vines and dry the bunches until January or February until they looked just right, not too shrivelled. Then we'd press them and put the juice into *damigiane* and they'd be left there for six or seven years.' Sadly the production of Vin Santo di Brognoligo, which can only be sold as an IGT wine, has dwindled since Recioto di

Soave was included in the Soave DOC discipline and became a more important focus of attention. In 2008, for example, the Dal Bosco family made just 108 litres of the wine divided between two demijohns. Tasted in spring 2016, the 2007 was still remarkably fresh, luscious and perfumed. A more studied example of Vin Santo is available commercially, albeit in minuscule quantities (250 bottles a year) from the well-known Ca Rugate winery. Michele Tessari outlined how their Corte Durlo is made: 'We dry carefully selected Garganega grapes on strings known as *picai* which are hung from the rafters for three or four months. We ferment in wooden casks and with some contact with the air so the wine develops a type of protective *flor* we call the *teralina*. Then we transfer the wine to smaller barrels to finish the fermentation. Finally we seal the bung hole with cement and leave it to mature for six years.' Corte Durlo is produced as a Veneto Bianco Passito IGT wine and only in favourable years. Proceeds from sales go to the parish of Brognoligo: 'When my great-grandfather died in 1918, the church was a great comfort to my family,' explains Tessari. 'Firstly my grandfather, then my father and now me, we've always honoured our debt of gratitude.' Azienda Agricola Portinari, another small Brognoligo-based winery, also produce a version of Vin Santo which the family refer to as a Passito d'Oro (golden Passito), named Anna Giulia after Umberto's granddaughter.

Meanwhile in wineries like Coffele and Pieropan it is still possible to see nets of drying bunches suspended from the rafters in the time-honoured manner (Pieropan also make use of the traditional *arele*). Here the question of *Botrytis cinerea* is also dealt with in a much more relaxed fashion: for example, Pieropan see noble rot as an important element in the production of their DOCG Recioto Le Colombare. A mid-2000s study carried out by E. Tosi, R. Verzillo, A. Marangon and G. Zapparoli – 'The effect of Botrytis cinera on the quality of Recioto di Soave' – was reported in the *Informatore Agrario* periodical in 2006. The researchers conducted a series of 'microvinifications' on musts obtained from both botrytized and 'non-infected' fruit with interesting results. Clear differences in the colour, smell and taste were recorded: the so-called 'clean' must producing a paler wine with fresher, less evolved fruit aromas and less evident richness and sweetness on the palate, whereas those containing proportions of must from 'infected' fruit were of a deeper golden colour, with more nuanced and honeyed aromas and a greater sensation of sweetness. A subsequent study by many of the same group published in 2013 came to similar conclusions, noting that noble rot had a marked effect on the volatile components of the wine (notably various esters, phenols and lactones) which in turn influence aroma, flavour and structure. The positive side of noble rot is, it must be pointed out, generally much more closely associated with white wines so a more obvious 'match' is immediately apparent. Relatively free from the pressure of commercial incentives and logistical considerations, wineries like those mentioned above can devote as much time as they see fit to the production of a truly authorial style of wine.

Aside from the issues of botrytis and drying methodology, and irrespective of the colour of the fruit, the primary effect of drying grapes is the substantial loss of weight which the process brings about.

It is estimated that the grapes will lose on average between about 40 to 60 per cent of their weight through evaporation during *appassimento* as the water content in the pulp and juice of the fruit is slowly lost. The production regulations that cover both Amarone and the two forms of Recioto all specify a strict maximum volume of wine, not exceeding 40 per cent (or 42 for the rare Recioto di Soave Spumante), which can be extracted from the original mass of fruit that has been set aside. Such a substantial decrease can only be arrived at over a considerable length of time: in both Soave and Valpolicella pressing the semi-dried fruit for conversion into the DOCG wines is not, under normal circumstances, permitted to take place before 1 December following the vintage, a minimum of around two months, though in real terms the process will frequently last much longer. Some may argue that the decision of when to press should be based on a more precise chemical analysis of the components of the fruit, but the rules enshrine a principle which most uphold: the idea that such a highly nuanced wine cannot be hurried and requires time in the cellar and patience on behalf of the producer in order to achieve its full potential. What distinguishes Recioto and Amarone from other *passito* wines made elsewhere is indeed the length of time for which the fruit is left to dry. Many wineries will, in the case of red varieties, delay pressing until the beginning of the New Year if possible (which equates to a period of approximately three months), whereas it is common with Garganega to put off the start of the winemaking process until March, or even in some extreme cases Easter, when the grapes will have been drying for six months and may have lost as much as 70 per cent of their original weight. The final decision will always be determined by a combination of climatic conditions and the level of 'readiness' of the concentrated fruit the winemaker is searching for. This is why the real success of a vintage in Verona cannot be measured merely in terms of the health of the fruit at harvest time: weather patterns during the autumn and early winter play a major part too and will either compromise or confirm the quality of the crop that has been set aside for drying.

The main changes brought about by *appassimento* are the increased levels of sugar and glycerol; the balance between glucose and fructose sugars is tilted in favour of the latter, which are sweeter tasting, as the glucose sugars are partly transformed into glycerine and gluconic acid. Many of the other components of the fruit such as aromatic substances, acid levels and colouring materials, are also affected. For example, as the ratio of skin to pulp will be higher – up to as much as 35 per cent in some cases by the end of process – so the level of normally stable anthocyanins increases proportionately as the water content diminishes. This same principle will apply to other constituent elements, one reason why the acidity levels in these wines give such a remarkable sense of freshness.

The speed of *appassimento*, as regulations recognize, is governed by the three variables of temperature, humidity and air circulation. Higher temperatures speed up the process, as does greater ventilation, while a rise in humidity levels will slow things down (with a correspondingly increased risk of grey rot infection). The production discipline is once again designed to cover these potentially contentious issues: where ventilation and dehumidification is practised, neither may take place at any other than ambient temperatures. Low temperatures are indeed vital for maintaining constant levels of polyphenols and anthocyanins which become less stable in warmer conditions when the added danger of ending up with slightly cooked or caramelized flavours also applies. For the record it should also be noted that the various grape varieties will react differently to the *appassimento* process. Corvina will dry more quickly than Corvinone, though it is also more susceptible to rot; Rondinella is by comparison much more resistant to rot; Molinara on the other hand lies somewhere between Rondinella and Corvina. With the white grapes, Garganega is again quite easily affected by rot; Trebbiano di Soave too though as we have seen, the fact that the bunches are typically quite compact makes the variety less of a suitable candidate. All in all, *appassimento* is an extremely complex process and managing the many variables discussed above means that the final months of the year in the winery are rarely tranquil ones!

VINS DOUX NATURELS

The fortified wines of Roussillon form the backbone of the region's wine reputation, and it would seem every producer has their own way of making these wines. In 2021's *The wines of Roussillon*, Rosemary George MW persuaded a few of them to share their winemaking secrets.

Vin Doux Naturel covers several different styles of wine. All are fortified, and the differences come with the ageing process, or indeed the lack of élevage. The oxidative wines are traditional, whereas the reductive winemaking for Rimage and Grenat is more modern; they are for the new generation, with freshness and fruit. As Victor Gardiés of Domaine Gardiés put it, vin sec is more demanding, whereas with Vin Doux Naturel, the sugar camouflages any faults. For him, 'it is a wine for *fainéants*', that is, for the lazy.

Mutage

The first thing to decide is the right moment to add the alcohol, the grape spirit, and stop the fermentation. There is a broad band of residual sugar allowed, anything between 75 and 130 grams per litre, but it is usually 80–100 grams per litre. If there is too much sugar, the wine will be heavy. Daniel Laffite at Domaine des Soulanes talked about sliding the tannins behind the sugar, so that you have ripe fruit balanced by a streak of tannin. For his Grenat he mutes at 87 grams per litre, observing that at 10 grams more of sugar per litre the tannins are masked. If you mute three days later, you will need less alcohol and the wine will be drier. It is all a question of balancing sugar and alcohol. The tannic streak can be quite refreshing. The volume of alcohol depends upon how ripe the grapes are. Ripe grapes need less alcohol, which usually accounts for about 8 to 10 per cent of the volume. Philippe Gard at Coume del Mas wants a dry style for his Rimage, with some tannin, and some barrel ageing for a few months. The wine is muted at 80 grams per litre, with the tannin balancing the sugar.

The other decision is whether to mute *sur juice*, or *sur grains*, before or after the juice is racked off the skins. It is more difficult to mute *sur grains* during the fermentation – it is harder to gauge the right time since you do not really know how much sugar there is in the skins. For this reason Alain Razungles described *mutage sur grains* as Russian roulette. The wine may be sweeter or drier than desired, so a solution is to make several batches and blend them. The advantage of *mutage sur grains* is that it gives more concentration and ageing potential, and makes for better integrated alcohol. In the past another factor in deciding when to mute was cost. It used to be cheaper to mute *sur jus*, as you had to pay the tax on the fortifying alcohol when you bought it. Now you pay the tax when the bottle is sold, with the result that today more people mute *sur grains*.

Ageing

Rimage and Grenat can have wonderfully ripe vibrant fruit, but there is no doubt that the true originality of Roussillon comes from the wines that have been aged for a number of years. For Hors d'Age that is at least five years, but very often much longer, so that the wines develop the most delicious *rancio* flavours. These are among the vinous treasures of France. *Bonbonnes,* foudres and barriques are all used for ageing Vin Doux Naturel, both inside and outside. The barrels for Vin Doux Naturel must be subject to the elements and to the changing seasons, with extremes of temperature. They are often stored in an attic, as they are at the cooperative in Fourques. The barrels are never topped up and over about 45 years with a 3 to 5 per cent evaporation they would be empty. The evolution is not linear; the winemakers taste regularly and decide what to bottle and what to continue ageing.

Philippe Gard has his barrels in his small cellar, on top of the vats, right under the roof. The barrels are not topped up as evaporation – the 'angels' share' – is a significant part of the process, and enhances the flavours of *rancio*. Barrels are often left outside so that they undergo a thermal shock, while those inside allow for less evaporation with a smaller angels' share. Bernard Rouby, a previous president of the cooperative of Maury, observed that in Maury, the angels are thirstier, as the atmosphere is drier than in Banyuls; the difference between mountain and sea. The Banyuls cooperative, Terres des Templiers sprays its barrels with water to avoid excessive evaporation. However, the angels' share is important; as the evaporation concentrates the wine. You can put Vin Doux Naturel in a barrel and simply forget about it, as many have.

Ageing in foudres at Mas Amiel

In old fashioned cellars like Château de Rey you will see enormous old foudres. They were the traditional vessel for Vin Doux Naturel. At Château de Rey, they are empty, but those at Mas Amiel are still used, as are those at Domaine Cazes and Terres des Templiers. There is more evaporation with a foudre as the surface area is so much larger.

Glass *bonbonnes* add another dimension, as they do not allow for any evaporation. However, the sun can also kill flavour, and two years is usually considered the maximum time for a wine to spend in a *bonbonne*. Barrels are gentler, with the wood adding more complexity. Mas Amiel still has a wonderful *parc de bonbonnes*, 800 of them, in which the *rancio* wines spend about 12 months, before being aged in foudres.

The solera is another aspect of the ageing process and often an important part of an Hors d'Age – and you will find old soleras in Roussillon. Domaine Madeloc has one begun in 1920 that was forgotten about in 1962 and only rediscovered when the current owners bought the estate in 2002. Olivier Saperas at Domaine Vial Magnères has a solera that his father started in 1968, with seven stages of barrels, which are kept inside. Some wine is bottled every couple of years or so. The essence of a solera depends on the younger wine taking on the characteristics of the older wine. It is a wine without a vintage, but with a minimum age of ten years, and many Hors d'Age are the result of a solera.

Cellars for Vin Doux Naturel are traditionally dry, so that the wine evaporates, leading to higher alcohol, rising from 17% abv to 20% abv, and making for a concentration of flavour. Georges Puig of Domaine Puig-Parahy insisted that you should never clean the barrels, though he might transfer the mother from one barrel into another. Victor Gardiés agreed that you do need a mother, the lees from a previous wine, and again you should never clean the barrel. Your nose will tell you if there is anything amiss.

Old vintages are part of the patrimony. It is not unusual to find wines that are 30 or 40 years old. Domaine de Rancy have made a speciality of their mature vintages, and Bruno Cazes went to great pains to save the stocks of the Cave de l'Etoile, with wines going back to 1947. More modestly, Mas Amiel still has a 1969.

*

The history of *rancio* wines in Roussillon is as old as winemaking in the region. Pliny refers to wines exposed to rain and sun and all the injuries of the air. In the nineteenth century *vi ranci* was widespread in Catalonia, and was served at a dinner in 1909 alongside Château Margaux and Château d'Yquem. But later in the twentieth century the oenologists waged a war on oxidation and *rancio* was sacrificed on the altar of modern winemaking.

Rancio Sec is quite different from Vin Doux Naturel as it is not muted, but instead is simply left in a barrel that is not topped up, so that it might develop a *flor*, or *voile*, with some deliciously incisive oxidative flavours. Some would say that as a wine it predates the fortified wines. Confusingly the term *rancio* can also apply to an oxidized fortified Vin Doux Naturel, as it describes a certain flavour of oxidation. Unfortified Rancio Sec very nearly disappeared from the repertoire of Roussillon, as it did not conform to any appellation regulations. Fortunately, the Slow Food movement helped change perceptions about Rancio Sec and a small group of wine growers began to make it again. With its revival in fortunes, it has been allowed for IGP Côtes Catalanes since 2012.

No one has ever asked for an appellation for Rancio Sec, so if the wine is not Côtes Catalanes, it is a Vin de France. The exemplary producer is Domaine de Rancy, with three different Rancios Secs, from Macabeo and Carignan, as well as a Syrah, which was made by mistake! They are also among the best producers of old Rivesaltes.

Bruno Ribière of Domaine Ferrer-Ribière talked passionately about *rancio*, saying that it is part of the Catalan fibre, and a tradition fundamental to society in the region, dating from a time when many families simply kept a barrel of old wine. A barrel that is not topped up will eventually turn *rancio* in character. They are 'les vins des papis et mamies, un vin d'apéro', which were drunk outside in the villages on summer evenings. They are also great for cooking. Bruno has a *rancio* solera, made from Macabeo, that he began in 2001.

In Roussillon, you will also find wines that are labelled Vin sous Voile, such as those from Domaine de la Rectorie and Domaine Boucabeille. Vin sous Voile has a layer of *flor*, which comes naturally when a wine is aged outside for two or three years. It is not fortified, since they do not want the alcohol to be too high, no more than 14.5% abv. Jean Boucabeille described his method as empirical. You need a sufficient amount of alcohol to avoid the development of any acetic bacteria and he keeps his barrels in the coolest part of the cellar so that the temperature is below 20°C. The *flor* occurs quite naturally. For Jean, the wine starts to become interesting when it is five years old, and becomes even more so at seven years. However, he emphasizes that it is not a *rancio*, but a good oxidative white wine.

*

In the past it was more usual to make Muscat de Rivesaltes with both Muscat d'Alexandrie and Muscat à Petits Grains, in equal proportions, but nowadays there is more flexibility. As a result there is more variation in flavour, depending on the proportions of each, or indeed the single variety, used. Muscat à Petits Grains is considered to perform better in the Agly Valley, whereas Muscat d'Alexandrie favours Les Aspres. Julien Jeannin picks his Muscat à Petits Grains at a low level of ripeness, so that it gives a more lemony flavour, and picks the Muscat d'Alexandrie when it is riper, which makes for more body. For him Muscat should have a fresh finish. In contrast, Marie-Pierre Piquemal likes to age a little Muscat each year.

The appellation regulations call for mutage at between 100 and 120 grams per litre of residual sugar, with the alcohol making up 10 per cent of the volume. Twenty years ago, the tendency was for 120, or even 125, grams per litre of residual sugar whereas these days 105–110 grams per litre is generally preferred. With lower sugar, more alcohol is added to produce 15% abv. For Victor Gardiés the balance is very complicated: if you have less sugar, the alcohol can give an impression of sweetness, but if the sugar is too low, the wine can seem heavy. Below 100 grams per litre residual sugar you do not obtain the right balance of sugar and acidity. A Rivesaltes at 45 grams per litre is simply not possible; the sums do not add up.

The mutage of Muscat depends on several factors. Serge Baux said that it ripens early in his vineyards but he has to wait for the *ban des vendanges* before picking, and if it is too ripe by that stage, 16% potential alcohol rather than 15%, the mutage is complicated. Grapes that are too ripe will lead to wine being classed as a *vin de liqueur*, for which the tax is higher. In terms of sugar, there is a big difference between 102 and 105 grams per litre. Serge wants fruit and finesse, otherwise it goes straight to your head, although in French they actually say that it falls to your ankles.

Muscat is so powerful that it can frighten people off with its intense perfume. Pierre Boudau feels that Muscat d' Alexandrie makes for more finesse, and his Muscat de Rivesaltes comes only from Alexandrie. He finds Muscat à Petits Grains is better for dry wine. The cooperative at Baixas always makes a point of having two Muscats, the fresh young Dom Brial and the more mature and complex Château les Pins, which demonstrates the perhaps unexpected ageability of Muscat de Rivesaltes.

One of the enigmas of Roussillon is the decline in its Vins Doux Naturels. The best, the Hors d'Age, which have spent at least five years in barrel, are truly wonderful original wines, and yet they have fallen from favour. Hopefully, there will be a revival in the reputation of the finer Vins Doux Naturels. I do hope so; the quality is undeniably there, and the aged *rancio* wines stand among the vinous treasures of France.

PORT TYPES

In this 2019 chapter from *Port and the Douro*, Richard Mayson explains the art of blending Port. The journey begins with the new wine in its winter home, huge vats in the Douro valley, and continues to the well-appointed tasting rooms in Vila Nova de Gaia, facing the city of Oporto.

The onset of winter transforms the Douro into a cold, soulless place. A thick blanket of icy fog sometimes hangs over the valley for weeks, blotting out the sun. Houses remain shuttered up and in the *armazém* the young wines seem to shut down in sympathy. As the heady aromas of the vintage fade, even the finest of Ports can seem to be something of a disappointment during the winter months. All Port wines spend their first winter in the Douro, during which time they 'fall bright' as minute yeast cells, grape solids and tartrates settle to the bottom of the vat, helped by the cold weather. Left in the wine, this sediment will absorb colour and could stimulate the growth of harmful bacteria.

A month or two after the vintage, the *lota* takes place. The young wines are racked or drawn off the sediment (lees), analysed and adjusted where necessary. It is not uncommon for a Port to be fortified initially up to 16% alcohol and an extra measure of *aguardente* is added to bring the level up to a minimum of 19% abv. This provides the opportunity for the first selection and classification. To a certain extent this is preordained. At the end of vintage, the origin, quality and quantity of the individual lots of wine will generally reflect a shipper's overall requirements. A large shipper marketing a complete range of different types of Port will end up with as many as 400 to 500 separate lots. Most large Port producers are therefore equipped with a variety of different storage vessels in the

Douro. These vary greatly in size. There are concrete *balões* (also known colloquially as '*mamas*' or '*ginas*' – after Gina Lollobrigida – because of their shape), each capable of holding up to 100,000 litres. Nowadays these are being superseded by stainless steel vats, some of which double up as vats for fermentation. Smaller producers use wooden *toneis* or even 550-litre pipes in which small parcels of high-quality wine can be kept separate for future appraisal. Some of the wine will remain in the custody of individual farmers throughout the winter months.

Balões … 'ginas', 'mamas', 'Lollobrigidas'

In the spring following the harvest, the colour begins to recover as the young Ports start to bind or 'close up'. This is the cue for much of the previous year's wine to be shipped down from the Douro to Vila Nova de Gaia before the onset of the summer heat. As the wines are prepared for shipment, they undergo a second racking from the lees, and levels of sulphur dioxide are adjusted to protect the wine from undue oxidation. The fraction of wine mixed in with the gross lees used to represent a considerable loss, amounting to as much as 10 per cent of total volume. In order to keep their losses to a minimum, producers would frequently empty the lees into canvas sacks, placing boards and stones on top to squeeze as much wine as possible from the solid matter. Nowadays, this troublesome and unhygienic practice has given way to the rotary vacuum filter, which separates clean wine from solid matter. The wine is kept to one side and blended later into lower-quality Ports.

For the best part of three centuries, the new wine was shipped downstream to Vila Nova de Gaia by *barco rabelo*. These distinctive Viking-inspired boats were gradually decommissioned following the construction of the railway in the 1870s and finally had to be abandoned altogether when the river was dammed in the 1960s. With an increasing amount of Port now being matured and bottled in the Douro, the region's winding roads are not quite so choked by spluttering articulated tankers from March through to May.

*

Listen to the daily weather forecast for Oporto and Vila Nova de Gaia and it often starts in much the same way. The *neblina matinal* (morning mist), which drifts in during the night from the Atlantic, often hangs around for much of the day during the winter months, obscuring the top of the Torre dos Clerigos, the tallest church tower in Portugal. An air of dampness pervades the city, penetrating buildings so that patches of mould grow on the walls if rooms are not regularly aired. This atmosphere is eminently suitable for the maturation of wine and it is here, rather than in the Douro, that the Port shippers inevitably chose to set up their cellars. They are not 'cellars' in the true sense of the word, for Port is generally aged above ground. The British shippers refer to their 'lodge', a term that derives from the Portuguese word '*loja*' meaning shop, store or cellar. The Portuguese themselves tend to use a more accurate term, *armazém* (plural *armazéns*), which translates as 'warehouse' or 'storehouse'.

The long, low red-roofed lodges or *armazéns* that stack up from the river bank in Vila Nova de Gaia serve both as headquarters for the majority of Port shippers and storehouses for a huge quantity of Port. Most of the wine ages in wooden vats and casks ranging in capacity from *balseiros*, vertical vats holding as much as 100,000 litres, to casks of around 600 litres (so-called 'lodge pipes'). They function as vessels for ageing where the permeability of the wood permits a gradual, controlled oxidation of the contents. Wines destined for bottling after two or three years – premium ruby, LBV and vintage – will be aged partly in *balseiros* and sometimes in stainless steel to preserve the primary character of the fruit. Wines set aside to become old tawnies are transferred to smaller lodge pipes to enhance the oxidative character of the wine.

Apart from a number of vats made from *macacauba* (Brazilian mahogany) and a few Italian chestnut casks, nearly all the wood utilized

Balseiros in the Graham's lodge used for ageing reserve, LBV and vintage Ports prior to bottling

for the maturation of Port is oak. This is favoured over other types of wood for its tighter grain, thereby reducing evaporation and enabling a more gradual oxidation. Much of the oak used for ageing Port originated from Memel and Stettin in the Baltic state of Lithuania before it was occupied by the former Soviet Union in 1939. More recently oak has been obtained from New Orleans in North America and from northern Portugal, although with no forest management policy to speak of, the latter is now almost non-existent. When new casks are required today, the oak is bought from the Limousin and Alliers forests in France and coopered in Portugal. New oak does not have a role to play in the maturation of Port. Unlike, say, a Californian Cabernet or classed growth claret, the merest hint of new oak can detract from the primary fruit character of a young Port. With a shortage of old wood, new Port producers occasionally resort to using new oak that imparts a strangely sweet, vanilla-like character to a naturally sweet wine. New casks should be well seasoned for a few years before they are put into use, usually with unfortified Douro wine.

Although some of the larger shippers still maintain their own coopers, the demand for wood is nowhere near as great as it was in the first half of the twentieth century when the majority of wine was still shipped in cask. Chestnut was generally used for shipping because it is cheaper and structurally more robust than oak, though it suffers from greater evaporation. The few chestnut casks that remain are left over from this period. Coopers are now retained on regular maintenance duty, repairing a pipe when a stave has been damaged or dismantling and rebuilding a vat when it has to be moved. The main shippers have a long-term programme of wood renewal. The recent closure and redevelopment of a number of lodges in Vila Nova de Gaia has created work for coopers as vats are dismantled, restored and reassembled.

Lesser Ports (white, ruby and inexpensive tawny) are generally stored in tanks made from stainless steel or cement. These wines have traditionally remained up in the Douro long after the premium-quality wines have been shipped down to Gaia, sometimes until they are called upon to make up the final shipping blend prior to bottling. Since the 1990s, there has been a gradual but important shift to the Douro with an increasing number of shippers maturing an ever greater proportion of their wine in purpose-built *armazéns*, mostly located on the *altos* at altitudes of 500 to 600 metres on the margins of the region. Quinta do Noval led this trend, moving lock, stock and barrel to the Douro after their lodges were destroyed by fire in 1981. With Vila Nova de Gaia becoming ever more congested and tourist-oriented a number of other shippers have followed, constructing well-insulated *armazéns* in the Douro. Gran Cruz, which vies with Symington Family Estates as the largest Port shipper and is by far the largest Port brand, plans to follow Noval by moving its lodges and bottling to the Douro in the near future. Sandeman, Symington Family Estates (Cockburn, Dow, Graham and Warre) and the Fladgate Partnership (Croft, Fonseca and Taylor) all maintain substantial stocks of Port in the Douro, especially stocks of aged tawny which develop well in humidity-controlled conditions without a hint of fabled 'Douro-bake'.

*

The process of racking (or *transfega* as it is known in Portuguese) is an important but extremely labour-intensive part of the annual cycle of cellar work. It involves separating the clear wine from the sediment or lees that have settled at the bottom of the cask or vat. Left in the wine, the lees will generate off-flavours and, apart from aiding the process of clarification, racking also provides aeration and helps to develop the flavour of the wine.

Racking regimens vary according to the shipper and the type of wine, but all Ports are typically racked three times in the first year, twice in the second and annually thereafter. Older wines like aged tawnies continue to precipitate solid matter as the anthocyanins (tannin and colouring matter) are deposited in the bottom of the cask. In this case pipes or casks (normally stacked four high) are decanted progressively, starting from the top row. The lees are left in the bottom of each pipe, which is then removed from the stack, cleaned and replaced. The stack is effectively entirely rebuilt, row by row. With labour saving in mind, some shippers have built new lodges with small cranes (many of these in the Douro) to shift and empty the pipes. The combination of ageing vessel, the amount of air in the head space and the frequency of racking provides the winemaker with an opportunity to influence the rate of maturation and has an important bearing on the style and character of the wine.

Racking alone is sufficient to eliminate heavier insoluble particles from a young Port but it does not remove inherently unstable material found in solution that could precipitate after the wine has been bottled. Most wines are therefore clarified further using fining agents such as gelatin, bentonite, egg white and casein. Young Ports are no exception and it is the winemaker's task to choose a fining agent appropriate to the type of wine. Gelatin and bentonite are normally used in tandem, with larger amounts added to round out the flavour and strip colour from a young wine (for example, a standard tawny which is supposed to be paler than a ruby). One or two shippers use centrifugation to hasten deposition. Some smaller producers continue to use gum arabic which prevents deposition and tends to produce wines with an opaque appearance and a dull colour. Casein-based products are used to stabilize and remove oxidative browning from white Ports. Unless there is a particular problem, old tawnies and bottle-matured wines like unfiltered LBVs and vintage Ports are rarely (if ever) fined.

Most rubies and young tawnies are cold stabilized to remove tartrates and colouring material, which could otherwise crystallize and precipitate in the bottle (particularly in colder climes like Canada and Scandinavia, both of which are important markets). Two systems are commonly used. The first involves the use of a heat exchanger to refrigerate the wine down to between -8 and -10°C followed by static settling for about a week in an insulated tank. Alternatively, most of the larger Port shippers have invested in continuous systems which chill the wine and pass it continually through a crystallizing tank. In each case, the wines are filtered after the stabilization process using diatomaceous earth followed by sheet and/or membrane filters. Smaller producers like single *quintas*, which lack the wherewithal to purchase such sophisticated equipment, tend to rely on metatartaric acid, which merely offers short-term protection against tartrate deposition. Since the increase in bacteriological problems during the 1980s (see below), shippers have resorted to flash pasteurization following cold treatment in order to achieve 'belt and braces' stability in volume ruby and tawny. Wine extracted from the lees is also pasteurized.

The methods of clarification and filtration outlined above inevitably strip a certain amount of character and flavour from a wine. Consequently, bottle-matured Ports are not cold stabilized and are rarely filtered, leading to the formation of a heavy deposit or 'crust'. These wines need to be decanted off the sediment before serving.

*

In the early and mid-1980s there was a rapid increase in the incidence of bacterial problems. Wines that appeared to be correct in the tasting room suddenly turned unpleasantly volatile (vinegary) in bottle. Lactic bacteria (*lactobacillus*), which flourish in the presence of small amounts of air, will transform naturally occurring malic acid into lactic acid and attack the glucose in the wine to form acetic acid. In dry red wines and some whites, this malolactic transformation is perfectly natural, leading to a reduction in the overall acidity of the wine. However, in Port, where glucose levels are high and acidity is generally low in the first place, the presence of lactic bacteria is always extremely detrimental to the wine. Until the 1980s many producers believed that these lactic bacteria were unable to tolerate high levels of alcohol and (particularly up in the Douro) hygiene was perhaps not accorded the highest priority.

Since a number of shippers were caught out with the 1985 vintage, hygiene and quality control have come to the fore. Technical requirements have to be adhered to and, in response to the decline and subsequent suspension of bulk shipments, the major shippers have all set up their own quality-control laboratories. The Instituto dos Vinhos do Douro e do Porto (IVDP) has a well-equipped laboratory and offers its services to smaller shippers. The IVDP also has its own rigorous quality-control procedures but I can think of a number of smaller shippers without their own laboratories who are still sitting on a potential bacterial time bomb.

The problem is most acute in the Douro where an increasing number of single *quintas* are shipping their own wine. (One property solved the problem of a tainted *tonel* by lining the inside with fibreglass to prevent the wine from coming into contact with the wood!) Despite the obligatory and rigorous assessment by the IVDP's Câmara de Provadores (tasting panel), a few inconsistent and occasionally downright faulty wines still occasionally reach export markets.

*

Every major Port shipper has a tasting room, often with a fabulous view. Huge plate glass windows look northwards over the River Douro and on to the kaleidoscopic city of Oporto beyond. Impressive as this sight is to visitors, there is a practical reason for capturing the panorama of Portugal's second city. Colour is axiomatic to Port and it is no coincidence that two of the most important types of Port, ruby and tawny, are named after different shades. A single glass held up and tilted against the cool north light may represent a blend of 1,000 or more pipes of Port. As soon as representative samples of the previous year's wines reach the shippers' lodges in Vila Nova de Gaia, they are reassessed. Each wine is given a name and/or number based on its origin and will be accompanied by an analysis detailing, among other things, its strength and sweetness. Relying on prior knowledge and experience, tasters have the future in their hands when they judge if a Port will stand up to ten, twenty or more years' ageing or whether it is destined to form part of a blend for early consumption. Following extensive replanting in the Douro in the 1980s, varietal *lotes* have added another variable into the already complex blending equation. With the notable exception of wines from a single year (vintage, LBV and colheita Ports), shippers generally seek to produce Port of a consistent style and age in keeping with their house style. This presents a formidable challenge, especially for younger, fruit-driven styles (ruby and reserve) where the variation in the character and quality of the wine from year to year has to be masked in the final blend. Although some of the same principles apply, there is no mechanism to blend Port by means of the *solera* system used for Sherry. Most brands of Port result from continuous blending, appraisal and reappraisal. Tasting is a question of memory as well as an inherent feeling for the style and character of the wines that have been put to one side. Samples are submitted by other producers (from small *quintas* to large cooperatives) but it is usual for shippers to have contracts with the same growers year after year in order to reinforce the continuity of style. Although colour, aroma and taste will always remain paramount, quantifiable colour analysis (spectrophotometry) and computer records provide a useful aide-memoire.

Shippers base their blends on a series of *lotes*. These are themselves blends of wines from different years held in reserve to feed a certain predetermined house style or brand. The *lote* is usually made up some time before it is required, and a proportion of the previous *lote* is usually included in the final blend to keep the wine consonant with the last bottling. Younger or older wines may be introduced accordingly and the final sweetness may be adjusted with *geropigas* or drier wines. Sometimes both are used in order to lend complexity to a particular blend. The standard blending unit for this fine-tuning is the *almude* (25.44 litres). With twenty-one *almudes* to a shipping pipe, this long-standing but apparently arbitrary measure represents the maximum amount that a person can be expected to carry on their head at any one time!

Wines destined to make up straightforward white, rosé, ruby and tawny blends tend to be classified early on and their *lotes* are made up first, usually within six months of the vintage. Many shippers purchase large volumes of wine from cooperatives, predominantly in the Baixo Corgo, in order to augment these wines. Later in the year blends of differing but complementary wines will be formed, perhaps with a particular reserve brand in mind. The small quantities of wine set aside to become old tawnies may remain for several years before further blending whereas potential vintage *lotes* are kept separate and classified as late as possible. They will be regularly reassessed before the decision is finally taken as to whether or not to declare a vintage eighteen months or so after the harvest.

REGIONAL
PERSPECTIVES

CÔTE-RÔTIE

Matt Walls paints a vivid portrait of one of the northern Rhône's famed appellations, exploring its history, terroir, vineyards, grape varieties and, of course, the wines they produce – the only reason anybody would attempt farming in such a punishing landscape. This originally appeared in *Wines of the Rhône* (2021).

Even to walk these vineyards is tiring; the smashed panes of schist slip and slide beneath your shoes. To spend day after day here in the beating sun, clearing woodland, building walls and tending vines is hard to imagine. If these craggy folds didn't produce a unique wine, there's no way people would still be farming here. But they do, and have done for over 2,000 years. When you look upon these irregular, rickety terraces, you can't help but ask questions: who started this extraordinary endeavour, when and why?

The northern Rhône inhabits the narrow eastern edge of the raised shelf of igneous and metamorphic rock known as the Massif Central. At its foot runs the Rhône, north to south. There are vineyards on the other side of the river, and even these consist in part of granite hewn off by the river. For many, granite is almost synonymous with the northern Rhône, but it's not the only rock here. At its southern pole there's limestone, and at the north, at Côte-Rôtie, schist and gneiss. The village of Ampuis is at the centre of the appellation, on the flat land close to the river. When the sun isn't shining it can feel a little dour; a village in need of a haircut and a new pair of shoes. It's the slopes beyond the houses that catch your eye, rising up abruptly from 180 metres to 325 metres altitude. It might not sound much, but the effect is dramatic.

From the heart of Ampuis, the schist runs north and the gneiss goes south. There is some granite here too, at the southern tip of the appellation at the border with Condrieu. Naturally, the real situation is more irregular and detailed; sometimes you see gneiss and schist in the same vineyard, there are thin bands of sparkling white flint, and even banks of small *galets roulés* at the far north of the appellation. The river flows mostly north to south in the northern Rhône, but between Vienne (just north of Ampuis on the other side of the river) and Condrieu, the river briefly flows north-east to south-west. A series of streams and rivers that tumble down from the plateau above have sliced into the edge of the rock as they snake their course to the Rhône, creating these corrugated, jagged vineyards. Most vineyards face east, south-east and south, but such is their chaotic state some even face south-west and west. These valleys are severe and difficult to cross – often you have to return to the village before taking alternative hairpins back up.

No doubt this terroir caught the eye of Roman winemakers on their journey up the river by boat. Wines were certainly produced here in Roman times, being mentioned by Pliny the Elder, among others. There are theories that viticulture may have been started here significantly earlier in fact, around 600 BC by Phocaean Greeks coming upriver from their settlement in Marseille. The wines from around Vienne at the time were known as *picatum*, meaning flavoured with pitch or resin – whether this came naturally or was an added flavouring remains unclear. Due to the punitive taxes on wine shipped via Burgundy, the wines only became better known throughout France from the seventeenth century, once the Loire was opened up as a shipping route (it runs closer to Ampuis than you might imagine, just 43 kilometres away at its closest point). Their early renown was cut short by phylloxera, which arrived around 1880, and by 1893 the vineyards were totally destroyed, with just a few solitary vines remaining according to contemporary reports. The vineyards were slowly rebuilt, but two successive world wars claimed the lives of many local vignerons. In 1949, Côte-Rôtie was fetching around 1 franc per litre and by 1973 there were just 72 hectares in production. Only the most dedicated stuck to the slopes, ignoring more comfortable, better paid jobs in the nearby factories of Vienne and Lyon. As recently as the 1960s, estates bottling large parts of their production were rare. It was only in the late 1970s and 1980s that the wider world began to take notice. Since then, plantings have increased rapidly.

It's often the coolest sites that can still successfully ripen a given grape variety that create its most compelling expression. On the fringes you see the subtle gradations of non-fruit aromas which define a grape variety. So it is with Syrah in Côte-Rôtie. It translates as 'roasted slope', and it's true that the south-facing slopes don't want for ripeness, but this is the most northerly appellation in the Rhône. Compared to Châteauneuf-du-Pape – or even Hermitage – the climate here is far from roasting. The result is a wine with multiple aromatic registers. There are floral notes, particularly violet. Herbs are common, especially juniper, thyme, rosemary and bay leaf, not to mention black olives. Smoky aromas sometimes curl from the glass, smoked meats like duck or bacon, wood smoke, tobacco. There is fruit of course, but it sometimes appears almost as an afterthought – raspberry, redcurrant, blackberry. White, black and pink peppercorns sometimes make an enlivening appearance, but as the climate gets warmer, they're not as common as they once were. It's a wine that is rarely heavy or solid and at its best is haunting, transparent, elegant and tender.

Some of this perfume is thanks to Viognier – up to 20 per cent is allowed in the blend. This is a well-known feature of Côte-Rôtie, but it's worth mentioning that other northern Rhône appellations can use a proportion of white grapes too: Saint-Joseph can contain up to 10 per cent of Marsanne and/or Roussanne in their reds, and Hermitage up to 15 per cent (but this is much rarer compared to Côte-Rôtie). Another source of this particular fragrance is down to using old local iterations of Syrah such as Serine. The historical basis for using Viognier in Côte-Rôtie is uncertain. It's been suggested that Condrieu and Côte-Rôtie both used to make red and white wines, but when appellation rules were drawn up in the 1930s, Condrieu was given white wine production and Côte-Rôtie red. Given the similarity of these terroirs, this is entirely believable. In fact, I've seen labels for white Côte-Rôtie (and even sparkling red Côte-Rôtie!) dating back to 1900. After these two appellations were established, presumably there were a lot of white plants remaining in the vineyards of Côte-Rôtie, hence the 20 per cent rule.

René Rostaing of Domaine Rostaing describes the 20 per cent rule as a 'tolerance' rather than a feature, and only his Côte Blonde contains any Viognier. He says it can be overly prominent in a wine and can 'denature' a Côte-Rôtie, making it flabby. It's rare to find any winemakers using the full tolerance, however – more than 10 per cent is rare, and even at this level it can feel destabilizing. According to the *cahier des charges*, any Viognier must be co-planted in the vineyard, and must be co-fermented. A problem with this is that Viognier ripens before Syrah. One option is to undertake a first pass through the vineyard to hand-pick the white bunches then store them at low temperature before co-fermentation – but this is labour-intensive and expensive. Viognier is much more commonly found in the southern vineyards of Côte-Rôtie, and is rare at its most northerly point.

The appellation is split into 73 *lieux-dits* across three communes. The original decree included just two: Ampuis and Tupin-et-Semons. The more northerly commune of Saint-Cyr-sur-le-Rhône was added in 1966. The two best-known *lieux-dits* are neighbouring sites Côte Blonde and Côte Brune. Occasionally, you might hear the whole of the southern part of Côte-Rôtie described as 'the Côte Blonde', and the northern half 'the Côte Brune'. This is unhelpful to outsiders trying to understand the appellation, but it is understandable: the soils south of Côte Blonde are paler, consisting largely of pale-yellow gneiss; the soils north of Côte Brune are a dark, brown-green schist.

It is the difference in soils of these two hallowed *lieux-dits* that gave rise to the somewhat hackneyed local legend about the two daughters. It goes something like this: once upon a time, a local nobleman called Maugiron lived in the Château d'Ampuis. He owned some of the best vineyards in Côte-Rôtie and gave half of them to each of his two daughters; the blonde daughter was given the Côte Blonde and the brunette was given the Côte Brune. The blonde daughter was very beautiful in youth (like the wines of *lieu-dit* Côte Blonde, which are highly perfumed and approachable young), whereas the brunette had hidden depths and took time to get to know (like the wines of *lieu-dit* Côte Brune, which are less perfumed and more structured). I'm inclined to agree with Jean-Paul Jamet of Domaine Jamet when he says, 'you need to forget this legend; it's for tourists.' To look at the soils in more de-tail, the paler soils are mostly made up of gneiss mixed with calcareous loess soils from the plateau. These give very perfumed, open and floral wines that are elegant and silky. The darker soils are from weathered micaschists, easily breakable and crumbly, with thin bands of clay with-in. They also have plentiful iron oxide, visible as crimson staining on the rock. The wines from these soils are darker and more intense, with weightier tannins, appearing more robust in youth but tending to age well. Those grown on granite tend towards a lighter style, but with a distinct saline freshness.

Due to the steepness of the slopes the soils need to be kept in place by drystone walls, here called *cheys*. The terraces that these walls create are known as *chaillés*. They collapse like drunken soldiers when it rains. 'You've never finished repairing the walls,' says Jean-Paul Jamet. 'You could spend your whole life doing it.' Though some vines are trained on wires on the flatter parts at the foot of the slopes and on the plateaux, the Syrah bush vines are traditionally trained on pairs of wooden stakes called *échalas*. It makes for a unique landscape. The scenery is further embellished with an ever-increasing number of billboards popping up among the vines. Since the end of the 1800s, certain producers have painted the larger walls in their vineyards with the names of their domaines and most prestigious cuvées, an early form of advertising to passing train passengers. There are now at least 20, of different shapes and sizes, some professionally painted on walls, others crudely daubed on planks. It doesn't exactly add to the natural beauty of the place. There is legislation being drawn up to prevent any more.

Planting en échalas *(wooden stakes) in* lieu-dit *La Landonne, Côte-Rotie*

Vineyards on steep slopes and narrow terraces are expensive to work – everything must be done by hand. In common with other Rhône estates, growers in Côte-Rôtie are turning towards organic viticulture, but while pesticides and some fungicides are relatively easy to forgo, finding a way to keep the weeds under control without recourse to herbicides is proving difficult. It can't be done mechanically in the more challenging vineyards, and finding the staff to do it by hand isn't easy – not to mention the significant added expense. Some producers such as Domaine Clusel-Roch, Domaine Georges Vernay and Domaine Pierre-Jean Villa are managing to work without herbicides, but compared to Hermitage and Cornas, progress in Côte-Rôtie is slow. Villa's domaine covers 17 hectares and he started going organic in 2011; by 2021 he should be certified. 'It's a question of investment,' he says, and taking it slowly rather than trying to convert all at the same time. Instead of spraying or ploughing he's been experimenting with using cover crops that don't compete for water around the base of vines, using local plants like mouse-ear hawkweed and sedum. Early experiments are encouraging. Regarding organics, Christine Vernay of Domaine Georges Vernay says 'Yes it's difficult. But it's possible. And terroir speaks more clearly when you take care of it.'

The traditional method of vinification in Côte-Rôtie was to use whole bunches – sometimes crushed, sometimes not – fermenting in large open-top wooden containers with punching down followed by submerging the cap under the surface of the juice. Wines would then be matured in old barrels, either 225-litre barriques, 600-litre demi-muids or larger foudres of various sizes. The 1980s and 1990s saw numerous new approaches. There was an influx of stainless-steel fermenters, the destemmer was introduced, and producers began using new oak barrels. This 'modern' style no doubt improved many of the more rustic wines at the time, and produced a more polished style of wine that was favoured by some of the powerful critics of the day. The Côte-Rôties of Guigal – mostly destemmed and matured in 100 per cent new oak barriques – quickly garnered high praise and high prices. Other producers adopted similar approaches, but not always with the same expertise. Overoaking in Côte-Rôtie became widespread, and remains a problem to this day, rubbing out the subtler details of terroir and adding drying, pinched tannins to the wines. The trend now is swinging back towards larger oak barrels, particularly demi-muids, and using a smaller proportion of new oak. Use of whole bunches is also increasing, which, when used sensitively, can add freshness, texture and aromatic interest. Mastering the use of stems will be increasingly important in creating balanced wines as the climate gets hotter.

Côte-Rôtie is a dynamic and exciting appellation, particularly in relation to Hermitage, which is considerably more static. There have been extensive new plantings over the past few decades, and there is still space to plant – both within the appellation, and on some exceptional land on the slopes which happens to be classified as AOC Côtes-du-Rhône. Côte-Rôtie can be expensive, and often overpriced. But find an excellent up-and-coming producer and, unlike regions such as Burgundy, there are spellbinding wines to be found without breaking the bank.

The changing climate is a challenge for the whole of the Rhône Valley, but Côte-Rôtie still appears relatively well placed: a northerly location, a variety of expositions, positive trends in both viticulture and vinification, talented young winemakers and a naturally exceptional terroir. There is still space for Côte-Rôtie to grow and improve: a mouthwatering prospect.

WHAT IS FAUGÈRES?

Rosemary George MW has been captivated by the wines of Faugères since tasting her first one in the 1980s. In 2016 this inspired her to pen *The wines of Faugères*. Here, she lays out the fundamentals of soil, grape varieties and climate that create the flavours of the appellation.

Unlike some appellations of the Languedoc, Faugères is a remarkably compact and homogeneous area, covering seven villages and a couple of hamlets, namely Faugères itself, Cabrerolles and the hamlets of Lenthéric and La Liquière, Caussiniojouls, Laurens, Fos, Autignac and Roquessels. The soil is schist, the climate that of the Mediterranean and the grape varieties are those that you find elsewhere in the Languedoc. So what makes Faugères special and different from the neighbouring appellations? Essentially, besides the hand of the *vigneron* who makes the wine, there are three main factors that determine the taste of a wine: the soil in which the grapes are grown, the grape varieties and the climate to which the vines are subjected.

Let's take soil first. There is no doubt that schist is the key characteristic of Faugères. In the Languedoc there is a band of schist that stretches from the north-eastern edge of the Minervois and through the northern half of St Chinian to encompass all of Faugères. It then peters out beyond Cabrières. But even in a small area, the schist is remarkably varied. You only have to visit the tasting *caveau* at the Château de Grézan to appreciate all the different types of schist, with a range of colours – grey, blue, yellow or ochre – all based on different soils and rocks, with schist *ardoisier* (slate) and its golden reflections in the sunlight, *gréseux* (sandstone), *argileux* (clay) or basalt. There is marble schist from around the quarry at Laurens, and all are on show at Grézan, alongside an appropriate bottle of wine. As Jean-Louis Pujol, the owner of the Château, observes, '*on tient au schiste, comme aux prunelles des yeux*', which translates more prosaically into English as 'we are as attached to schist as we are to the pupils of our eyes'.

So what is schist? Often translated as 'shale' in English, schist is a met-amorphic rock that was shaped by intensive heat and pressure from com-pressed clay, and that is hard and compact. The name comes originally from a Greek word that means 'split', making reference to the foliated nature of schist. You only need to drive through the vineyards of Faugères to see a bank of schist that illustrates this point. The layers between the schist are important as they are where the roots, water and organic mat-ter filter through. Usually they are vertical or sloping layers, which allow for the roots of the vines to travel down deep. Schist accounts for 10 per cent of the world's vineyards. It is one of the most distinctive of soils, and is generally considered to be one of the great vineyard soils.

The schist of Faugères, squeezed between the Pyrenees and the Massif Central, is 350 million years old, making it 100 million years older than the schist of neighbouring St Chinian. In Faugères the layer of schist is perforated by limestone, like a Roquefort cheese, and is quite different from that of St Chinian, Cabrières and Berlou, and more like that of Roquebrun. Schist is acid, but the pH is not too low. The soil is quite mixed: there is clay and sandstone as well as schist. The schist crumbles and the sandstone forms pebbles, so the soil is very stony and drains well.

There are other vineyards in the south that are based on schist, such as Maury, one of the villages of Roussillon. The vineyards there are on an island of black schist in the middle of a sea of clay and limestone, some seventeen kilometres by three. The vineyards of nearby Banyuls are planted steep terraces of schist. Olivier Gil, one of the new *vignerons* of Faugères, has also worked at Domaine la Tour Vieille in Collioure and observes that the schist there is quite different. In Collioure the schist is red and not as degraded as in Faugères, so the soil is very shal-low and you need to use dynamite to plant vines. In Faugères the schist is older blue schist and is more degraded so that it retains water better, resulting in more freshness in the wine. And, as it also retains heat, the grapes carry on ripening at night.

Schist is also the distinguishing feature of the vineyards of Priorat in northern Spain. Pierre Jacquet of Domaine Binet-Jacquet sees similari-ties with Priorat, not only from the point of view of soil, but also with regard to altitude and climate, the position of the sea and the use of some of the same grape varieties, notably Grenache Noir. In Portugal you find schist particularly in the dramatic vineyards of the Douro, and the Portuguese-French producers Roquette e Cazes even make a wine that is labelled Xisto, the Portuguese for schist. The Moselle is another vineyard area based on schist, again with fabulous scenery. The Valais in French-speaking Switzerland has schist, and in New Zealand Nick Mills at Rippon Vineyard, that most photogenic of all vineyards on the shores of Lake Wanaka in Central Otago, attributes the quality of his Pinot Noir to schist.

Ask the *vignerons* of Faugères about typicity, and what really determines the character and taste of their wines, and schist will feature in most of their responses, for it is schist that is the bedrock of Faugères and a key component in the flavour profile. Curiously, although schist is high in acid, and although Faugères has relatively high acidity for a wine from the Languedoc, that acidity does not come from the soil. The acidity level in the wine is linked to the nutrients in the soil, with a high level of potassium in the soil resulting in a wine with less acidity. Any wine grower worth their salt in Faugères will have an opinion about schist. Catherine Roque of Mas d'Alezon observes that schist is very fragile and more sensitive to drought than her vineyards of *argilocalcaire*, limestone and clay, at Clovallon outside Bédarieux. She is convinced that schist has a fantastic and as yet untapped potential for white wine; Clairette on schist will be '*géant*', producing wonderful minerality. Simon Coulshaw of Domaine des Trinités is adamant that Faugères is about schist. 'Do not mess around with it and it will give you fruit, spice and freshness'. For Vincent Vallat of Château Sauvanès, schist makes for concentration in the wine, whereas limestone gives freshness. And for Brigitte Chevalier of Domaine de Cébène, schist canalizes the *côté virile* of Mourvèdre, a grape variety that she particularly likes. When searching for her vineyards, she looked particularly for schist combined with altitude. There is no doubt that schist has many useful qualities for vineyard soil. It provides good drainage. It is poor soil, so the yields are low and, according to Arnaud Barthès of Château des Estanilles, it produces wines with fresh minerality and pepper.

The appellation regulations recognize three red '*cépages principaux*', namely Grenache Noir, Mourvèdre and Syrah, while Carignan is considered to be a *cépage complémentaire* and Cinsaut a *cépage accessoire*. In this context, Lledoner Pelut, which is closely related to Grenache Noir, is included in the regulations for Grenache Noir. And the appellation regulations lay down very precisely the required percentages in the vine-yard, but not necessarily in the wine. A red Faugères should contain at least two grape varieties, but I can think of at least one *vigneron* who gave me the blend of one of his wines as 50 per cent Syrah and … 50 per cent Syrah. So in the vineyard the three *cépages principaux* must amount to a minimum of 50 per cent, with no maximum percentage laid down, and within that 50 per cent there must be at least 20 per cent Grenache Noir, 15 per cent Syrah and 5 per cent Mourvèdre. Carignan, as a *cépage complémentaire,* must account for between 10 per cent and 40 per cent of the vineyard, and Cinsaut must be less than 20 per cent. But in the cellar, quite frankly, the wine growers can pretty much do what they like, and that is where the fun starts. There are as many views and opinions about grape varieties as there are *vignerons* in Faugères, and even with just five varieties, there is infinite scope and variation in the artist's blending palette.

When Faugères was recognized as a VDQS or Vin Délimité de Qualité Supérieure in 1955 the vineyards were mainly planted with Carignan and Cinsaut, as well as some Grenache Noir, and not to men-tion Aramon and Alicante Bouschet, which were not allowed in the VDQS. Although Aramon and Alicante Bouschet are now firmly ex-cluded from the appellations of the Languedoc, you do still occasion-ally find odd pockets of them, such as the Aramon belonging to André Balliccioni in Autignac, and also to Clos Fantine in Lenthéric.

It could be argued that the original typicity of Faugères came from Carignan. The 1970s and 1980s saw a distinct shift, with the planting of more Grenache Noir and the introduction of Syrah and Mourvèdre as the three *cépages améliorateurs.* It is quite difficult to ascertain who actu-ally planted the very first Syrah. Gilbert Alquier (Domaine Alquier) was certainly innovative, planting Syrah as early as 1963 and, when I met him in 1987 on my very first visit to Faugères, he said that his father had planted the very first *cépages améliorateurs* in the appellation, just after the Second World War, so that he had Grenache Noir which was then nearly forty years old. He also thought, then, that no more Carignan would be planted, so despised was the variety, and also Cinsaut. But these days the balance has shifted again, and there is a renewed appre-ciation of the quality of Carignan (and Cinsaut too), especially from old vines, and the realization that these grape varieties cope much better with heat and water stress than either Syrah or Mourvèdre. Centennial vines are not uncommon. As Didier Barral observes, the mistake of the

Languedoc is to plant early ripening varieties, as their acidity is burnt in August; Carignan and Mourvèdre ripen much later and therefore retain their acidity. And Bernard Vidal from Château la Liquière explains, describing himself as *un grand amoureux du* Carignan, 'the quality of the *terroir* of Faugères was recognized, but we were told that the grape varieties were not suitable and that if we had more Grenache Noir and more Syrah, the quality would improve. But nobody thought to ask: can we improve Carignan? Instead we were advised to pull it up and plant Syrah and Mourvèdre. The INAO said we needed Mourvèdre and Syrah and we believed them, so Faugères started to resemble the other wines based on Syrah, like St Chinian and Pic St Loup. If only we had been encouraged to keep Carignan, Faugères would have had another identity.'

Carignan was criticized for its rusticity, but an improvement in its flavour has come with the development of better vineyard and cellar techniques, such as carbonic maceration. People are now replanting Carignan but face the problem that the vines take several years to come into their own, so they are really planting Carignan for their children, or even their grandchildren. In the vineyard, Carignan is a late ripener, and a particular characteristic of Carignan is a tough skin, which means that rain is less of a problem than with other, softer-skinned, varieties. Those who like Carignan often think it deserves better than carbonic maceration and, with gentle handling, find that it gives body and structure and also ageing potential, and that the rustic fruit is softened by barrel ageing. Not everyone would have agreed fifteen years ago that Carignan could age. Boris Feigel of Domaine des Prés-Lasses, who has 8 hectares of Carignan that are between sixty and ninety years old, is very definite on the subject. 'Carignan may be more complicated than Syrah, but it retains acidity and really represents the *terroir*, and it is as good as Mourvèdre for structure.' Didier Barral of Domaine Léon Barral also enthuses about Carignan, observing that it performs well in Faugères. Pierre Jacquet talks about the grainy, *granuleux mais en finesse* tannins of Carignan, providing the base of the pyramid while the tannins of the other varieties complete the picture, so that each variety contributes something and no single variety dominates the wine.

In contrast with neighbouring St Chinian, in Faugères growers must have a small amount of Mourvèdre, and nobody is quite sure why. Maybe it enhances the ageing potential, or possibly the idea was to provide a tangible difference between Faugères and St Chinian. This meant that, when the appellation was created in 1982, there was a rush to plant Mourvèdre among the people who did not already have it, and that consequently quite a lot was planted on sites that are not really suitable for this temperamental variety. Mourvèdre is generally considered to be the fussiest of grape varieties. In Bandol, where it is at its most expressive, they say that it likes its head in the sun and its feet in the damp. Ideally it likes to see the sea, which is why it performs so well in Bandol. It is a late-ripening variety, even on good sites, and virtually always the last one to be picked. Catherine Roque observes that it only ripens one year in three in her coolest vineyards, but says she has learned to like Mourvèdre. Brigitte Chevalier of Domaine de Cébène is more emphatic – *'J'adore Mourvèdre'* – and it accounts for a high percentage of her Cuvée Felgaria. She finds that it has 'a unique aromatic range, with soft spices, that are not at all aggressive'.

Frederic Albaret from Domaine St Antonin also likes Mourvèdre, but he does note that it can be difficult to ripen and needs work in the vineyard; it gives *finesse* to a wine, but is not easy, because it is capricious and late. For Pierre Jacquet Mourvèdre is his Cabernet Sauvignon; the grape variety that gives structure and ageing potential. Jean-Claude Estève of Domaine des Adouzes suggests that a green harvest helps ripen Mourvèdre, but adds that it must be planted in a good spot in the first place, preferably somewhere west facing, for it to ripen properly. According to Antoine Rigaud of Domaine Anglade, a good year for Mourvèdre is one that is not too hot, with regular rain. In short, it can be the best and the worst variety. It has a difficult reputation – but the people who like it, really like it.

Both Grenache Noir and Syrah are deemed to be more reliable than Mourvèdre. A lot of Grenache was planted in the 1960s, and then people discovered Syrah. And while Lledoner Pelut is a variant of Grenache Noir, it has one significant difference: it ripens much more slowly than Grenache Noir, as it has hairs on the underside of its leaves which enable it to cope with drought more easily; consequently it is lower in alcohol than Grenache Noir. Grenache Noir can reach a heady 15% abv and is less structured, so that it provides richer fruit and body. However, it does not keep as well as Syrah. It is seen as a more fluid variety in the glass.

The earliest plantings took place in the 1960s but these days the enthusiasm for Syrah is widespread. For Luc Salvestre, director of the cooperative, Syrah is quite simply magnificent; for Philippe Borda at Domaine du Rouge Gorge, it is Syrah that makes Faugères, and half

View of the village of Faugères

his vineyards are planted with Syrah because he finds it more stable and more reliable.

There are various expressions of Syrah. It can be more floral, more exuberant and more peppery. However, it is not always simple. Syrah is affected by drought and there is a view that it performs better on cooler, north-facing slopes. In the cellar it needs oxygen, as it can easily suffer from reduction. However, it is generally accepted that the structure of Syrah is easier to get right than Carignan and Mourvèdre, which are much more complicated. The general view is that it is more reliable than Mourvèdre or Carignan. Pierre Jacquet very thoughtfully sums up some of the differences: 'Carignan is fundamental to Faugères. Syrah is easier, but it can be a trap, a *piège*, when there is not enough acidity. Grenache is tricky and capricious. Mourvèdre is the worst, if the year does not suit it.'

And then there is Cinsaut, which among other things can provide a solution for lowering the alcohol level, as it is ripe at 12% abv. In Faugères it is used particularly for rosé. Mas Onésime has a rosé that is as much as 90 per cent Cinsaut from 70-year-old vines, with a little Grenache Noir. But there is also a growing appreciation of its quality as a red wine. One new example, though not officially Faugères, is L'Etranger from Domaine des Trinités, with 90 per cent Cinsaut and some Syrah, and a modest 13.5% abv. The flavour is delicious, with ripe but refreshing cherry fruit. Le Producteur de Plaisir from Montgros is also largely Cinsaut, with some Grenache Noir and Syrah. Cinsaut is another relatively late ripener, and although it can cope with drought, it does appreciate a little water at the end of the growing season in order to ripen fully.

For the much more recent appellation of Faugères Blanc, two grape varieties are required. Grenache Blanc, Marsanne, Roussanne and Rolle are considered *cépages principaux* and individually may not exceed 70 per cent of the blend. Clairette and Viognier are *cépages accessoires* and are limited to 10 per cent, either together or separately.

Marsanne and Roussanne have been successfully introduced to the Languedoc from the northern Rhône valley, where they perform particularly well in Hermitage Blanc. The first experimental plantings in Faugères were done at the beginning of the 1990s by people such as Jean-Michel Alquier, Bernard Vidal, Michel Louison, Luc Ollier and Genevieve Libes who went on to persuade the INAO of the validity of white Faugères. Roussanne and Marsanne naturally complement each other, but Roussanne is generally considered to be more interesting, nicely filling out the palate, with a touch of white blossom. For Simon Coulshaw, who makes a pure Roussanne *vin de pays*, it is so much more than a simple blending wine, but has a real character all of its own. Françoise Ollier dismisses Marsanne as being too soft and uninteresting, and finds Grenache Blanc too alcoholic.

Rolle (or Vermentino, for its Italian synonym is often used) is a grape variety that is found along the Mediterranean from the Languedoc through Provence to Tuscany, and taking in the islands of Sardinia and Corsica. Luc Ollier of Domaine Ollier-Taillefer was one of the first to plant it in 1991, grafting cuttings obtained from the pioneering François Guy at Château de Coujan in St Chinian on to some forty-year-old Carignan Blanc. Generally Rolle adds a fresh, sappy note to white wine, with some natural freshness and herbal flavours.

Although Viognier is allowed in white Faugères, it does have a very distinctive character and as little as 5 per cent in a blend can quite dramatically change the style of a wine, and even overwhelm the flavour with rich peachy-textured notes. At Ollier-Taillefer they planted some in 1995, and pulled it up ten years later, as they found the flavours too soft. Those who have Viognier usually prefer to make it as a varietal *vin de pays*.

Clairette, on the other hand, is a traditional grape variety of the Languedoc, with the oldest white appellation, Clairette du Languedoc, created in 1948, bearing witness to this. Essentially Clairette is a grape variety that can be short on flavour, but it does perform well in the warm climate of the Midi. Catherine Roque is convinced that Clairette could produce wonderful results on schist. Curiously, although Grenache Blanc is allowed in white Faugères, Grenache Gris can only be used for *vin de pays;* possibly there was simply not enough planted at the time when the white appellation was being established for it to merit the attention of the INAO. One of the most diverse examples of white Faugères comes from La Grange de l'Aïn, which has seven different varieties, namely Grenache Blanc, Vermentino, Marsanne, Roussanne, Clairette, Viognier and Bourboulenc. The interest is in the blending and the result is intriguing.

As elsewhere in the Languedoc, people are taking a new look at some of the older varieties which were initially dismissed as worthless. There is a suggestion that Terret Blanc should be allowed in the appellation, and what about Macabeo and Carignan Blanc? Boris Feigel at Domaine des Prés-Lasses suggests that Carignan Blanc preserves acidity and also represents the *terroir.* Then there is Bourboulenc, which is characteristic of La Clape, but very little remains in the vineyards of Faugères. When he was at Château des Estanilles, Michel Louison experimented with Chenin Blanc but found it to be too heavy. Somebody else had the temerity to suggest Petit Manseng, but the INAO firmly stamped on that idea for being '*hors region*' and therefore completely unacceptable. Quite often a white will be *vin de pays* or Coteaux du Languedoc rather than Faugères as the wine is a single variety or includes a variety such as Carignan Blanc.

With the development of white wine in the Languedoc there is a general feeling that there is more to be learned about the white varieties and even the *gris* varieties, those grapes that have a pale pink skin when ripe. Thierry Rodriguez of Mas Gabinèle considers Grenache Gris much more interesting than Grenache Blanc, saying that it is more complex with better acidity and better ageing potential. He is planning a small vineyard around his new cellar for *gris* varieties, 100 to 120 plants of each of varieties such as Pinot Gris, Picpoul Gris, Sauvignon Gris, Carignan, Muscat à petits grains, Gewurztraminer, Clairette and Ribeyrenc.

The climate of Faugères is dominated by the mountains of the Espinouse, the foothills of the Cevennes, which form a backdrop to the vineyards and protect them from the prevailing north winds. There is a significant difference in temperature between the village of Faugères and the small town of Bédarieux, which is in the valley of the Orb on the other side of the hills. Within the appellation of Faugères there is again a big difference in altitude, and therefore also in temperature. The northern villages are Faugères itself, La Liquière, Roquessels, Fos and Caussiniojouls and Cabrerolles. There the nights are cooler in summer, and in the winter they may well even have snow in Faugères while there is none in Laurens. Happily spring frosts are very rarely a problem. In the northern part of the appellation the grapes tend to ripen later, by as much as seven to ten days, and consequently the wines are more *aerien*, fresher and long lasting.

In contrast, Laurens and Autignac are lower in altitude and therefore warmer, with more sheltered vineyards, producing wines that are riper and more opulent. In Autignac the vines are at an average of 140 metres, rising to 300 metres in Faugères, while the highest vines of the appellation are at around 450 metres. Some disparage Autignac as '*Faugères de la plaine*' but there are some fine wines from here. However, there is no doubt that the backdrop of hills helps to provide the conditions which make for an important element of freshness in the red wines, not to mention the significant potential for white wines.

It would be a very unusual year if there were insufficient sunshine and warmth to ripen the grapes. It is really rainfall that accounts for the key vintage variations, with the average annual rainfall totalling around 500 to 600 millimetres. The Mediterranean climate dictates warm, dry summers and mild, wet winters, implying that most of the rainfall occurs during the autumn, winter and spring, but that pattern is in fact far from regular. Ideally the water reserves are replenished during the winter, but the spring of 2013 was one of the driest since records began, while July 2013 was one of the wettest ever. The weather conditions during the 2014 harvest posed problems with heavy rainfall in the second half of September. Even if the summer is dry, ideally the vines would enjoy some rain around 14 July and 15 August, the two public holidays of the summer. But that is far from predictable, and seems to be becoming increasingly so. Jean-Michel Mégé at Domaine de la Reynardière observes that the weather between 15 August and 15 September is the most critical. A heavy rainstorm on 15 August is good, but the humidity must not continue. Drying north winds, the Tramontane, are essential after the storm, but the *vent marin* from the south brings humidity and – potentially – disease. Geneviève Libes of Domaine du Météore remarks that the disturbing effect of the equinox in late September is most worrying, especially if you are still harvesting.

I like to think of Faugères as a homogeneous whole with a more consistent identity than many of the other appellations of the Languedoc, but within the appellation there is nonetheless a mosaic of different grape varieties, villages and *vignerons,* each with their own individual style, experience and philosophy.

VINHO VERDE

On the Atlantic coast, in the north of Portugal, sits Vinho Verde, a distinctive wine region the name of which you've almost certainly been pronouncing incorrectly. In this regional profile from 2020's *The wines of Portugal*, Richard Mayson depicts the landscape and its vineyards, detailing the subregions and styles of wine produced.

The coastline north of Oporto is aptly named the Costa Verde (Green Coast). Behind the surf and white sandy beaches, a barrier of aromatic pine and eucalyptus yields to a riot of vegetation like a kitchen garden gone to seed. Go into a restaurant on the Costa Verde and you will find *caldo verde*, 'green broth' made from local cabbages that are capable of growing six feet high. Once casting a shadow over cabbage patch fields, paths and byways was a giant network of pergola-trained vines producing Portugal's most singular wine: Vinho Verde (pronounced *veeng-yo vaird* – the 'e' on the end is silent).

When I first visited the region in the late 1970s it came as something of a shock to find that most of the production of Vinho Verde was red. (In 1980 production of red was still double that of white.) The 'green' in the name originates neither from the colour of the wine nor from the often repeated 'fact' that it is made from unripe grapes. The 'verde' is partly an expression of the local landscape but mostly an instruction to drink Vinho Verde (red or white) young, while it is still 'green' and in its first flush of youth. Restaurant wine lists in Portugal used to make the broad distinction between *vinhos maduros* (so-called 'mature' wines) and Vinhos Verdes, a tradition harking back to the days when Vinho Verde was the only fresh, early drinking style of wine available in Portugal. Improvements in winemaking technology and technique mean that fresh fruit-driven white wines can now be made almost anywhere in Portugal, even the far south. But the Vinho Verde region has kept its identity and greatly enhanced its image in recent years. The insipid, spritzy, carbon dioxide-injected whites, frequently sweetened and heavily sulphured for export markets, are largely a thing of the past. When this sort of wine lost its popular appeal in the 1990s the region began to reinvent itself. There is a minimum alcohol level of 8% abv but for most of the region there is no longer a maximum, which gives the region's better grape varieties a chance to express themselves. Yields remain high (up to a legal maximum of 80 hectolitres per hectare) and alcohol levels are typically around 12% abv. This is part of the appeal of Vinho Verde to increasingly alcohol-conscious drinkers in a world where Chardonnay can reach the same strength as Sherry. These days a good Alvarinho can ripen to 13% or more. But the key to a good wine is about finding a balance of natural acidity and acuity of flavour, something that could not be said of Vinho Verde a generation ago.

The region producing Vinho Verde is the largest DOC in Portugal. It stretches from Monção and Melgaço on the River Minho, all the way down the coast, through Oporto, almost to the banks of the River Vouga south of Vale de Cambra. Most of the region corresponds to the historic province of Entre-Douro-e-Minho ('between the Douro and Minho'), an area now sweepingly referred to as 'Minho', the name of which has been adopted for the Vinho Regional. Vineyards are mostly to be found along the broad river valleys that drain the mountains of Trás-os-Montes inland. From north to south these are the Minho (forming the frontier with Galicia in Spain), Lima, Cavado, Ave, Douro and its tributaries the Tamega and Paiva. Vines peter out above 700 metres or so and the high country is mostly given over to forest.

Vinho Verde country is the cradle of Portugal: Guimarães 50 kilometres north-east of Oporto was the nation's first capital. The Minho was also one of the first tracts of mainland Portugal to produce wine for export. When the English shied away from all things French in the sixteenth century, they sourced wines from Monção and Viana do Castelo, the Portuguese seaports closest to London. Finding wines unpalatably light and acidic they quickly turned to Oporto and the Douro instead. The strong link between the people and the land in north-west Portugal makes for a conservative attitude. Chapels and churches ring out all over the countryside, a mark of the deep Catholicism that pervades in these parts. The left-wing military officers who briefly ran the country from Lisbon during 1975 received short shrift from the folk of the Minho when they attempted a programme of 'cultural dynamization'. The anticommunist backlash began here with the burning of the Communist Party headquarters in Vila Nova de Famalicão in August, and ended with the country's first free elections in April 1976.

With the economic recovery that followed the revolution and Portugal's accession to the EU, the landscape of Vinho Verde has become increasingly disordered. This is the most densely populated part of rural Portugal with nearly three million people distributed between the districts of Viana do Castelo, Braga and Oporto (nearly a third of Portugal's population). The region now includes some of the most industrialized areas of the country cheek-by-jowl with some of the most Arcadian. In the south of the region, agriculture vies for space with houses and light industry. Textiles, shoes, timber and furniture are the mainstay of the local economy, alongside a polyculture of different crops. Maize, cabbages, a cow, a goat and some vines can still sometimes be seen co-existing on the same tiny plot. This is the legacy of self-sufficient peasant agriculture in which vines, eking the last drop of goodness from the generally poor granite-based soils, seemed to take up every last inch of space. Vines once formed hedgerows between fields, grew along railway lines and over roads and infiltrated back gardens.

In 2019 the Minho region officially encompassed 21,000 hectares of vineyard, a considerable decrease from nearly 40,000 hectares at the end of the 1990s. There has been a rapid retreat from the traditional smallholding or *minifundio*, where wines were made for domestic consumption or grapes delivered to the local cooperative to be turned into wine. Nonetheless, with 19,000 registered growers, the average size of a holding is only just over a hectare.

The move from away from self-sufficiency has also had an important bearing on the training methods used in the vineyards and consequently the style of the wines and the character of the landscape. In the past, to make the most of the available space, vines were trained to grow high above the ground, leaving space for other forms of land use underneath. Vines would be trained to climb like beanstalks up the trunks of chestnut, elm, cherry or poplar trees, the canopy of the vine draped from one tree to another. This impractical method of cultivation known as *enforcado* ('hanging') has largely been abandoned but it is still possible, often in unexpected places, to see an extension of this system known as

The patchwork landscape of the Vinho Verde region. Vines trained on pergolas are mixed with cordon trained vines as well as other crops

arejão or *arjoado* ('aired' or 'ventilated'). Four or five wires are stretched between small trees or tall pillars and vines planted 2 or 3 metres apart grow vertically to form a dense screen, up to 6 metres in height. One or two growers are making a feature of this tradition in their wines. More widespread are the pergola-trained vines known as *vinha ramada*. Stout granite posts around 3 metres in height support a horizontal wire trellis. This in turn supports the vine canopy and the heavy bunches of grapes that hang beneath. *Vinha ramada* has a distinctly ornamental look, resulting from the fact that during the Salazar era, when feeding the nation became a priority, vines could only be planted in the Vinho Verde region for 'decorative purposes'. This drove smallholders to coax as much yield as they could from their supposedly 'decorative' vines and did nothing to advance the quality of Vinho Verde.

Apart from maximizing the use of space, high-trained vines had a number of other advantages. The climate in Vinho Verde country is challenging for growers. The humid westerlies that sail over the Atlantic are forced to rise and condense when they reach the Iberian landmass. Annual average rainfall varies from 1,200 millimetres on the coast to well over 2,000 millimetres on the *serras* of Peneda and Gerês inland (to put this into perspective London receives an average of 600 millimetres of precipitation a year and Manchester, in the north of England, an average of 900 millimetres, while New York averages 1,200 millimetres a year). Most of the rain falls in the winter months (for example Viana do Castelo typically receives 900 millimetres between October and March), but the occasional wet spring and early summer has the potential to create havoc during flowering and necessitates regular treatment against mildew and oidium. The summer warmth which creates the conditions for olive trees, kiwis and oranges to flourish alongside vines also provokes fungal disease. Raising the canopy above the ground helps the air to circulate freely and reduces the risk of rot or, in the mountain valleys, damage from late spring frosts. But these practical advantages are increasingly outweighed by problems. After the phylloxera epidemic in the late nineteenth century, vine varieties were selected for their resistance to disease, vigour and yield rather than the intrinsic quality of their fruit. Vigorous plants (including many direct producers and hybrids) produced a heavy crop of grapes that were low in sugar and high in acidity.

In the 1970s (with the relaxation in the 'decorative' legislation that followed the revolution) growers began to abandon the labour-intensive pergolas in favour of lower forms of training. This was the era of the *cruzeta*. In this system, four vines are planted around the base of a wooden, cement or granite pole, 2 metres or so in height. A crossbar (hence the name *cruzeta*) 1.5 to 1.8 metres in width supports two lateral wires along which the vine's fruit-bearing arms are trained to give the plant a semblance of order and shape. Planted in rows and spaced to allow tractors to pass in between, *cruzetas* permit a certain amount of mechanization but they proved unpopular with growers, who find them troublesome and expensive to maintain. Most growers have now moved on to a more straightforward system of training, *cordão simples*, with vines supported on a vertical cordon 1.5 metres in height. This facilitates mechanization to the extent that some larger estates are now harvested by machine. Planted at a density of 2,000 vines per hectare (compared to the fewer than 500 vines per hectare common in the past), cordon planting has helped to improve the quality of the fruit. A focus on better varieties, along with increased exposure, has produced grapes with higher levels of sugar and lower acidity. Initially, when the maximum permitted level of alcohol for Vinho Verde was 11.5% abv, this brought some growers into conflict with the authorities.

Subregions

The Vinho Verde region divides into nine officially recognized subregions, each of which produces a distinct style of wine based on a different terroir and a different mix of grapes. Most of the Vinho Verde DOC is covered by these regions, with the exception of the area around Viana do Castelo, the city of Oporto and the area in the south bordering Lafões.

In the extreme north along the River Minho, **Monção–Melgaço** takes in the municipalities of the same name. This subregion is sufficiently well sheltered from the Atlantic to make it ideal for Alvarinho, the same grape as Albariño, which is cultivated in Rias Baixas in Galicia, immediately to the north. In fact growers here became so possessive about the Alvarinho grape that the authorities effectively prohibited it from being planted elsewhere in the Vinhos Verdes. However, in what could prove to be a game-changer for the region, from 2020 Alvarinho can be used to make Vinho Verde anywhere in the DOC. But the Monção–Melgaço subregion still has a dynamic all of its own and Alvarinho wines (technically categorized as Vinhos Verdes) enjoy a certain amount of autonomy from the rest of the region. Alvarinho typically ripens to produce wines with 12.5 or 13% abv, although the Trajadura grape is also planted in the region and the two varieties are sometimes blended to produce a distinctive but less fragrant style of wine. Two distinct styles of pure, varietal Alvarinho have emerged. Those from the stony, alluvial soils tend to be the richest and most aromatic whereas those from granite are more subdued. Although no distinction is made on the label, Alvarinho from Melgaço, upstream, tends to have more nervy acidity whereas that from Monção produces wine which is softer and more rounded. The well-managed cooperative at Monção blends wines from both districts. A small quantity of red and rosé Vinho Verde is also produced from Pedral and Alvarelhão grapes in the subregion.

The **Lima** subregion covers the municipalities Ponte de Lima, Arcos de Valdevez and Ponte de Barca and part of Viana do Castelo, on either side of the River Lima. Ponte de Barca is now one of the most productive parts of the entire Vinho Verde region. Cut off from the urban areas to the south by the foothills of the Serra Amarela, the Lima is the most rural part of the Vinho Verde region. Pergola-trained vines still thread their way through the countryside, gradually petering out as they ascend the Serra da Peneda. Precipitation is high here, with annual totals often well in excess of 1,200 millimetres. The municipality of Ponte de Lima is the heart of the region and home to an excellent local cooperative. The leading vineyards are planted with Loureiro, a grape that produces wonderfully elegant, fragrant varietal Vinho Verde. Arinto (known locally as Pedernã) and Trajadura are also planted here as well as Vinhão and Borraçal for red wines. Wines from the few outcrops of schist south of the Lima tend to be finer and more aromatic than the lighter wines from the granite-based soils that predominate throughout the Vinho Verde region. Ponte da Barca and Arcos de Valdevez make a speciality of red Vinho Verde from the Vinhão grape.

Cávado, to the south, takes in the municipalities of Esposende, Barcelos, Braga, Vila Verde, Amares and Terras de Bouro, all of which span the Cavado Valley. This area has been steadily urbanized (Braga is Portugal's third largest city) and the area towards the coast has lost much of its agriculture. Arinto, Loureiro and Trajadura are the principal white grapes with some Azal. Vinhão and Borraçal are used for reds and rosés. The region was traditionally dominated by cooperatives but there are also some substantial family estates (some linked to the local textile industry), many of which have been revitalized.

Ave is the largest but most urbanized of all the subregions, taking in the industrial towns north of Oporto, namely Vila Nova de Famalicão, Fafe, Guimarães, Santo Tirso, and Trofa, as well as Póvoa de Lanhoso, Vieira do Minho, Póvoa de Varzim, Vila do Conde and part of the municipality of Vizela. Where vines are still grown, this is an area for white wines, predominantly from Arinto and Loureiro with some Trajadura.

Basto, due east of Braga, takes in the upper Tâmega Valley, upstream from Amarante, as well as the lower slopes of the Serra do Alvão. Off the beaten track this, the most mountainous Vinho Verde subregion, is also one of the most attractive to visit, with terraced smallholdings and vines strung out between the trees. Four municipalities make up Basto: Celerico de Basto, Cabaceiras de Basto, Mondim de Basto and Ribeira de Pena. The climate is more continental here with cold, wet winters and hot, dry summers. White wines are traditionally based on early ripening Azal, along with Batoca and Pedernã, but there is still a large quantity of red emanating from Borraçal, Espadeiro, Padeiro-Basto, Rabo de Ovelha and Vinhão.

The subregion of **Sousa** takes in the municipalities of Penafiel, Lousada, Paredes, Felgueiras, Paços de Ferreira and part of Vizela. The region, which covers the valley of the River Sousa and lower reaches of the River Tâmega, is now quite urbanized and similar to the Ave and Cávado. Azal and Arinto are the traditional white grape varieties with Loureiro, Trajadura and Avesso planted in newer vineyards. Amaral, Borraçal, Espadeiro and Vinhão make up the red. The region includes Quinta de Aveleda, which is located close to Penafiel, and the huge

Felgueiras cooperative, Caves de Felgueiras, which is part of an association of cooperative *adegas* called Vercoope.

Located inland, the **Amarante** subregion covers the municipalities of Amarante and Marco de Canaveses (birthplace of Carmen Miranda) in the middle reaches of the River Tâmega. It is well protected from the Atlantic. Azal and Avesso are the favoured white grape varieties with Vinhão, Amaral and Espadeiro for reds. There is still a large quantity of red wine produced here.

The **Baião** subregion spans the Douro valley and covers the municipalities of Baião, north of the river, and part of Resende and Cinfães to the south. It has become known euphemistically as the 'Douro Verde'. The climate here is warmer than in the rest of the Vinho Verde region and tends to produce wines with higher levels of alcohol, mostly from the Avesso grape. Avesso means 'contrary' which explains the style of wine in relation to the rest of the region.

Paiva is the smallest and most southerly of all the subregions, covering Castelo de Paiva and part of Cinfães south of the River Douro. Reds are favoured here, mostly from Amaral and Vinhão. Avesso, Arinto, Loureiro and Trajadura produce fuller flavoured white wines.

Styles of wine

September slows the narrow lanes of Vinho Verde country to a crawl as carts and trailers groaning with grapes wend their way to the nearest winery. In the past, 5 October marked the height of the harvest. This coincides with a national holiday (*Dia da Republica*), allowing entire families to go back to their rural roots and pick grapes. Helped by better viticultural practices and the need to conserve natural acidity in the grapes and possibly by climate change, the harvest is now taking place earlier, from early to mid-September. This also reduces the risk of the crop being diluted by early autumn rains.

Until the 1950s and the advent of the cooperatives, Vinho Verde was largely a cottage industry where wines were made in small, stone *adegas* or back parlours all over the region. An unknown quantity of wine is still made on this scale, with the grapes trodden and fermented in stone *lagares*, after which the wine (mostly red) is run off into old wooden casks. Shortly after the end of the alcoholic fermentation or in the spring after the harvest, the malolactic begins, converting harsh malic acid into softer lactic acidity. Carbon dioxide is generated by this process and some of this is retained in the wine, giving it a natural spritz or sparkle. The wine would be bottled in mid-November, traditionally around the Dia de São Martinho (11 November). According to custom: 'É dia de São Martinho; comem-se castanhas, prova-se o vinho' (On St Martin's Day, you eat chestnuts, you taste the wine). This is the origin of Vinho Verde: an astringent, hazy, rustic style of wine that is also inherently unstable. It can still be found served fresh and frothing from the cask in private houses or roadside *tascas* in the more remote parts of the region.

With the drive to make wine for export in the 1950s and 1960s, Vinho Verde came to be made on a much larger scale. In the cooperatives, which mostly date from this era, the grapes are crushed or pressed mechanically (often in continuous presses) and the must is fermented either in lined cement vats or, since money flowed in from the EU, in temperature-controlled stainless steel. Once the sugar in the grapes has fermented to alcohol, all white wines are dosed with sulphur dioxide (SO_2) to prevent the malolactic from taking place. This not only helps to prevent oxidation but also preserves much of the primary fruit character and acidity that would otherwise be lost during the malolactic. With this in mind, bottling takes place early, during either the winter or early spring. The characteristic spritz comes from an injection of carbon dioxide (CO_2) shortly before the wine is bottled.

Since the late 1980s, the move towards single estate (*quinta*) Vinho Verde has meant that much more care is taken in winemaking, from the separation of different grape varieties in the winery to bottling with much lower levels of sulphur and retaining natural carbon dioxide to give the wines just a touch of petillance rather than outright spritz. Whereas in the past, Vinho Verde was often sweetened for export (to mask the naturally high acidity) most Vinhos Verdes (even the larger brands) are now bottled dry or off-dry. And while at one time Vinho Verde was bottled to be drunk in the year after harvest (and few wines carried a vintage date as a result), Vinho Verde is now being made in a multitude of different ways with some wines (notably those made from Alvarinho) capable of age in bottle for up to five years. An increasing number of producers apply *batonnage* for a few months, leading to a slightly fuller, more complex *sur lie* style of wine. Some producers have also been tempted to experiment with fermentation and/or ageing and *batonnage* in new oak. This, to my way of thinking, is a technique that rarely enhances the wine, the oak merely detracting from the gentle beauty of the fruit.

Red Vinho Verde is something of an acquired taste but is still popular in the Minho, where it cuts through the richness of the local food. A number of producers are attempting to make an international name with red Vinho Verde, particularly from the Vinhão grape, the same variety as the increasingly well-respected Sousão in the neighbouring Douro. Rosé and espumante Vinhos Verdes are also finding a market. All Vinho Verde is bottled with a seal of origin, now mostly found on the back label, which was first granted by the Comissão de Viticultura da Região dos Vinhos Verdes (CRVV) in 1959.

RIOJA: A WORLD WITHIN A WORLD

Rioja is surely Spain's best-known wine region. But while there have been changes in winemaking, other regions such as Bierzo and Priorat have been pushing ahead, introducing quality classifications. Can Rioja afford to be left behind? In this discussion from her 2018 book *The wines of northern Spain*, Sarah Jane Evans MW discovers what may be coming to the region.

What's the best way to arrive in Rioja? For me, it's coming from Bilbao, taking the road through the mountains and watching Rioja as it unfolds before you. The mountains are majestic, and in between is undulating countryside with rivers running through and hilltop towns spread about. There's a lot to be said for arriving by rail, too. Take the train from Zaragoza. The last section, Logroño–Haro, meanders past the Ebro and vineyards. For the people who lived here in previous centuries Rioja must have seemed a blessed enclave. Any time is good to come: autumn is particularly beautiful; winter brings snow (and sometimes problems driving); in spring there's blossom on the trees and in the summer it's hot, but with plenty of cool places to enjoy wine in the evening. Too many wine regions can be flat monocultures of vines. Come to Rioja, it's altogether more human.

When phylloxera came to France, the producers cast around for vine-growing land. Spain was conveniently close and with the opening of the railway line from Logroño to Bilbao via Haro in 1880, Rioja was an ideal source. Thus it was that Haro's Barrio de la Estación came into being, with wineries clustered around the railway. The first to arrive was R. López de Heredía y Landeta in 1877, followed by CVNE in 1879,

Duque de Montezuma and J. Gómez Cruzado in 1890, La Rioja Alta in 1890 and Bodegas Bilbaínas in 1901. (To complete the contemporary set, Muga moved from Haro town in 1970, and in 1987 came RODA.) In those early years the bodegas jostled with factories making brandies, soaps and fertilizers. While some of the Haro bodegas may seem today the epitome of classical wines, Haro was cutting-edge in its day – the first town in Spain to have electric street lighting.

Phylloxera came to Rioja, inevitably, in 1899. The first outbreak was in a vineyard in Sajazarra. The region recovered reasonably quickly as by then the wine world had discovered that the solution was to graft vines on to much more resistant American labrusca rootstocks.

For a number of years Rioja continued to define itself like so many parts of the world in terms of French wines, for instance by selling 'cepa Borgoña' (intended to mean 'Burgundy style') wines. The really significant change, after Spain's entrance to Europe, was Rioja's elevation to DOCa status, denominación de origen calificada, a first in Spain in 1991. While regulation can be criticized for too much policing and of the wrong kind, it has to be noted that a DOCa should never be about selling any wine at bargain basement prices. The very nature of being a DOCa should protect it from that unsustainable marketing. Yet when the DOCa was introduced it was a generic blanket for all Rioja wines to satisfy all interested parties: grower, small producer, cooperative and multinational. Hence Rioja can be sold too cheaply. Surely the wine world has changed? One size (or type of classification) need not fit all. This has led to a number of leading wine producers releasing a manifesto questioning the validity of the current DO system.

Before we go any further, this is the place to run through the ever-growing list of possibilities behind the naming of the region. There is a River Oja, which surely must be the reason for Rioja's name. But this is a little trickle compared to the grandeur of the Ebro, and its dominance in the landscape. Then there's a possibility it refers to a local tribe called in Latin, Ruccones. Another source suggests that the source is Erriotxa or a similar spelling, which means 'bread country' in Basque. The US writer Ana Fabiano suggests that it might come from Rialia, describing a collection of small tributaries in Rioja Alta around the River Oja. She also speculates that it could come from the Basque Arrioixa, or 'land of rocks'. And thus, the debate continues.

Those who like to define Rioja in terms of Burgundy, will note that in geographical terms there are similarities. Imagine Rioja turned upright, clockwise through 45 degrees, and there you have Burgundy. It is approximately 35 kilometres wide by 120 kilometres long, running from north-east to south-west, tucked in between mountain ranges. Administratively it is composed of three provinces: La Rioja (43,885 hectares of vineyards, 118 municipalities), Álava, the southern tip of the Basque country (12,934 hectares, 18 municipalities), and to the east, Navarra (6,774 hectares, 8 municipalities). All in all, there are 14,300 growers and 799 wineries. There is also one bodega to the far west of Rioja that is in Castilla y León. Climatically there are strong differences. Nothing is straightforward about the soils, either, a complex blend of chalky clay, ferrous clay and alluvial types. Add to this the differing aspects and elevations – up to 700 metres, and in a few cases up to 900 metres. Blend in the grape varieties. To finish, there are the decisions of the producers, each serving diverse customer tastes.

The River Ebro, which decants to the Mediterranean, winds through Rioja and into it flow seven significant small rivers – significant in terroir terms, that is, each offering different aspects and soils. All of these come down from the Iberian system of mountains to the south. Starting in the west, the River Oja rises to the south of Rioja in the San Lorenzo mountains and flows down to Haro. The snows and cold of the Sierra Demanda above the river valley have a strong influence on the higher altitude vineyards. Next comes the Najerilla river valley. Again, it rises in the San Lorenzo mountains and comes down to the Ebro with many terraces of vineyards on both sides. The Iregua valley to the east of it flows down to Logroño, creating fertile conditions for plenty of market garden produce and olives. The River Leza joins the Jubera before arriving at Agoncillo by the Ebro, and is distinctive for its cliffs and canyons. Great for walkers, both rivers are distinctive for the difference from the elegant beauty of some of the Rioja Alta landscapes. Finally, the Cidacos valley winds at length down past the Monte Yerga, and the high Garnacha-dominant vineyards of Quel and Arnedo till it comes to the Ebro just after Calahorra.

Rioja's story is all about diversity. As Ana Fabiano notes, Rioja contains 36 per cent of all the plant biodiversity in Spain. Furthermore when vineyard sites range from 300 to 700 metres, the climate really varies, and that's before one takes in considerations of slope, aspect and soil. That's why the vintage assessments beloved of fine wine retailers and auction houses are so difficult. Take the terrible frosts of April 2017. They wiped out 100 per cent of some vineyards, but others

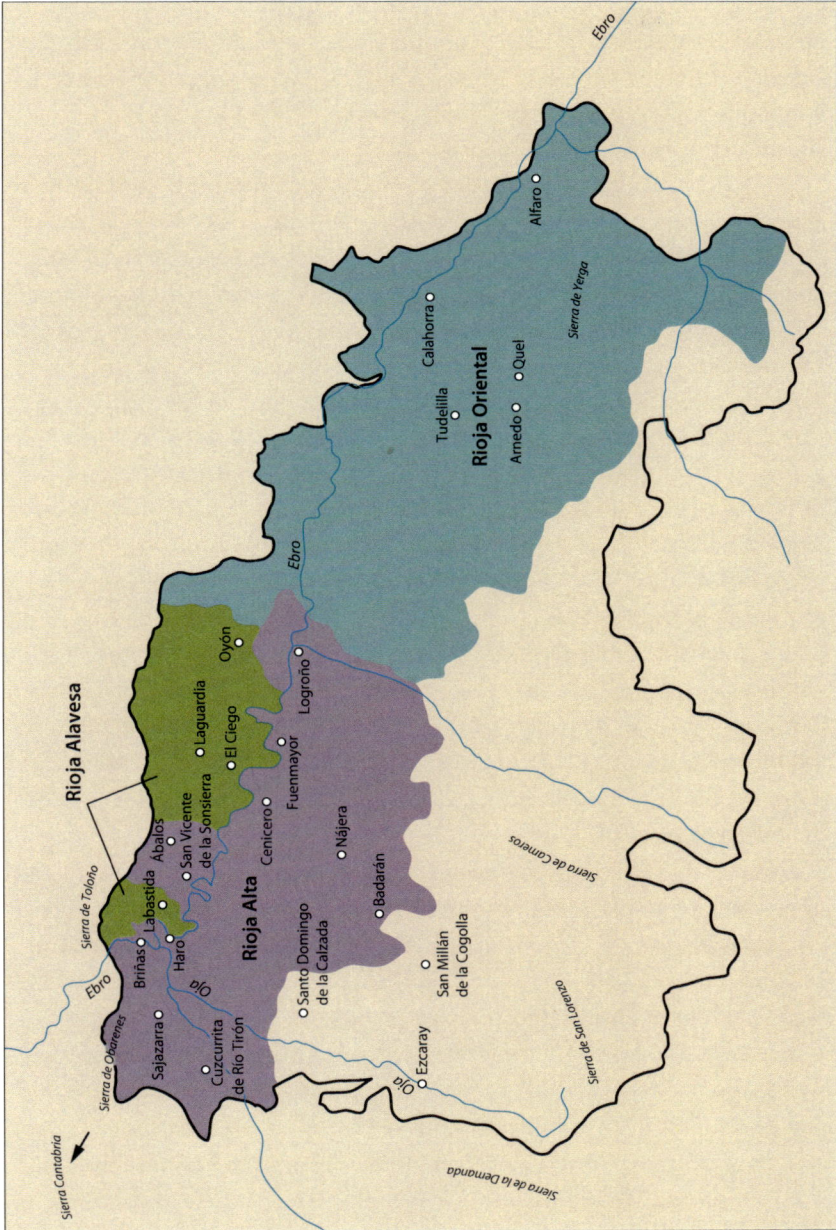

Rioja Oriental

Calahorra

Tudelilla

Arnedo ○ ○ Quel

Alfaro

Sierra de Yerga

Ebro

Ebro

Oyón

Laguardia

El Ciego

Logroño

Rioja Alavesa

San Vicente
de la Sonsierra

Abalós

Labastida

Briñas

Haro

Fuenmayor

Cenicero

Nájera

Rioja Alta

Badarán

Santo Domingo
de la Calzada

San Millán
de la Cogolla

Sajazarra

Cuzcurita
de Río Tirón

Ezcaray

Sierra de Toloño

Sierra de Obarenes

Sierra Cantabria

Ebro

Río

Río

Sierra de Cameros

Sierra de San Lorenzo

Sierra de la Demanda

escaped completely. In terms of climatic influences, at the north-west end, Rioja is little more than 100 kilometres from the Atlantic, which gives the producers of Rioja Alta a good reason to describe their cooler vintages as Atlantic. The Sierra Cantabria is some protection from the Atlantic extremes. To the south the frequently snow-capped Sierra de la Demanda and the Sierra de Cameros protect the valleys of Rioja from strong winds from the south-west.

The CRDOCa recognizes three distinct viticultural sub-zones. Rioja Alta, where the climate is mainly Atlantic, with soils that are chalky clay, ferrous clay, or alluvial; Rioja Alavesa, where the climate is Atlantic, and the soils are chalky clay, broken up in terraces and small plots; and Rioja Baja, with alluvial and ferrous clay soils, which has a drier, warmer climate, with strong Mediterranean influences. These categories are long established, but are quite crude divisions of such an exceptional wine-producing region. Growers who have worked in Rioja for a long time know the subtleties. To advance the lively debate about if or how Rioja should segment its wines by sub-zone, the consultant José 'Pepe' Hidalgo, whose connections with the wines of Rioja are long and deep, has made a very constructive map. He points out that there are too many villages – 144 of them – to permit the sensible naming and management of village wines as Burgundy has done. The problem is compounded if you add in estate or vineyard wines. He advises that the work should begin by recognizing the correct sub-zones, beyond simply the historical ones of Rioja Alta, Rioja Alavesa and Rioja Baja. Now that there is so much understanding of the soils and vineyards, it is time to define them more clearly.

His sketch map identifies nine comarcas or zones. Each zone name opposite is written in bold type and the rivers are shown with fine lines. Hidalgo's plan neatly summarizes many actual assumptions about Rioja – Monte Yerga and Alto Najerilla for instance are well-known – while finding a logical pathway through the puzzle of some of the others.

Hidalgo's proposed La Sonsierra is what is currently Rioja Alavesa, as well as the few areas of Rioja Alta which are on the north side of the Ebro and geographically – if not politically – belong to Alavesa. The soils are calcareous clay, and this is practically the only part of Rioja where these soils are found. Rainfall is 400–500 millimetres and the annual average temperature 12–13°C. Moving east from La Sonsierra he identifies Ribera Oriental del Ebro, the eastern bank of the River Ebro, a large section which runs all the way down to Álfaro in the east. What unites this

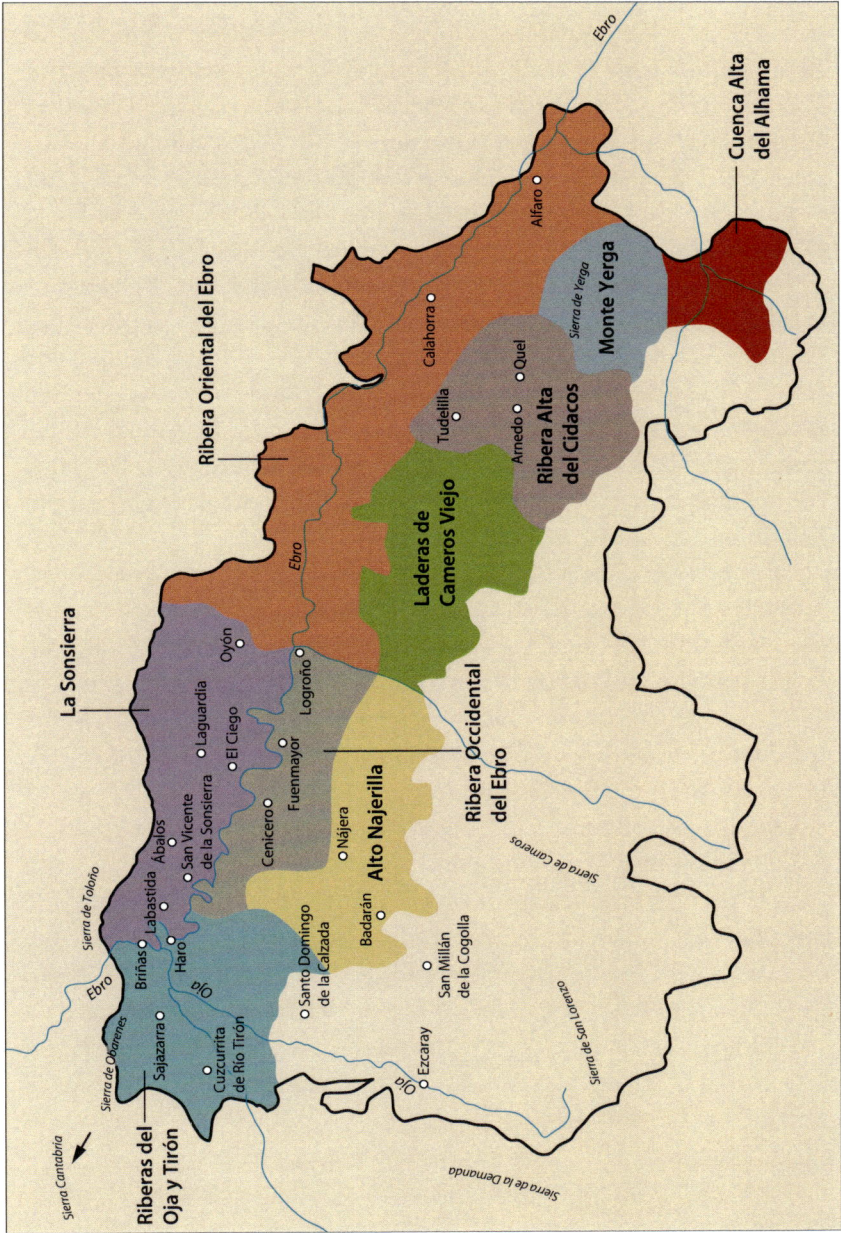

Cuenca Alta del Alhama

Ribera Oriental del Ebro

Monte Yerga

Sierra de Yerga

Alfaro

Calahorra

Quel

Tudelilla

Amedo

Ribera Alta del Cidacos

Laderas de Cameros Viejo

Oyón

La Sonsierra

Laguardia

El Ciego

Logroño

Ebro

Fuenmayor

Ribera Occidental del Ebro

Cenicero

San Vicente de la Sonsierra

Nájera

Alto Najerilla

Ábalos

Labastida

Santo Domingo de la Calzada

Badarán

Sierra de Cameros

Briñas

Haro

Sierra de Toloño

Oja

San Millán de la Cogolla

Sajazarra

Cuzcurrita de Río Tirón

Ezcaray

Sierra de San Lorenzo

Sierra de Obarenes

Ebro

Oja

Riberas del Oja y Tirón

Sierra de la Demanda

Sierra Cantabria

zone are the mainly alluvial soils, with some ferrous clay also. There's less rain, at 300–400 millimetres annually and it's warmer at 13–14°C. The wines from here have higher alcohol levels, and are less fresh, but much more deeply coloured and fruity. To the west is the Ribera Occidental del Ebro, the west bank of the Ebro with the river as its northern boundary. There are three main types of soil here: alluvial by the rivers, red-coloured ferrous clays, and also a smaller amount of calcareous clay. It's a cooler zone, 12–13°C and a little rainier at 400–500 millimetres.

Furthest west Hidalgo proposes Riberas del Oja y Tirón, the banks of the rivers Oja and Tirón. The northern boundaries here are the Ebro and the Obarenes mountains, and the southern is the Sierra de la Demanda. There are three types of soil here: on the slopes of the Obarenes mountains it is brown limestone, closer to Haro, Briones and Ollauri it's calcareous clay and in the southernmost part, ferrous clay. It's cooler here, often much cooler, at 11–12°C, and the annual rainfall varies, depending on the site, from 400 to 600 millimetres. The wines are well coloured, perhaps the most Atlantic in style, with greatest potential for long ageing in bottle.

The zone of Alto Najerilla is undoubtedly the freshest and most humid of the DOCa, given its altitude of 700 metres. The Serradero mountain at 1,495 metres looms over it, and the rivers Najerilla and Iregua segment and define it. The climatic data illustrate this well: 10–12°C average temperature and rainfall between 400 and 600 millimetres depending on the site. The riverside soils are alluvial, but the rest are ferrous clay. This is the zone of very pale reds, the claretes riojanos, of refreshing reds and some fine Garnachas. The Laderas de Cameros Viejo is altogether different: a mountainous zone at 700–1,000 metres, with average temperatures at 10–13°C and rainfall at 500–600 millimetres. The wines are well-built, full-bodied and long-lasting. The Ribera Alta del Cidacos is the proposed region on the bank of the Upper Cidacos river. This rises from 500 to 1,000 metres, with the peak of Peña Isasa at 1,456 metres. The average temperature falls as the altitude rises, from 13°C to 10°C, while rainfall is 400–500 millimetres. There are alluvial soils by the river, and ferrous clay to the north, with brown limestone in the highest parts. The best wines having long ageing potential.

The eighth proposed region, Monte Yerga, is already well accepted. The Yerga mountain rises to 1,101 metres, and many of the vineyards are clustered at 500 metres, with others rising much further. Monte Yerga has become very fashionable as the popularity of Garnacha has risen, and the vineyards at 600–700 metres and higher are extremely promising. The climate changes with the altitude, with temperatures from 13–11°C and rainfall at 400–500 millimetres. The final suggested zone is Cuenca Alta del Alhama, literally, the high basin of Alhama. Hidalgo comments that it's probably the smallest and least known of Rioja's sub-zones. It's reasonably high at 500–700 metres, with average temperatures of 12–13°C and rainfall at 400–500 millimetres. The brown limestone soils here are excellent for Garnacha and there are some old vine reminders of the Garnachas that once grew here.

Until such time as the CRDOCa introduces a really clear system, this simple sketch map of Hidalgo's is a measured, constructive introduction to the diversity of Rioja. In the meantime, Rioja continues to be divided into Rioja Alta, Rioja Alavesa and Rioja Baja. Álava has always been a special case, as it is part of a separate province with a very strong political identity. As Europe in general becomes more interested in separatism Álava's interest in her differences from the rest of Rioja have also become more acute. It's not just the language that is so obvious on all the road signs the moment you cross into Álava. Nor is it simply the style of winemaking, with a continued tradition in partial or total carbonic maceration for young wines. It's not just the genuine beauty of the region: the villages and towns that stand out against the vineyards, the Ebro, and the Sierras de Toloño and Cantabria. These are special places. The region was always known for the quality of its produce. In 1164 King Sancho el Sabio (the Wise) ordered that vines should be planted in the region, which gave rise to the villages of Labastida, Labraza and Salinillas. They were definitely appreciated by the far-sighted Queen Isabella la Católica who ordered in 1504 that Alavesa wines should be taxed at a lower rate than those from the surrounding regions. The pilgrims in search of sustenance en route to Santiago de Compostela must have been delighted.

Fast forward to 2016 and 40 producers came together to propose the creation of Viñedos de Álava. This was not well received in the CRDOCa. They were already having to contain any repercussions from Juan Carlos López de Lacalle having taken the Artadi winery out of the DOCa just a few months earlier. In a flurry of activity in 2017, the CRDOCa managed to restore calm, and the Álava producers withdrew their plan. There are now two new proposals from the Consejo Regulador, which have to be ratified at a governmental level. This will take time, but in essence the proposals are as follows.

For wine to be able to declare that it comes from a Viñedo Singular, the vineyard has to have demonstrable boundaries and ownership for a minimum of ten years. The vineyard must be more than 35 years old, and it can be made up of several plots or vineyards together if they are connected. The yield must be at least 20 per cent below the regional requirement. The vineyards must be well-balanced with limited vigour, hand-harvested, and managed with respect for the environment. In terms of finished wine it must show traceability, undergo quality assessment both initially and before sale, and have an 'Excellent' rating.

Will this be enough to satisfy the critics? One exporter of Spanish wines was blunt: 'I cannot see how it will help the consumer; a shoddy single vineyard wine will still be a shoddy wine but it will now be backed by an official recognition as "something special".' On the other hand, a leading winemaker was more optimistic: 'Rioja is now in the perfect moment to show all its diversity regarding terroir, knowledge and origin … That's the beauty of this initiative. Whether the choice is single vineyard or Reserva and Gran Reserva will depend on the type of wine, the style of the house, the style of the winemaker, but they can be totally complementary.'

At the time of writing there are many owners of famous vineyards who are not keen to go to the trouble of registration when their wines are already known. On the other hand there is a surprisingly high number of others who are looking forward to the extra recognition that the label could provide when the legislation passes. Will they deliver the superior quality the words Viñedo Singular suggest?

The second decision taken in 2016 was to allow village wines to be declared as such on the label. At last! Rioja is taking the Burgundian route. Not entirely. The critics are unhappy here, too: the CRDOCa requirement is now that the winery must be in the same village as the vineyard. This prevents people with multiple single vineyards in different villages making multiple village wines, unless they go to the expense of constructing a winery for each. These producers argue that nowadays roads are good, and chilling available, that grapes can be brought quickly and safely from one end of Rioja to the other. Adding fuel to the fire of the critics, the new regulation will permit producers to include up to 15 per cent of non-village fruit from neighbouring vineyards outside the village boundary. Critics say that these two decisions play into the hands of the large producers, who have the strongest voices in the DOCa. Is this proposal undermining the very nature of village wine, as they say, or is it merely practical? At this stage these two decisions look as if they have been made in haste, to satisfy producers who are threatening to break away, and may be regretted at leisure. Undoubtedly revisions will be needed, as well as a generally more flexible approach by the regulatory body.

There are now so many styles of Rioja – modern, vino de autor, single vineyard, carbonic maceration, as well as subzonal variations of terroir and tradition – and so many strongly held opinions that it is easy to lose sight of one important quality in many fine Riojas. Namely, that they are blends. There are historical reasons for this. Many producers did not own their own vineyards, and there are commercial brands who still don't. They rely on the growers for supply, growers from right across Rioja. Then there are also producers who wanted to make classical blends of two or more varieties, of Tempranillo with Graciano or Mazuelo, for instance, who own vineyards or buy their grapes from the best places, but not necessarily close to the winery. Rioja Alta producers sourced and still source their Garnacha grapes from Tudelilla in Rioja Baja. This was never an issue, until the debate promoting single vineyard wines became so excessively heated.

Which is better: a cross-DOCa blend of the best grapes, or a single vineyard where perhaps only one variety flourishes? This is the same debate over the merits of Penfold's Grange and Henschke's Hill of Grace in Australia. One is a multi-regional blend, the other a historic single vineyard. Different styles, different consumers, equal pleasure. Everyone has different views: my current notebook is filled with diagrams of Burgundian-style pyramids (Bierzo proposals), interlocking circles (neighbouring village proposals) and criss-crossing rectangles (the CRDOCa vision). Speaking at RODA, director general and all-round viticultural expert Agustín Santolaya pleaded: 'Don't Burgundify Rioja'. RODA is the newbie in the Barrio de la Estación, having only been founded in 1989. Santolaya's mission is to make the best wine from a blend of the best vineyards; the traditional approach, though perhaps in a modern way. Look back at history, he says: 'Traditionally Rioja blended its wines from great vineyards; there were practically no single vineyard wines made.'

*

A decade ago, perhaps less, white Rioja had a really terrible reputation. The general view was that it was made from only one variety – Viura – and that Viura was flabby and boring. Yet in just a few years white Rioja has returned to favour. It may still only account for some 6–7 per cent of Rioja production but from that low base its market share has been increasing by some 20 per cent year on year. There are a number of reasons for this. They include: climate change, improved distribution, the requirements of export markets and the creativity of individual winemakers, while maintaining respect for the old ways and the classics. The launch of the latest Castillo Ygay 1986 white from Marqués de Murrieta with some 30 years of age hit the fine wine headlines and helped to bolster the profile of white Rioja as something exceptional. Of course, like the Viña Tondonia Gran Reserva white, it is a one-off, an original. In general, today's white Riojas are – many of them – beautifully balanced, with subtle oak, and complex. They could not be further from the oxidized, tired wines of the past.

White Rioja is not just made from Viura – though it remains the dominant variety. Malvasía de Rioja (known in Catalunya as Subirat Parent), with its distinctive reddish, yellowish bunches, plays a small but significant part. Garnacha Blanca again amounts for a tiny percentage of the vineyard, but is making some finely textured wines. The Consejo Regulador wobbled a little when it permitted the introduction of Chardonnay and Sauvignon Blanc to an already fine line-up of varieties. An understandable step, an attempt to give their wines an international appeal, but the future for a DOCa lies in making great terroir wines with local varieties.

New varieties are appearing. Tempranillo Blanco made the headlines first. This is a genetic mutation; a single plant with white grapes was found in 1988 in Rioja, in Murillo del Río Leza. It's a late budding variety, but like the red Tempranillo it ripens early. It can show citrus and floral notes and has been popular because of its relationship to Tempranillo itself. Another of the 'new' varieties is in fact an old variety, rescued and revived. Maturana Blanca is the oldest known grape variety in Rioja, and may have been referred to in 1622. The fact that it is sensitive to botrytis will have helped it fall out of favour. In character it has bright acidity, a tendency to warm alcohol, and a hint of bitterness on the finish. Another 'new' variety is Turruntés de Rioja, no relative of the Galician Turruntés or the Argentine Torrontes. Instead it is similar to Albillo Mayor, found in Castilla y León. It is low in alcohol, with a welcome high acidity, offering crisp apple notes. For a taste of these traditional and new white varieties, look to Abel Mendoza, and to Juan Carlos Sancha, the university lecturer and bodeguero, who has also fostered these rarities.

SANTORINI

In his 2018 book *The wines of Greece*, Konstantinos Lazarakis argues that the volcanic island of Santorini is the shining star among Greek quality wine designations. Explaining its unique training system, its natural immunity to a certain vineyard pest and its traditional and modern wine styles, he puts the case for Santorini's special status.

Santorini is one of the most remarkable and beautiful places in the world. People travel from all around the globe to see the beauties of Santorini and watch the sunset. Sometimes people actually applaud when the sun disappears, as if thanking Nature for the spectacular performance. There are no words to describe Santorini's magnificence – one has to see it, and most of all, feel it for oneself.

Its wines are also among the best in Europe, and it is almost a sad fact that these two qualities coexist on the same plot of land. Over the last decade, Santorini has clearly emerged as the throughbred able to pull Greek wine out of anonymity, removing the curse of belonging to 'the others'. For many professionals around the globe, Greek wine *is* Santorini. The quality of the wines produced is indisputable. In terms of individuality of regional style, as the wine world stands right now, it belongs without a shadow of doubt in the top five.

Santorini and its small sister island of Thirassia exist on a dormant volcano. During its last eruption, in 1500 BC, much of it collapsed, forming an inverted cone that starts from the cliffs of Santorini and plunges under the sea: this is the caldera. The eruption was connected to the destruction of the Minoan civilization in Crete, located more than 100 kilometres (60 miles) to the south. Tsunamis and earthquakes created a catastrophe of epic proportions, leading many to speculate that Santorini could have been the Atlantis of legend. Two small islets have been created over the centuries in the space between Thirassia and Santorini, called Nea Kameni and Palea Kameni. Palea Kameni, 'Old Burnt', was formed less than 2,000 years ago, while Nea Kameni, 'Young Burnt', or simply 'The Volcano' as locals refer to it, started becoming visible around 1580 AD.

There have been constant signs of activity since, but without the violence of thirty-five centuries ago. There were small-scale eruptions in 1649 and 1650, and as recently as the 1920s. In 1956 there was some activity, followed by a devastating earthquake that made many locals seek refuge in Piraeus and Athens. During this eruption, new lava was added to Nea Kameni, making it the youngest volcanic earth in the eastern Mediterranean. The volcano has never been completely silent, and sulphurous smoke can be seen coming out of Nea Kameni every day. The Greek Army has a plan in place, enabling the complete evacuation of Santorini in less than forty-eight hours, even at the peak of the summer season.

The island has very complex, young volcanic soil, superimposing schist, limestone, lava and ferric dusts. There is little organic matter or water; even *Vitis vinifera* finds it difficult to live here. Rainfall is next to zero during the summer, and springs are so rare and precious that they are usually not used for irrigation. To decrease competition between vines, the average density is very low, less than 2,500 vines per hectare. Even weeds are inhibited by the dryness and infertility.

Wind is another serious problem. It can disrupt flowering and berry-set, or increase the water stress in July and August. Basket vines are the most used form, offering protection from the wind and preserving humidity. However, Sigalas, in wind sheltered Oia, has been experimenting with Guyot training for almost a decade with promising results. So far, he also escaped crucifixion by the locals for doing so.

The eastern side of the island, facing away from the caldera, is fairly flat and the only side where beaches can be found. Moving westward, the island starts a steady incline and then reaches a plateau, which in turn is cut off abruptly by the cliffs forming the caldera. Vineyards can be found in most areas but are more usual in the central and western parts. Ripening patterns vary across the island, and quality-oriented producers must follow these closely and be able to harvest fruit at very short notice.

Santorini has its own quality-wine designation, a PDO, the legal maximum yield for which is about 60 hectolitres per hectare, making it the lowest in Greece. However, in reality yields are much lower; only a few vineyards, in the most plentiful vintages, manage over 40 hectolitres per hectare, and most producers are content with half this. Roughly two years in every decade, most vineyards produce 7–10 hectolitres per hectare. But these low yields don't necessarily make for higher quality. On the contrary, most growers believe that increased yields of around 30 hectolitres per hectare would give better quality – as well as being more financially viable.

The soil, the vines of Santorini, and their shaping should be taught at every serious university dealing with viticulture. The facts seem unreal unless you hear them from an authority. The shape of vines in Santorini is one of the most imposing synergies between nature, plants and people that exists, not just in the world of wine.

Vines in Santorini trained into the traditional basket shape

Santorini is very windy, apart from a few sheltered areas, and any form of vegetation with a height of half a metre or more (1.6 feet) is bound to have a hard time. So the vines had to be trained low on the ground and a basket shape was selected. The vine shoots are woven around the canes of the previous seasons and, slowly, a round basket is formed, called *kouloura*. There are also permutations of this, such as *klada*. Instead of having one big horizontal basket, the trunk is allowed to grow slightly higher and a number of smaller vertical baskets are formed, one from each cane. Pioneering Santorini winemaker Paris Sigalas believes that this peculiar form of vine training was just another form of artistic expression for the locals, reflecting 'a need for beauty'.

These shapes have several advantages, most of which completely contradict what can be found in a viticultural handbook. The shape protects only the flowers inside the basket, with all others torn apart by the wind. This leads to an intense crop thinning, not that these vines needed it. Usually vines have to develop well above ground, to be protected from weeds and insects but Santorini lacks either. The emerging bunches on the inside are protected from the blazing sun and the sandblasts. The basket shape also traps humidity, a malady in most vine growing areas. Not in Santorini however – the climate is extremely arid but every morning mist rises from the volcano and falls onto the island, causing poor visibility and making driving difficult. This most sophisticated drip irrigation offers a little precious humidity, which must be trapped by the vines to ensure survival.

Pruning of basket-trained vines is a specialized and time-consuming job

The basket system is very expensive and time consuming to cultivate, and needs specialized skills. All work in the vineyard is done on the knees. Harvesting takes four times longer than in Guyot trained vineyards; pruning almost ten times. Even with grape prices reaching

champagne-like heights, grape-growing in Santorini is still more a labour of love, and a very hard one. A possible way out of this, in Sigalas'
mind, is planting, where you can, vertical vineyards. Upon suggesting
this he was immediately denounced as a sort of viticultural Antichrist,
demolishing the very identity of Santorini in one single stroke. He was
threatened with legal proceedings, and worse. The dispute came to a
deadlock, but was possibly dissolved with one short comment made by
the, at the time, 85-year-old Dr Kourakou-Dragona, the great modern-
izer of Greek wine, during a viticulture symposium in Athens, when the
situation became tense: 'There is only one priority, making viticulture
in Santorini financially viable. If basket training is not helpful towards
that, then it defeats the purpose. If vertically trained vines can be a solution let's try them out. Create a Heritage Viticultural Park, to show how
we used to do things, and let people do what they think they can do
best.' Brilliance is a lifelong quality.

The vine shape is not the only weird thing about the island's vineyards. Santorini is not only phylloxera-free but phylloxera-immune.
Phylloxera vastatrix needs at least 5 per cent clay to spread in a vineyard
– it cannot crawl in clay-free soils, and once it reaches its winged phase
it stops reproduction. The young volcanic soils of Santorini have zero
clay. Releasing a couple of the bugs in the middle of Barossa would, giv-
en time, completely ruin the vineyards of the whole region. Dropping
a whole bucket of bugs on top of a vine in Santorini would leave even
that very root intact.

Free from phylloxera concerns, vines are propagated by layering and
a new basket is started. When a basket becomes too bulky to work with,
every twenty years or so, the basket is cut off, used as decoration in
houses on the island, and a cane at the bottom of the trunk is used to
generate a new basket. Vines in Santorini have been found to be ten
or twenty years old above ground and several centuries old below. For
some, 400-year-old root system is considered a conservative estimation.
This also proves that, at least in Santorini, the old vine character is derived from the age and size of what is below ground.

The vineyards are dominated by four varieties. Assyrtiko covers about
70 per cent of the total area and Mandilaria about 20 per cent, followed
by the white versions of Athiri and Aidani. Yet the remaining small
proportion of the island's vineyards contains a remarkable diversity of
vines. It is commonly stated that a century ago, the total number of varieties cultivated was approaching 100. In a diminishing vineyard, a lot

of varieties vanished for ever. Currently there appear to be around 30 varieties in fairly common usage.

Along with the loss of varieties went the loss of expertise. Yiannis Paraskevopoulos claims that, in his first days as a winemaker on the island in the early 1990s, older vine-growers could walk with him around the vineyards and identify the most obscure varieties from ten paces, while no obvious differences were discernible to the untrained eye. In addition, these people, in their late eighties, were able to suggest particular ways of getting the best fruit from these vines. Most of these people are now gone, and young people tend to be better at differentiating between styles of Margaritas than at knowing their Platani from their Mavrathiro.

Assyrtiko is arguably the best white Santorini variety and one of the finest in the Mediterranean. It is not aromatic but can produce an excellent combination of steely structure, minerality, extract, depth, high alcohol and high acidity. In Santorini, a wine with 13.5% abv, a pH of three or less, red-wine-like levels of dry extract and an aromatic expression that is closer to the Loire than to a hot climate is not uncommon. This intense personality is toned down by the roundness of Aidani and the more expressive Athiri.

The list of local varieties makes interesting reading. Platani is another white vine, lesser in significance than those already mentioned, but still of high quality; it can reach high sugar levels with moderate acidity. Thrapsathiri used to be considered a clone of Athiri but has been proved to be a separate variety. It is one of the most aromatic to be found on the island. Flask Assyrtiko was considered, also incorrectly, to be a clone of Assyrtiko. It has high sugars, and acidity below 4.7 grams per litre. Flaska is not related to Flask Assyrtiko, and is less productive, giving higher acidity.

Gaidouria is one of the oldest varieties of the Cyclades and one of the most vigorous vines of Santorini, but it is still only moderately productive. It gives high sugar levels and moderate acidity. Kritiko declares in its name that it comes from Crete, but so far there is no evidence that it is grown beyond Santorini and a few other Cycladic islands. Glikadi is possibly Glikerithra, found in the Peloponnese. In Santorini it is rare, producing high sugar readings and very low acidity. Agrioglikadi – 'wild Glikadi' – might well turn out to be genetically linked to Glikerithra and Glikadi. It is a very rare vine, producing high sugar and low alcohol. Katsano is close in style and habits to

Agrioglikadi. Finally, very few plants of Santorini's Asprouda must exist by now. It is a moderately vigorous and moderately productive vine that reaches high ripeness levels.

Mandilaria covers about 20 per cent of the cultivated area and is used for dry rosés, dry reds and some rosé dessert wines made from sun-dried grapes. There are a number of other red varieties, but they're not as numerous as the whites. Aidani Mavro is present, together with Mavrathiro, a high-quality grape that matures in the first half of September and gives rich colour, high sugar and moderate acidity. Voidomatis is grown in other Greek regions as well, and in Santorini it matures in mid-August, at least twenty days earlier than it does elsewhere. It produces deep colour, high sugar levels and low acidity. Stavrohiotiko is one of the rarest red varieties in Santorini. It ripens in mid-September, giving rich sugars, but very low colour and low acidity.

The island has no lack of traditional styles of wine. The oldest, and currently the most famous, is *vinsanto*, not to be confused with the Tuscan speciality, *vin santo*. Assyrtiko and Aidani are left on the vine to reach high levels of ripeness, ideally above 16° Baumé. After picking, they are sun-dried for between six and fourteen days. Sun-drying increases the volatile acidity and some producers, including Gaia and Argyros, tried drying the grapes on stacked trays, so that half the fruit was dried in the shade. But rather than being a fault, controlled volatility can add complexity to *vinsanto*. A more traditional approach to minimizing the negative effects of sun-drying is to harvest the fruit as late as possible. The sugar level is higher and fewer days are needed in the heat of the sun to reach the desired concentration.

After the drying, the grapes are crushed and fermented, mostly on their skins. It takes 10 kilograms of raisins to produce a litre of *vinsanto*. Fermentation is finished before Christmas, and the usual levels of residual sugar are between 200 and 300g/l. A vinsanto has to be aged by law for two years in oak before release, but many producers age it for longer, in older barriques, traditional 500-litre or larger casks. Topping-up is done with care, sometimes with wines from younger vintages, while racking is rare. Each barrel is usually treated as a separate personality. Many old-style *vinsantos* finished their alcoholic fermentation at low strengths, below 9% abv, so some producers used to fortify them with high-strength tsipouro (the grape spirit), to 13% abv. In the last decade, however, most high-quality producers have preferred to use yeast strains that will continue fermentation to give a natural strength of over 13% abv.

Mezzo is a style close to *vinsanto*. It is produced much in the same way, but only red grapes are used, mainly Mandilaria. *Mezzo* clusters are sun-dried for less time; usually fewer than ten days. Sugar levels are not high, since there is less dehydration, and Mandilaria grapes at harvest are not as sweet as Assyrtiko. Most *mezzos* are aged in oak for more than a year. The alcohol level is over 13% abv and residual sugar is below 200g/l.

There are two other traditional styles made on the island. The first, *brusco*, derives its name from the Venetian period, from the word for 'coarse'. And coarse it was: because vineyards were fragmented, yields were low and picking grapes was physically demanding, the locals were not able to gather large quantities of fruit in a day. Each day's crop was put into a shallow vat, on top of the previous day's harvest. When enough had been picked, the grapes were trodden and the must drawn off. The whole process could take up to a week, during which time the juice would start fermenting and macerating of its own accord. The oxidation and extraction of phenolics were intense. *Brusco* could be white, rosé or red, but was always fiercely tannic and acidic, with alcohol levels over 15% abv, sometimes as much as 17% abv. *Brusco* can still occasionally be found in Santorini these days, but not commercially. However, Mystirio from Artemis Karamolegos, Santorini's first orange wine, bows in that direction.

If *brusco* was the product of an unsophisticated winemaking approach, *nykteri* offers a complete contrast. The grapes destined for *nykteri* had to be ripe, but not as ripe as for *brusco*, and had to be picked before dawn and pressed and drawn off the must within a day. Presumably it was a long day, since the name means 'working the night away' in Greek. This passionate effort was aiming at the creation of the finest wine, with minimum extraction of colour and contact with air. *Nykteri* had to be aged in oak for long periods, sometimes for as long as *vinsanto*. Traditionally there is some slight maderization, but usually the character is not obtrusive. *Nykteri* is popular nowadays, with most producers making one, usually aged in oak. Alcohol levels in modern *nykteris* range from 13.5–15% abv or more.

What made Santorini famous among Greek wine-lovers is not these traditional styles, but a more modern approach championed in the 1990s by Boutari and the pioneering co-op, Santo Wines. Picking is done earlier, bringing potential alcohol down to around 13 per cent. Pressing is faster, with pneumatic presses playing an important role, and the fermentation temperature is cool, in stainless steel. This 'new era' Santorini may lack some of the character of the more traditional styles, but displays the grace of Assyrtiko in a less extreme form.

Another turning point was the creation of Kallisti by Boutari in 1988, the first oak-aged Santorini. The use of oak is even now hotly debated among wine producers and consumers. One side claims that oak can only subtract from the racy minerality of Assyrtiko. Others believe that oak can add complexity and longevity. Both camps are right and wrong. Although there are some wines that lack any synergy between the grape and the oak, the well balanced examples, usually with low-key oak, can compete with *grand cru* Chablis in all aspects but price.

There is only one appellation on the island, PDO Santorini, which encompasses all styles, from dry to sweet. The appellation includes the Thirassia islet. Sweet wines can be called *vinsanto* and can be produced by all three methods to become *vin naturellement doux, vin doux naturel* and *vin doux*. The second approach is the occasional addition of spirit after fermentation has stopped naturally.

With the tourist sector in Santorini going from strength to strength and viticulture being financially unattractive, the decline of vineyard acreage seems inevitable. The co-op has done much to protect growers, but private producers starting their own ventures have been and will be the only hope. Wine tourism is becoming more and more important, yet pessimists argue that the future could see viticulture here becoming a distant memory. This would be an immense loss. The real aim today should be not just to preserve Santorini but to realize its full potential.

ARIZONA: CLIMATE, REGIONS AND CHALLENGES

Why would you grow grapes in the desert? In this regional profile from *The wines of Southwest U.S.A.*, Jessica Dupuy explains that it's not all cactuses and tumbleweeds and that while the climate may suffer from extremes, this state is producing some of America's most exciting wines and showing real promise when it comes to quality.

While most people associate this sunny state with the wild west, picturing cactus-riddled desert vistas and the iconic Grand Canyon, in recent years Arizona has witnessed a new awakening with glimpses of excellent wine. To date, the state has just over 115 wineries and more than 1,200 acres (485.6 hectares) of vineyards in production. Its wine industry is reported to have an economic impact of more than $56.2 million, attracting more than 600,000 visitors to the vineyards and tasting rooms of the state's three primary wine regions.

Arizona's varied landscape is unique in its ability to experience wide temperature variations during the growing season – the diurnal range can swing by as much as 50°F (27.7°C) in ripening season. Another key growing factor for Arizona vineyards is that most of them are planted at elevations of 3,500 to 5,500 feet (1,067 to 1,676 metres) above sea level.

Of its three primary viticultural regions, two have official AVA designation. Sonoita, about 161 miles (259 kilometres) south-east of Phoenix, is a rolling landscape that is home to myriad cattle ranches. The Willcox Playa, or Willcox Bench, is home to a large dry-lake basin with the Chiricahua Mountains and Dos Cabezas Mountains to the east and the Dragoon Mountains and Cochise Stronghold to the west. The northern Verde Valley constitutes the third wine-growing area in the state. Though not an official AVA, the region is on the list for its AVA designation and is expected to be approved within the next year or two. Located about two hours north of Phoenix by car, with vineyard sites planted at roughly 3,000 to 5,500 feet (914 to 1,676 metres) in elevation, the area is sprinkled with nearly two dozen producers amid a handful of small-town communities.

Arizona is part of the desert Basin and Range Province, which is a physiographic region spanning the inland south-western part of the United States and northern Mexico. Arizona's expansive, barren landscape is scattered with drought-tolerant scrub-brush and cactus, though a surprising 27 per cent of the state is forest land. In fact, the world's most massive Ponderosa pine tree is located in the Prescott National Forest. The majority of the state's topography, which encompasses a total of 113,998 square miles (295,255 square kilometres), was shaped by prehistoric volcanism resulting in a uniquely diverse geography. It is renowned for its jagged, narrow mountain chains, flat valleys, deep canyons, high elevations, low-lying deserts, and dramatic red-hued rock formations. The result is an almost confounding array of soils, from rocky and sandy, to red, iron-rich loam, clay and calcium-rich caliche. The high bicarbonate levels found in these caliche layers bring a particular minerality to the wines that offsets the high pH levels also found in the soils.

With such variations in elevation in any given part of the state, Arizona is unique among the south-west's wine regions in having a wide variety of localized climate conditions. In general, the climate can be sweltering in the summers, particularly in the south-central capital city of Phoenix, which is situated at a lower elevation of about 1,086 feet (331 metres), in the bottom of a bowl-shaped depression of the state. Here, temperatures can reach more than 106°F (41°C) in summer, while in other parts of the state temperatures are lower, though still averaging well above 90°F (32°C). Winters are generally mild, with lows reaching close to 45°F (7°C) in Phoenix and 17°F (-8°C) further north in Flagstaff. The more mountainous northern portion of the state, with its significantly higher altitudes, offers an appreciably cooler climate, with cold winters and mild summers.

While the average rainfall is nearly 13 inches (330 millimetres), the majority of the year is severely dry and arid, except for two specific rainy seasons. The first is in the winter, with cold fronts influenced by the

Pacific Ocean to the west, and the second is the monsoon season, which pulls tropical moisture up from Mexico to make for significant rains during the late summer – often in the thick of grape harvest. The higher humidity combined with the scorching summer heat brings lightning, thunderstorms, wind, and torrential downpours.

Late summer rains mean growers can't afford to be laissez-faire in the vineyards if they want to maintain quality fruit. Instead, canopy management, proper spraying, and the management of airflow through the vineyards are critical during the growing season. As winegrowers have found in recent decades, Arizona's climate is generally conducive to yielding grapes with desired ripeness and structure – more so with certain varieties than with others. However, maintaining the balance between acidity and ripeness remains a persistent challenge throughout the state, especially when the threat of heavy rain often guides the decision to pick during the most crucial part of the season.

But rainfall later in the growing season isn't the only potential problem for wine growing. As with most of the south-western states, late spring and early autumn frosts are a perpetual threat. Many winegrowers have invested in wind machines to help mitigate frost, but it's not always a guaranteed safeguard.

The northern and southern parts of the state feature elevation gains resulting in much cooler wine-growing regions. In the southern part of the state, in the Chiricahua Mountains near Willcox, vineyard sites are planted at elevations upward of 5,300 feet (1,615 metres). Further west, in Sonoita, sites range between 4,000 and 5,000 feet (1,219 and 1,524 metres), and in the Verde Valley to the north, some of the region's highest plantings are at around 5,000 feet (1,524 metres). Despite Arizona's searing summer heat, these higher elevation sites, among the highest in the world, benefit from the dramatic shift in evening temperatures, which help slow vine respiration, allowing the grapes to retain acidity. These conditions also aid in tannin development, resulting in wines with good ageing potential despite elevated pH levels. In the vineyards, growers work to combat high pH levels with a healthy canopy-to-fruit ratio that provides ripeness without any hang time necessary. Making a pass during the mid-season for shoot-thinning can also help. When yields are managed at between two and four tons per acre (4,483–8,966 kilos per hectare), the pH levels are rarely too high. Despite these efforts, acidulation in the winery is relatively standard, particularly for red wine (although some producers are choosing to live with higher pHs, in the 3.9–4.0 range).

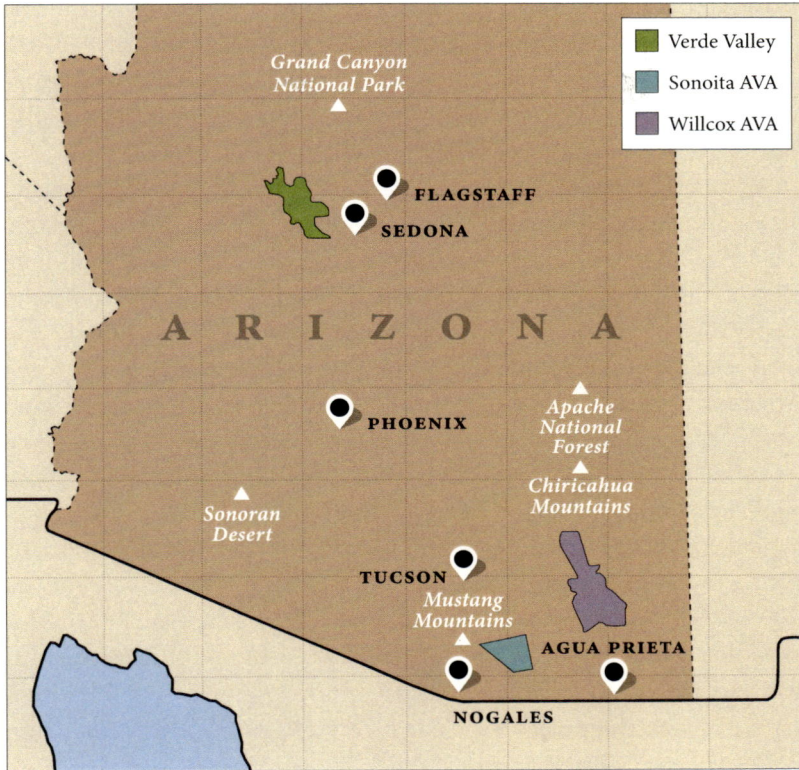

Arizona is home to three specified growing regions, though only two of them, Sonoita and Willcox, have official AVA designations. The third, Verde Valley, has an application pending approval as of publication date.

Sonoita AVA

Though most people pronounce it son-oy-ta, the Spanish pronunciation, soy-no-ita, is perhaps more revealing about this idyllic landscape. Meaning 'I am not little', with a tone of endearment, Sonoita is a region of undulating grasslands that blanket the rolling hills, peppered by the outstretched canopies of native oaks and embraced from every direction by the Santa Rita, Mustang, Whetstone and Huachuca Mountains. Indeed, with a landscape reminiscent of Alentejo, Tuscany, or Paso Robles, when it comes to its potential as a winegrowing region, there's nothing little about it. Once home to vast cattle ranches, the plentiful rainfall and well-draining soils prompted several winegrowing pioneers to plant vineyards here in the 1970s. Located about an hour south-east of Tucson, in the south-eastern corner of the state, Sonoita was the first AVA in Arizona, receiving its designation in 1984. Though it resembles a valley, the region is more of a basin comprising the headwaters for three distinct drainages, including the Sonoita Creek to the south, Cienega Creek to the north, and the Babocaman River to the east.

Surrounded by the popular tourist towns of Sonoita, Patagonia and Elgin, Sonoita's geography sits at elevations between 2,500 and 5,000 feet (762–1,524 metres). It is heavily influenced by its nearby mountain ranges, with a unique mixture of iron-rich reddish loam soils. Compared to the Willcox region to the east, Sonoita's soils tend to be thinner and more shallow, forcing vines to take longer to get established. For grape growers, the early years of a vineyard are a game of patience. Once established, yields tend to be lower, but the quality of the fruit tends to reveal more structure and concentration. During the growing season, high temperatures range between 80 and 90°F (27–32°C), and average rainfall is 15–20 inches (380–500 millimetres), most of which occurs during monsoon season.

Some of the state's most revered vineyards are located in Sonoita, including Callaghan Vineyards and Sonoita Vineyards. The region is home to more than a dozen wineries and tasting rooms of note, including Callaghan Vineyards, Dos Cabezas WineWorks, Rune Wines, Deep Sky Vineyards, and the new Los Milics Winery.

Willcox AVA

East of Sonoita, near the south-eastern border of the state, the arid, dusty mesa of the Willcox region is a cornerstone for Arizona wine. Though it only received its official AVA designation in 2016, the district has long been one of the most productive growing regions of the state. Currently, it accounts for more than 70 per cent of Arizona's grape production. A large percentage of these grapes are planted on the 'Willcox Bench', an alluvial fan that elevates the vineyards along the historical Kansas Settlement farmland. The result: excellent grape-growing conditions.

The AVA covers a total area of 526,000 acres (212,864.6 hectares) within Graham and Cochise Counties, including the town of Willcox along with Kansas Settlement, Turkey Creek and Pearce. The area is a shallow 'closed basin', separated from neighbouring valleys by the Pinaleño, Dragoon, Chiricahua and Dos Cabezas mountain ranges. Most of the region's vineyards are planted in the Sulfur Springs Valley and along the bases of the mountains in the area, at between 4,000 and

5,500 feet (1,219–1,674 metres). At this elevation, vineyards in the area can experience up to a 50°F variance (27.7°C) in diurnal temperature during the growing season. This basin is reliant on its average rainfall of 13–18 inches (330–457 millimetres), most of which comes from heavy summer monsoons, to recharge its underlying aquifer. In contrast, the area surrounding it has year-round creeks and streams. The dry, desert climate benefits the grapevines by placing stress on them during the growing season, slowing the vegetative growth and adding complexity to the grapes.

The soils of the Willcox AVA are mainly alluvial and colluvial and composed of loam made up of nearly equal parts sand, silt and clay. These loamy soils retain enough water to hydrate the vines while allowing sufficient drainage through to the aquifer. The soils are referred to as the Tubac, Sonoita, Forrest and Frye soil types, and are not found to a great extent in the area surrounding the AVA. Compared to Sonoita, Willcox's soils are generally more productive, though there is a high degree of variation from site to site.

Most vineyards in the Willcox AVA are harvested by machine

Willcox is home to roughly 1,000 acres (404.7 hectares) of vineyard, including the Al Buhl Memorial Vineyard, planted by Arizona wine pioneer Robert Webb in 1984, and now owned by Maynard James Keenan of Caduceus Cellars and Merkin Vineyards. Nearly two dozen wineries and tasting rooms are scattered throughout the region, including

Bodega Pierce, Pillsbury Wine Company, Sand-Reckoner Winery and Keeling-Schaeffer Vineyards.

For years, the Willcox area has been a rural agricultural area devoid of much tourism infrastructure. In fact, the primary road leading to the majority of vineyard sites wasn't even paved until a couple of years ago. Producers and visitors alike had to make their way along open dirt roads that fast became muddy pits, where vehicles without four-wheel-drive would often get stuck. (Access improvements came thanks to for-ward-thinking producers, including Barbara and Dan Pierce of Bodega Pierce, who worked with the county to have the road paved.) More res-taurants and guesthouses have sprung up in and around Willcox with the hope that they will transform the region into a weekend destination for visitors.

Verde Valley

Though the Verde Valley is not yet an official AVA, its location in the north-west part of the state boasts high elevations and ideal growing conditions, with ample water from the Verde River and well-draining soils. Located in the red-rocked canyon lands of northern Arizona, about two hours north of Phoenix by car, the region is home to the towns of Sedona, Jerome, Camp Verde, Cottonwood, Clarkdale and Cornville, the geographic heartland of Arizona. The Verde Valley is part of Yavapai County, bordered in the north-east by the red-hued rock formations of Sedona, with the craggy rise of the Black Hills mountain range to the south and, to the west, a rolling landscape peppered with the towering pines of the Prescott National Forest.

The region is home to a range of volcanic soils at higher elevations, leading to sandy and clay loam soils throughout the valley along with alluvial deposits near Oak Creek and the Verde River. The common thread for the Verde Valley with its compatriot wine-growing regions to the south is a layer of calcium-rich caliche deep beneath the topsoil. Vineyards in the Verde Valley can be found hugging the foothills of mountain rises at elevations hovering around 5,000 feet (1,524 metres) or near the valley areas of Oak Creek and the Verde River at around 3,400 feet (1,036 metres). Compared to Sonoita and Willcox, the Verde Valley is considered a lush, verdant desert region, with an abundant wa-ter source from its two primary rivers as well as a higher percentage of rainfall, which averages about 16–18 inches (404–457 millimetres) per year – mostly during monsoon season.

Winegrowing began taking off in the Verde Valley just after the turn of the millennium, starting with just a handful of vineyards and evolving to include more than two dozen wineries and tasting rooms spread throughout its 450 square miles (1,165 square kilometres). Though an application for AVA designation is still pending, the past decade has seen an increase in wine tourism that has revived the area's small towns with new restaurants, shops and accommodations. Its proximity to Sedona, in particular, has made it a perennial tourist favourite for wine-tasting excursions. Among the region's top tasting rooms are Chateau Tumbleweed, Merkin Vineyards Osteria, Bodega Pierce, Caduceus Cellars, Page Springs Cellars, and the Southwest Wine Center.

Although the three central growing regions of the state are relatively well defined, several other growers and producers have been experimenting in other parts of the landscape. These vineyard sites can be found on the outskirts of valleys and mountain areas, such as the Chino Valley, Young, Kingman, Williams and Portal, and the Chiricahua Mountains. Considered to be on the frontier of wine growing for Arizona, this contingent of producers has become known locally as the 'mavericks and pioneers'.

*

As can be expected with any fledgling wine industry, Arizona faced many early challenges, ranging from plant diseases such as cotton root rot to devastating hail storms. But the common theme throughout the Southwest in terms of viticultural challenges is late spring frosts. In Arizona, the rise and fall of elevations make it easy for pockets of cold air to settle into certain vineyard sites. As in Texas and New Mexico, wind machines and burning hay bales seem to be the most common lines of defence among grape growers.

Arizona is unique in having a monsoon season, which arrives in August and can last until October, just as harvest season begins. As a result, grape growers have learned to manage vineyards with this expectation in mind. Canopies are now being trained up and open, and vineyard managers are learning to be careful not to set too much fruit.

Regardless of the region, picking a site with decent air drainage is a critical factor in avoiding winter kill and spring frost. Even a couple of feet of elevation can make the difference between a great site and an impossible one. Indeed, with each new vintage, growers are learning to manage their inputs to mitigate the results of these threats better.

Aside from the viticultural challenges, the industry has spent the past decade working to determine the best grape varieties for each region. Equally important has been the effort to foster a better public perception among consumers. As is the case with most emerging wine regions throughout the country, the hardest consumers to convince to support the industry are the ones closest to it.

Perhaps one of Arizona wine's most significant hurdles is its inability to grow beyond a specific production size. As of the date of publishing, Arizona wineries are legally prohibited from making more than 40,000 U.S. gallons (151,417 litres), or about 200,000 750-millilitre bottles, without impeding their retail licences. The largest single producer, Arizona Stronghold, makes about 36,000 gallons (136,275 litres) annually, but it is not able to produce beyond that quantity under its existing permit. In the past few years, many of the state's more progressive producers, including Callaghan Vineyards, Dos Cabezas WineWorks, Caduceus Cellars and Chateau Tumbleweed have led the effort to change the regulations. In February 2020, legislation was introduced to the Arizona State Legislature to reduce unnecessary regulation on Arizona wineries and allow small farming operations the opportunity to grow and compete with neighbouring states such as California. The legislation has yet to pass, but the topic remains pressing among producers who are hopeful of seeing progress in the coming legislative sessions.

THE WINES OF JAPAN

Although its wines may only recently have become worthy of note, Japan's history of grape cultivation is surprisingly long. In this review from 2018's *Sake and the wines of Japan* Anthony Rose assesses the progress made in Japanese wine over the last decade or so and discusses what the future may hold in store.

Until the 1980s there was one world of wine. It wasn't called the Old World then because it had no rivals or parallels. If you had an ear to the ground, you might have picked up a distant tremor from north of San Francisco in the wake of the seminal Judgment of Paris of 1976. Napa Valley was on the march and by the mid-1980s, California was followed by Chile and Australia. The domino effect was such that by the 1990s there were two wine worlds in collision – an Old and a New World. It seemed not to be an ever-expanding universe and so that, we thought, was that. But it wasn't.

Inspired by the remarkable success of the New World, along came a new band of 'emerging' wine countries hungry for a slice of the action: England, Canada, Uruguay, Turkey, Israel, Lebanon, China. On to the stage, politely and quietly, came Japan. Japan? If you'd asked me a decade ago, I would have told you that there was little to write home about in Koshu grapes grown at more than 20 tonnes to the hectare. And there wasn't a lot else, unless you count Niagara, Delaware, Concord, the oddly-named Muscat Bailey A, and other exotic hybrids of which we knew little and cared less.

Traditionally Japan has looked to the West for the wines that it drinks and equally the West has looked to Japan as an appreciative market for its wines. For reasons of health and status initially, the classic regions of Europe, Bordeaux, Burgundy and Champagne in particular, became the latest must-have fashion accessory. The Japanese developed a taste for fine wine and most of the bottles drunk in the restaurants of Tokyo, Osaka and Kyoto were imported, with little thought to their own home-grown product. After a boom in the early to mid-1990s, the market for the European classics slowed as the millennium approached.

Thanks to the vision of a handful of companies and individuals, a fledgling Japanese wine industry was already flexing its muscles, albeit beset by problems of a challenging climate and high production costs. In a decade, it has changed out of all recognition. Coinciding with the improvements in both quality and variety, the past decade has seen a surge of genuine pride and interest in, and enjoyment of, real Japanese wine.

Since 2012, I have been invited to be a judge at the Japan Wine Competition, organized by the four major wine prefectures of Yamanashi, Nagano, Yamagata and Hokkaidō together with the Japan Wineries Association and the University of Yamanashi. A Japan-wine only event taking place in the charming Yamanashi countryside, it puts up more than 700 wines from 200 or more Japanese wineries and all the wines to be judged are made from Japan-grown grapes only.

I was initially entrusted with the task of judging wines from *Vitis vinifera*, consisting mostly of Chardonnay and the other French globe-trotters, Merlot and Cabernet Sauvignon. And I was impressed with much of the quality. Having been invited to judge the Koshu section on a couple of recent occasions, what has surprised me most is the speed at which progress has been made in the quality of Japan's native Koshu. Not all Koshu. But whereas on my first visits to Japan, I struggled, succeeding years have seen the development of a critical mass of high quality, eminently drinkable Koshu.

Despite this steep gradient of progress, less than 5 per cent of wines produced in Japan are made from fresh grapes. Around half of those are made from hybrid varieties resistant to the vagaries of a challenging Japanese climate, in particular, humidity and substantial rainfall including typhoons throughout the growing season. The remaining 19 in 20 bottles produced for sale in Japan are processed from imports of cheap wine and grape concentrate must in bulk and then sold with a Japanese label stuck to the bottle.

From 30 October 2018, a new law aimed at improvement in the quality, authenticity and image of Japanese wine requires wineries to distinguish on the label 'Japan Wine' from wine processed from imported raw materials, or 'domestic manufactured wine'. An area name can't be used if the grapes aren't harvested or the wines not made in the area. For the label of a particular grape variety, vintage or area, at least 85 per cent of that wine must be from that variety, vintage or area. Gradually, the main prefectures are moving towards a seal of origin to guarantee the authenticity of the grape source.

Despite the many challenges still facing Japanese wine, there is a new air of optimism in the industry and spirit of adventure among consumers. Instead of shunning, or at best grinning and bearing them, wine drinkers are happily buying Japanese wine out of choice. The light, refreshingly drinkable wines of Japan are being avidly consumed by thirsty Japanese and visitors alike. At this rate, if Japan starts to follow the example of the Swiss, who hoover up practically all the wine they can make, we may well see fewer, not more, high-quality homegrown wines leaving Japanese shores.

*

Legend has it that when in 718 AD the hermit Gyōki had a vision of the Buddha Nyorai holding a bunch of grapes, he established the Daizenji Temple and planted vines there. Visitors came from far and wide to study the culture of the grapevine. In another legend – this *is* Japan – Amemiya is supposed to have discovered Koshu Budo in 1186 outside Kamiiwasaki village where he lived. In medieval times, grapes were grown principally for medicinal purposes. Katsunuma, whose climate and soils were ill-suited to rice growing, became home to the Koshu grape, which is thought to have been either introduced from Eurasia or cross-bred in Japan from two *vinifera* parents.

Not a lot more is known about wine in Japan until St Francis Xavier, the Portuguese Jesuit missionary, arrived bearing gifts of vines for the *daimyō* (feudal lords) of Kyūshū in 1545. The wine made from it was called *tinta-shu* or, simply, red wine. Even before the prosperous Edo period got under way in 1603, there was little wine around, and what there was of it was most likely made for medicinal or religious purposes.

The missionaries were sent packing by the insular Tokugawa shogunate operating out of Edo. Though they weren't wine drinkers, the shogunate's partiality to its delicacy as a table grape enabled Koshu to survive and prosper. With its vineyards and tea houses lining the Koshu

Road, the old post-town of Katsunuma Juku was a favourite watering hole for travellers on their way to the capital. It took three days for the grapes to reach Edo from Yamanashi. A prominent Japanese doctor, Kai no Tokuhon, ensured Katsunuma's popularity as a sun-drenched haven for growing the variety with the establishment of a trellising system known as Tanashiki-saibai. Classified as a *Vitis vinifera*, albeit containing a proportion of the Asian wild grape *Vitis davidii*, the thick, pink-skinned Koshu, with mouthwateringly crisp acidity and subtle flavours, was basically cultivated for eating.

It wasn't until Japan emerged from its shell in 1868 that winemaking came back into the frame. Attempts were made by a local merchant in 1874 to produce wine on a commercial scale from local grapes in Yamanashi. In 1877 the Dai-Nihon Yamanashi Budoshu-Gaisha (Great Yamanashi Wine Company) dispatched Ryuken Tsuchiya, aged 19, and Masanari Takano, aged 25, the sons of wealthy farmers, to Troyes in Champagne's Aube region, and elsewhere in France, to study viticulture and winemaking. On their return in 1879, local chestnut trees and bamboo forests were requisitioned to make an overhead pergola trellising system and the Great Japan Yamanashi Wine Company was soon up and running.

At around the same time, the prominent Akayu personality, Yasō Sakai, was inspired by an Englishman, Charles H. Dallas, to make wine from Koshu in Yamagata to go with his Yonezawa beef. It was made there for the first time in 1892 – as a sweet wine. None of these early pioneering efforts were helped, however, by the arrival of the vampire-like phylloxera louse in 1882. However, it wasn't so much the phylloxera that contributed to a slow decline in wine after this, as a lack of enthusiasm for the product by the Japanese themselves.

Meanwhile, local authorities began to permit the importation of *vinifera* and American vines for plantation and Delaware and Campbell Early became the most popular vine varieties, while Muscat of Alexandria was cultivated in greenhouses in Okayama. In 1951, Goichi Hayashi, the owner of Hayashi Nouen, brought Merlot cuttings from Akayu and planted the first vinifera grape in Kikyōgahara in Nagano. In 1962, the Izutsu winery in Nagano introduced Merlot, Cabernet Sauvignon and Sémillon to complement its vineyards of Concord and Niagara.

For the most part though, the Japanese showed a strong predilection for sweetened port-style wines, which were produced in large volumes from hybrid varieties supplied from Kikyōgahara and from

Izutsu Vineyard, 70-year-old Kyoho vine, Nagano

Mogamigawa in Yamagata. By 1967, the equivalent of 44 million bottles of these sweet wines were being lapped up by the sweet-toothed Japanese. It didn't bode well for the future of a quality wine industry.

As visitors went on daily excursions from Tokyo to Yamanashi during the Shōwa Era to see 'the haven of the grape', growers increased their efforts to make their vineyards visitor-friendly. Yet delicious as Koshu may have been to eat, it was labour-intensive and challenging to grow, and with limited financial incentives, the grower cooperatives making, and drinking, wine turned to more lucrative, high quality table grapes. As often as not, the grapes the wineries received were unsold, inferior quality table grapes.

The lack of incentive was at the same time aggravated by the abolition of customs duties on the importation of overseas wines in 1970 and the growing strength of the Japanese yen. Thanks to the Tokyo Olympic Games in 1964 and the Japan World Exposition in Osaka in 1970, the Japanese taste for overseas wines grew along with their purchasing power and an interest inspired by overseas travel.

From the first surge of the 1980s (consumption was 0.5 litres per head in 1985) to a bigger, second boom in the mid-1990s, serious wine meant prestige imported brands in contrast to the sweet port-style homegrown product made from disease-resistant hybrids such as Concord and Niagara. This taste for overseas wines was boosted thanks to lax regulations allowing Japanese wine companies to produce wines made from bulk imports of overseas wines and grape concentrate. With little incentive, there was a widespread feeling that perhaps the whole idea of trying to make quality wine was a chimera.

Yet even though the cultivation of Koshu for wine declined, a few wineries kept the flame alight because of their attachment to it as part of the culture of Katsunuma and a belief that with the right care and attention, it could produce superior wine. Despite the challenging conditions of Japan's climate, a few pioneering risk-takers, mainly in Yamanashi, decided it was worth having a stab at European *vinifera* such as Chardonnay, Merlot and Cabernet Sauvignon, while Hokkaidō hung its hat on Zweigelt.

Illustrious Bordelais names such as Denis Dubourdieu, Paul Pontallier and Bernard Magrez were enlisted as consultants to assist in the new initiative. Around the same time, in the belief that European varieties could be the saviours of Japanese wine, the relatively cool Kikyōgahara and Chikumagawa Valleys in Nagano, and the Mogamigawa region of Yamagata Prefecture were emerging as potentially viable locations for classic European grape varieties. With accompanying European technology and a change in cultivation methods to those for wine rather than table grapes, a foundation for a modern industry was gradually being laid.

*

Pop down to the basement of the Mitsukoshi Department Store in Ginza and you can see immediately that Japan is capable of growing the most delicious grapes known to humankind. With more than a third of Japan's acreage under vine, the big, sweet, juicy, dark-skinned Kyohō is Japan's most popular table grape variety. Pione and Shain Muscat, monster grapes as big as small plums, burst juicily on to the tongue. It's obvious that Japan can grow grapes brilliantly, but what's juicy as a table grape doesn't necessarily translate into a great wine grape.

Kyohō, literally, 'giant mountain grape', is a local cross between the American Ishiharawase (*Vitis labrusca*) and the European Centennial (*Vitis vinifera*), but with only 1.9 per cent of Japan's total wine production, its popularity as an eating grape is not matched by its merit as a wine grape. It takes its humble place below a number of more common hybrids, most notably the white grapes Niagara and Delaware, and the red Muscat Bailey A, Concord and Campbell Early. To give it its due, it pips a number of other hybrid and wild grape varieties grown in

Japan to the post: white wine's Seibel 9110 and Portland, and red wine's Black Queen, Yama Sauvignon, a crossing of Yamabudo and Cabernet Sauvignon, and the elegantly-named Yamatonadeshiko, also known as Ryugan and Zenkoji.

Japan's back story with hybrid varieties is based on their tolerance of wet climates and resistance to diseases, and Japan has both, in spades. Over the years, the Japanese have developed a taste (a tolerance some might say) for the sweet and often confected character that most of them have. Despite an increase in planting of European varieties, hybrids still account for a little over 50 per cent of Japanese wine grape production. Even wineries that have greatly expanded their production of wines made from vinifera will often retain some hybrids as an insurance policy and because the locals like it.

From this hotchpotch, the one hybrid variety with a claim to quality is Muscat Bailey A. A crossing of Bailey and Muscat of Hamburg, Muscat Bailey A was created in 1927 by Zenbei Kawakami, the so-called 'father of Japanese viticulture', at his Iwanohara Winery in Niigata. As a late budder and early ripener, it was resistant to the problematic spring frosts of the region and to mildew and rot. Today, a handful of wineries are starting to take it seriously. Château Mercian has a smoky-oaky version. Suntory ages it in both Japanese and French oak to good effect (I prefer the French oak version). Takeda's Noriko Kishidaira in Yamagata produces an almost Pinot Noir like red from it with not a whisper of confection.

The native grape that the Japanese have championed in recent years is the pink-skinned Koshu, and perhaps it's its Asian genes and a thick skin, literally, that bring a certain level of protection from the extremes of the Japanese climate. Its table wine credentials meant that until the 1980s, wine made from it was pretty much produced as an afterthought, when growers found that they had table grape surpluses for which they had no other outlet. Koshu accounts for 16 per cent, the biggest varietal percentage, of Japanese wine production, although even today, fewer than 500 hectares are planted in Japan, 95 per cent of which are in Yamanashi.

For anyone accustomed to neat rows of vineyards in Europe, the sight of Koshu growing in Yamanashi comes as a viticulture shock. Koshu is grown on high pergolas, known as Tanazukuri. With each hectare populated by 100 vines or fewer, the vine looks like a small tree. Its spreadeagled branches are trained some five to six feet above ground to optimize ventilation and allow waxed paper mini-umbrellas to be

Hundreds of waxed paper mini-umbrellas tied by hand to ripe bunches of grapes in Yamanashi to keep off the rain

tied to bunches, as many as 800 per vine, before the harvest rains. It grows vigorously in Yamanashi's soils, so much so that the multiplicity of bunches that hang decoratively from this hovering magic green carpet can produce more than 20 tonnes to the hectare. Quality producers looking for Koshu gold have to take to the hills.

Left to its own devices, Koshu would probably have languished for a few more centuries before anyone took serious notice of its potential as a quality variety. It was adopted, perhaps initially for sentimentally patriotic reasons, by a handful of pioneering growers who thought that by harnessing it to modern viticultural and winemaking techniques, aided and abetted by some overseas savoir faire, it might just work for them. And to an extent it has. In a variety of dry, sweet, barrel-fermented, orange and sparkling styles, Koshu is, as Jancis Robinson says in *Wine Grapes*, 'starting to gain international recognition … for wines that have a certain zen-like purity about them'.

Given the opportunity to taste over 100 Koshus at the Japan Wine Competition in 2013, it became clear that many wines suffered from excessive dilution, off-flavours, oxidation and overuse of oak. A promising few were clean, fresh and pure. By 2016 a substantial improvement had taken place, with better textures, fruit concentration and finely balanced acidity, bringing elegance and a bone dry, mineral, saline quality to the fruit. I was probably less surprised than many at a blind tasting at the 67 Pall Mall Club in London in February 2018. Hosted by Lynne Sherriff MW and Ronan Sayburn MS, with a Chablis Premier Cru Vaillons teasingly inserted, the Koshus more than held their own with many tasters impressed by their delicacy, purity and intensity.

One of Koshu's strong points is that there's nothing else to compare it with and so, as Japan's national wine grape, it has a handy USP all its own. The same cannot be said for the array of international grape varieties that have been increasingly adopted by the Japanese wine industry. This new focus on classic varieties occurred as a shift in wine consumption towards the European classics piqued the interest of an industry that had become reliant on hybrids.

As early as the late 1950s and 1960s, some of the bigger Japanese wine companies believed that the introduction of classic European grape varieties was a prerequisite if Japanese wine was to achieve any kind of international kudos. Among them, Suntory, Manns and Mercian began to explore the possibilities with trial plantings of French varieties in Yamanashi and other regions. After considerable trial and error, a blueprint has begun to emerge as to which varieties are most suited to Japan's hugely varied terrain and climatic conditions.

Chardonnay is the only French white variety with a critical planting mass but it still only accounts for 5 per cent of Japanese wine production. Given the Chardonnay section to judge one year at the Japan Wine Competition, I was surprised at the quality at least of the wines that made it to the second round stage, with styles varying from delicately unoaked to more 'Burgundian' barrel-fermented examples. Many of these were from the Hokushin area of Nagano but, on a more recent trip, I also found convincing examples from Yamagata and Hokkaidō.

To a more limited extent, Japan has taken a sheaf of Germanic white varieties on board, notably Kerner, the biggest by some distance, followed by Müller-Thurgau, Gewürztraminer and Bacchus. This legacy is due in part to the Hokkaidō Wine Company's Akiyoshi Shimamura, who, with the assistance of his mentor, Germany's Gustav Grün, planted vines in the cold climate of Hokkaidō in the mid-1970s. The best red counterpart to the Germanic whites introduced in the 1970s is Austria's Zweigelt.

Among classic European red grape varieties, Merlot is far and away the most popular, but like Chardonnay, it still only accounts for 5 per cent of all Japanese wine grape production. Merlot was given a helping hand by Manns, which started making wine in the Tōshin area of Nagano from plantings of Merlot, as well as Cabernet Sauvignon. The cool climate, high altitude region of Nagano suits the production of Merlot in a medium-bodied, textured and elegant style not a million miles from those of its right bank Bordeaux counterpart. Enthusiasm for Merlot has seen it adopted in other prefectures, most notably Yamanashi and Yamagata, as well as Niigata and Iwate.

As yet, Cabernet Sauvignon only accounts for 2 per cent of Japan's wine production, and unless and until climate change sees a dramatic shift in temperatures, much of Japan is either too cold, or too wet, to sustain any great expansion. There's even less Cabernet Franc in Japan, which is a shame because, as an earlier ripener, the limited results to date suggest that it might well be better suited to the climate.

Although also negligible in terms of plantings, the two classic red grape varieties starting to cause ripples of excitement are Pinot Noir and Syrah. Pinot Noir at its best needs a marginal climate and the two prefectures that fit the bill are Nagano, with its high altitude, cool climate, and Hokkaidō, whose cold climate sees the vines buried under up to 2 metres of snow in winter. Neither yet feature in the production list of Japan's top ten red wine grapes, but judging by the some of the perfumed, delicate Pinots and spicy Syrahs emerging, these two varieties look set to grow substantially in volume, and in quality.

In addition to these varieties, the list is growing with smatterings of Sauvignon Blanc, Sémillon, Pinot Blanc, Pinot Gris, Petit Manseng, Riesling, Viognier, Fiano and isolated pockets of Barbera, Tempranillo, Tannat, Petit Verdot, Rondo and Regent. With good examples now coming out of Niigata, Nagano, Toyama and Ōita, the one so-called 'alternative variety' that does seem to be gaining traction is the Galician variety Albariño. None of these varieties are on the statistical radar as yet, but as the industry's growing confidence in its own homegrown product increases in line with consumer loyalty and curiosity, I suspect it won't be long before that picture changes.

SOME WINES
OF NOTE

TAVEL

For centuries Tavel was France's foremost rosé wine; favoured by popes and kings, it was among the first appellations created. In this extract from 2018's *Rosé*, Elizabeth Gabay MW describes the vineyards and winemaking techniques and reflects on how both the popularity of pale, Provence-style rosés and climate change may affect Tavel's future.

Tavel, despite its small production, has been the most famous rosé for almost 200 years. Even with the growth in Provence rosé, Tavel still holds on to its pre-eminent reputation. Its vineyards lie on the sun-baked undulating hills of the west bank of the southern Rhône around the small town of Tavel. The town shows evidence of once greater prosperity, with large, old buildings made of the local white stone. Today it is more of a backwater, but close enough to the city of Avignon, on the eastern shore of the Rhone, to be a dormitory village.

Vines were originally cultivated in the area by the Greeks, and later grown by the Romans. Tavel was located on a major communication route between the *oppidum* in Roquemaure and Nîmes, and lies near the major trading route of the Rhône. King Philip IV, le Bel, supposedly travelled through Tavel on a tour of the kingdom, where he was offered a glass. He emptied this without getting off his horse, and afterwards proclaimed Tavel the only good wine in the world. His dispute with the papacy led to Avignon becoming a papal seat during the fourteenth century, when Pope Innocent VI kept Tavel from the Prieuré de Montézargues in his private cellar. The wines continued to find success. The Sun King, Louis XIV (1643–1715), is supposed to have been fond of the wine (and many others around the kingdom) which helped maintain its reputation.

Until the early nineteenth century, the vineyards of Tavel were concentrated on the sandy alluvial soils to the south of the village. These were easier to cultivate than the forested limestone soils to the north or the rocky hills to the east. In the early 1800s, the forests were turned over to agriculture, including some vines. These sandy and limestone soils produced very fresh, light wines.

In *The American Farmer* (1826) Tavel was described as having a 'Bright rose colour, flavour and aroma, delicate.' In 1834, a poetic 'epistle' on Tavel by William Stewart Rose says '… liquid ruby, Tavel; / The juice of paler grape which loves the gravel, / Or that which runs in purer stream, which gushed / From clusters richer, riper, and uncrushed.' George Hodder Tinsley reminisced about drinking Tavel in the 1860s when, 'In ordering his dinner his great fancy was for *quelque chose appétissante*, as he called the lighter form of entrées, and a bottle of Tavel.'

The wine list at the restaurant Les Trois Provençaux in the nineteeth century, includes Tavel among the red wines of Burgundy. In 1872 the wines were described as 'First Class: Red wines, not vatted. Tavel: Very dry, very light-coloured wine; improves much by age … Lirac: Very dry wine, more firm than Tavel, of a lively rose-colour.' Modern producers say that the light colour is because the original vine-growing area of Tavel was on the sandy soils south of the village, a terroir which typically results in lighter wines.

The fortunes of Tavel declined when, in the 1860s, the railway bypassed the town. Worse followed. In 1870, the owner of Château Clary in the neighbouring village of Roquemaure made the unusual decision to replant his vineyards with American vines. Unbeknown to him, these were infected with the phylloxera bug, which spread rapidly round the region, making Tavel one of the first hit areas in France. By 1873, 'the rose colour wines of the Côtes du Rhône, such as the dry and insiduous Tavel, the firm and generous Lirac, and the robust Roquemaure, with the luscious Chusclan and St Geniés, and pleasant sparkling Laudau, the majority made [by] default, [had been] more or less overrun by the *Phylloxera vastatrix*.' The reference to 'rose colour' does not mean this was a rosé wine but more a dark rose petal pink and the 'default' may refer to the grapes not fully ripening, leading to wines of a weaker colour. Many vineyards were abandoned and not replanted for some years, as viticulturists struggled to keep up with demand, supplying vineyards with vines grafted on to American rootstocks.

To survive, winemakers discovered they had to group together. In 1902, Tavel vineyard owners and winemakers formed a union, the *Syndicat des Propriétaires Viticulteurs de Tavel*. To promote their wines, members participated in national and international fairs, including those in Lyon, Marseille, Strasbourg and Liège. The sandy soils were the first to be replanted, followed by the stoney limestone plateau by the early years of the twentieth century.

The First World War decimated agricultural communities across Europe, as manpower was diminished and rural areas depopulated. Demand for wine from the nearby urban centres along the Rhône rescued Tavel. The current estate of Château d'Aqueria was founded in 1919 and Domaine Mejan-Taulier (now Florence Mejan) in 1920. Upon the suggestion of Baron Pierre Le Roy de Boiseaumarié, in 1927, the Chairman of the *Syndicat*, Aimé Roudil, and forty winemakers of Tavel, petitioned the Gard courts to officially define the production area.

In *Les Grands Vins de France* (1931) the wines of Tavel were recorded as being an amazing dark pink colour, similar to the great wines of the Côtes du Rhône. The vineyards were described as lying in the recently defined region, in a warm and sheltered amphitheatre among the hills on chalk and limestone soils, surrounded by forests of evergreen oaks and aromatic *garrigue*. It was acknowledged that the definition of vineyard territory was essential to prevent wines of a lower quality from being produced. With only 2,500 hectolitres actually produced annually, much that was claimed as Tavel was from further afield. Variable quality did exist, so the right estates needed to be selected. Tavel wines were cultivated by numerous small producers, primarily from Grenache, blended with Clairette, Cinsault, Carignan and Bourboulenc. Among the best was Château d'Aquéiria, a 20-hectare estate owned by M. Jean Olivier. Other top producers included M. Héraud, M. Roudil, M. Fraissinet and Château Montézargues.

Particularly interesting is the detailed description of the wines. Tavel rosés had a 'quick' maceration of twelve to twenty-four hours in order to achieve the required colour, a little darker than the final desired colour. The wines then rested in *barrique* for at least one year, often two. They were regarded as having good ageing potential, lasting up to forty years! However, they lost their pink colour with ageing and became the colour of yellow quartz. At three to five years of age, they still had all their Tavel qualities, *'capiteux et corsés'* (heady and full-bodied), with high alcohol of 13–15% abv. At this age, the colour was a beautiful golden pink, ruby with hints of topaz, not dissimilar to the wines of Arbois. Aromas of wild strawberries and iris developed with age. The wines were described as very dry, soft and delicate. They were best drunk cooled rather than at room temperature, and were an excellent accompaniment to bouillabaise and oysters.

When the first wine appellations were created in 1936, Tavel was among them, which preserved their traditional *clairet* style of rosé winemaking (neighbouring Lirac rosé is not made the same way). The early definition written up in the appellation differs slightly from the 1931 description, which noted that the light red wine style found on the sandy soils was the essential character of the wines. Gael Petit, chairman of the Tavel union in 2017, is a lawyer and amateur historian who has researched the archives looking for descriptions and references to Tavel. He noted that while Tavel has evolved, the appellation regulations have slowed down the evolution of the style.

In 1938 the cooperative was opened, with its rooftop slogan proclaiming '*Tavel, 1er rosé de France*' (Tavel, first rosé of France). After the Second World War, Tavel was able to take advantage of its appellation status. New domaines were created, such as Domaine Lafond 'Roc Epine'. In 1948 d'Aqueira started to export to America, through Kobrand, a working relationship which has continued for nearly seventy years.

Ernest Hemingway claimed he could not have lunch without a bottle of Tavel, and frequently mentioned it being served with meals. '"What I want to be when I am old is a wise old man who won't bore," he said, then paused while the waiter set a plate of asparagus and an artichoke before him and poured the Tavel,' wrote Lillian Ross in her interview with Hemingway in the *New Yorker* in May 1950. In a letter to Hemingway, his friend A. E. Hotchner wrote in 1955, 'The turtle steaks preserved beautifully and were consumed with cold Tavel and nothing repeat nothing, can go up against that. What makes Tavel so much better than any other rosé? Just the soil or is there some other secret like a special bee, indigenous to the area, who shits on each grape.' In *The Garden of Eden*, Hemingway calls Tavel the 'wine of Love'. In 1960 he wrote of his journey in Valdepeñas in Spain, where he describes the wine as the 'poor man's Tavel but it does not need to be chilled [unlike Tavel]'. The Valdepeñas is a 'wine with no pretensions. It tastes roughly smooth and clean ... it grew and was pressed to be drunk at all temperatures and it travels in a wineskin.'

The popularity of Tavel, and indeed of rosé, during the 1950s encouraged producers to think of expanding production. In the mid-1960s the chalk and limestone hills were once again cleared of forest and prepared for growing vines.

In 1965 Allen Sichel wrote that, 'Unlike the general run of rosé wines, both Tavel and Lirac are made from a mixture of red and white grapes, fermented together. The poorness of the soil on which the vines grow assures the finesse of flavour … they age well in bottle, particularly Tavel.' Before the 1970s, Tavel was fermented in *foudres*, which gave colour, but without temperature control the wines had more of a red wine style.

In 1977, Maynard Amerine appeared to be the first to voice criticism over the quality of Tavel wines. He mentioned that the colour of these long oak-aged wines was 'out of kilter' with that of other pink wines being made. He noted that Tavel, which was 'well known in France and occasionally exported to the United States', had winemaking issues, as did Provence, with the high degree of sulphur required to stop the Grenache-based wine from oxidizing and turning brown. Higher alcohol levels were also a problem. The more expensive rosés were still well regarded (*Black Enterprise Magazine* 1982): 'While France produces many fine rosés, most of the better ones are rather expensive … for picnic drinking. If price is no object, Château d'Aqueria Tavel Rosé, Domaines Ott Bandol Cuvée Marine [Château Romassan] and Château de Selle Coeur de Grain [Domaines Ott, Côtes de Provence] are excellent choices.' Nevertheless, the American market was changing, and Victor de Pez, of Château d'Aquéria, noted that the trade to the United States started declining, especially after 1984, as Zinfandel blush became popular.

In a forerunner to some of today's trends for rosés aged in oak, made to age, or go with food, Tavel was described as able to age well compared to other rosés. In 1986, Maureen Ashley MW commented that 'The 1985 Château d'Acquéria from Le Chemin des Vignes, while warm and ripe on the nose was still young and raw on the palate and will need some time to show its colours.' '*Tavel* is the only Grand Cru of rosé, yielding a spicy, solid, aromatic wine that can stand up to food', wrote André Gayot in *Gault et Millau* (1996).

The 1990s saw improvements in quality, with the introduction of technology, tanks and temperature control. As the pale Provence rosé has grown more successful, some producers have attempted to compete with it, with earlier harvesting and shorter maceration. De Pez says there is currently a big discussion among producers in Tavel on whether they should become more like Provence rosé or should keep their uniqueness. De Pez supports the traditional style, which he feels can be marketed all year, not just in summer, and noted that since quality started to improve, from 2012, Tavel has begun to regain its popularity.

Tavel wines have moved on from being the 'solid' wines of 1996 to being generally fresh and fruity, with a structure which appeals to red-wine drinkers. Ripe red fruit (sour Griotte cherries, black cherries, strawberries and raspberries), sometimes with notes of bitter almond (d'Aqueira has notes of cherry and almond), often with a mineral or spice core, is typical. The wines have a hint of silky tannic structure, and long, fresh acidity, with a vibrancy of wild hedgerow fruit. Some have a touch of perfumed, floral character, especially those from vines from the sandy soils. Depending on the length and temperature of maceration, the wines can have quite a chewy structural character.

The weight and intensity varies between domaines, terroirs and vintages. Wines made from a blend of the three soils will differ depending on varieties and maceration. Some wines are made from a single terroir, such as Mordorée's Reine de Bois, which uses the white varieties Clairette and Bourboulenc for freshness and acidity and red Cinsault for delicacy, to balance the ripe Grenache and Syrah and give a classic quality Tavel with restrained sour cherry, raspberry and strawberry red fruit and freshness, a firm, mineral structure and a hint of tannin.

Some take advantage of the greater ripeness and structure of recent years and are making wood-aged *cuvées*.

The climate is Mediterranean but not maritime, with the northerly mistral the prevailing wind. The cold cevenol wind blows from the Massif Central at the end of September, which shuts the grapes down but generally guarantees a dry harvest. The range of grape varieties is also typically Mediterranean.

The main varieties are Grenache (red, white, grey), Cinsault, Bourboulenc, Clairette (pink and white) and Picpoul (black, white, grey). Together, they have to make up the major part of the blend, but in reality, Grenache is the main variety. Mourvèdre and Syrah were added in 1969 to replace Carignan and Calitor, which cannot be more than 10 per cent. Grenache provides fruit, sweetness and volume, Cinsault finesse, Syrah colour, Clairette fruit and Mourvèdre stability of colour (and structure). A small amount of Carignan can bring freshness, as can the addition of white varieties.

The geology varies significantly throughout the appellation. Blending from these different sites is important, although some wines are made from single sites.

The original area in the south comprises flat, sandy, rocky fields, chalky with little gravel, which are easy to cultivate and good for ripening. Although poor for water retention, with sufficient depth of soil, the vines do better in drought years. The grapes from this area give finesse and elegance, due to the large diurnal temperature variation, which helps restrain the sugar in Grenache. Grapes from the sand and *terres blanches* sites give good balance for alcohol and acidity.

To the north of the village is an alluvial area formed by the Rhône, whose deposits cover the lower and middle terraces of the Lirac and Tavel AOCs. These deposits are rarely very deep and overlay limestone bedrock. The large *galets* (river-rolled rocks), as in Châteauneuf-du-Pape, act as storage heaters, ensuring great ripeness. However, since 2003 there has been a noticeable increase in hot summers, and now this extra ripening is not so important. This terroir gives very structured, complex red wines, so care must be taken in using wines from this part for rosé. On *galets* the vines suffer in drought, but the extra ripeness contributes to greater weight and structure. Richard Maby of Domaine Maby's single vineyard Prima Donna, planted on the *galets* with old vine Grenache and Cinsault, illustrates the distinctive character of this terroir. The natural extra ripeness of the terroir is balanced by fractionally longer maceration for greater structure. The wine has opulent, ripe raspberry, blackberry and black cherry and hints of silky tannins. Maby has also tried an oak-aged version with grapes from this terroir.

To the west of the village, lie the Terre Blanches, notable for marl limestone deposits. *Lauze* (flagstone), found in the valleys, is very stony with hard limestone. The quality of cultivation depends on the depth of the hard subsoil. Here, low-yielding vines produce deep, aromatic wines. Grapes from the *lauze* have finesse, elegance and fruit.

Global warming has affected the wines of the region, with 2003 marking a divide. In the 1930s, the highest alcohol levels were around 12.5% abv. While relatively high alcohol fits the Tavel style, contributing to roundness, too much can lead to imbalance and goes against the current trend of lighter alcohol rosés. Before 2003, harvest was in early October for maximum ripeness, with some chaptalization in one in every three years. Since 2003, chaptalization has not been required and the harvest occurs in mid-September; harvesting any later causing the wines to exceed 15% abv.

Since the 1980s, malolactic fermentation has been stopped by most producers, although Demoulin of Trinquevedel, whose vines are on sandy soils, believes these soils can give sufficient freshness to allow malolactic fermentation. Biodynamic producer Eric Pfifferling of Domaine de l'Anglore also does malolactic fermentation.

Balancing acidity, lower alcohol, ripeness and structure is vital for rosés such as Tavel. If producers want the extended maceration for the fruit and structure *and* need the fresh acidity, greater work is required in the vineyards, making sure the soil is well turned over and removing leaves to reduce over-production of sugar. The skins and pips must be fully ripe to avoid bitter greenness, which could be extracted during the extended maceration. Maceration time can range from six to seventy-two hours. Typically it is between ten and thirty-six hours. The time depends on the winemaker's choice of colour and style. Trinquevedel's wines, from sandy soils, with twelve- to twenty-four-hour maceration are on the lighter side of traditional Tavel, with paler colour and more floral and strawberry fruit than traditionally. Producers who choose to make a paler Tavel, macerating for just six hours, can pick earlier for greater acidity, but this is atypical of Tavel.

After the maceration, the juice is bled off (*saignée*). Sometimes, as is the case with Trinquevedel's Autrement *cuvée*, some of the must is kept with the skins longer, then blended into the lighter must.

The term *méthode Taveloise,* is preferred to describe the method for making Tavel, including the maceration, but largely referring to the bleeding off of the juice in its entirety, avoiding the term *saignée* which suggests that the juice is bled off to concentrate red wine.

Despite Tavel's reputed ability for ageing well, the wine has suffered from the reputation of lighter, less concentrated rosés, which age less well. Evidently the wine matures, evolving from more explosive fruit to greater spice (cinnamon, nutmeg and cloves), intense dried fruits (sour cherries, black cherries and cranberries) and savoury notes (dried orange peel and some rich, gamey notes). The extra maceration in the wines of Tavel contributes to the ageing capacity of these wines.

MANZANILLA

Manzanilla is made only in the coastal town of Sanlúcar de Barrameda. In this entertaining chapter from 2019's *Sherry* (now in its sixth edition) Julian Jeffs relates the history of the town and its wine, explaining how the peculiarities of Sanlúcar's climate are essential to the wine's style, and adding a health warning for anybody tempted to overindulge.

Manzanilla comes from Sanlúcar de Barrameda. The British connection with Sanlúcar goes back many years, long before manzanilla was heard of. There were certainly British merchants there at the beginning of the sixteenth century, and their church of St George was founded in the reign of Henry VIII, when the town was the main port and metropolis of the sherry district, but that story has already been told. Sanlúcar is a delightful town that still retains traces of the days when it was a busy port; the Conquistadors sailed from there to discover the New World. There are some good houses and even a royal palace. In the 1950s and 1960s it seemed enchantingly asleep, but now all that is changed: the world has found out that it likes manzanilla and it has become especially popular on the Spanish market. The town has woken up to what appears, compared with the old days, frenzied activity.

In the summer the air of Sanlúcar is noticeably more agreeable than in Jerez, thanks to cool breezes and the proximity of the river. Jerezanos drive down after work or at weekends to get out of the sweltering heat of summer. The people are charming and happy; flamenco is sung and danced spontaneously in the streets, and there is something delightfully informal about it all.

The town is very ancient, perhaps even older than Cadiz, and the pagan temple of the Morning Star once stood there, hidden in a dense wood. Fragments of old buildings and many ancient coins are still found: the site is now known as *Sanlúcar el Viejo*. *Barrameda* is said to be a modern word. Just outside the harbour, there is a hidden reef, or *barra*, that is very dangerous to shipping, and there used to be, on the bank of the river, a convent of the Jeronimite fathers, whose walls served as a landmark to guide pilots past the reef. There was also an enormous pine tree near the convent, called *el pino de la marca*; it was so wide that two men could not span it, but it was blown down in a gale many years ago. Inside the convent was an image of Our Lady, and it was called Santa María de Barrameda, because its divine powers delivered sailors from the reef. Soon the two names were combined and corrupted to give the modern Sanlúcar de Barrameda. That is the accepted story, but the following passage from Steven's translation of Mariana's *History of Spain* (1592) would suggest an alternative derivation:

> *After a siege of 6 months, the Moors raised their camp from before Xerez, being in want of all necessaries, and fearing lest King Sancho should offer them Battel. After they had pass'd the River Guadalete, rather in the nature of Flight, than a Retreat, one ask'd of the Moorish king the Reason why he sho'd so much Fear, and he answer'd: 'I am the first that rais'd the Family of Bar-ameda to the Regal Dignity; my enemy is descended from above 40 Kings, which in Battle would have been a great Terror to me, and a mighty Incouragement to him.'*

So it seems possible that the name is really Moorish.

For many years Sanlúcar was very prosperous and an important provincial centre. Francisco Pacheco, the master and father-in-law of Velazquez, was born there in 1564. But the fortunes of Sanlúcar began to decline when the great Indies trade was diverted to Seville and Cadiz in the seventeenth century, and the shipping business for the wine trade also gradually migrated, first to El Puerto de Santa María and then likewise to Cadiz. By 1762 J. Hinxman was able to write: 'The town declines daily, and its principal trade is in salt.' By the time George Borrow called there in 1839, on one of his hot-gospelling missions, it had become noted for its thieves, rogues and smugglers. Nevertheless, he actually succeeded in selling prohibited books (Bibles in Spanish and Gitano) in the customs house, of all places. Unfortunately he had no taste for sherry.

Perhaps owing to its antiquity and geographical position, Sanlúcar is mentioned in English travel books more often than either of the other sherry towns. Henry Swinburne, writing in 1810, described how it was a quiet and pleasant town without much business. But when the arch-disparager Richard Ford went there in 1858, he described it thus:

White and glittering, it is an ill-paved, dull, decaying place; pop. 16,000 … San Lucar exists by its wine-trade, and is the mart of the inferior and adulterated vintages which are foisted off in England as sherries. Nota bene, here, at least, drink manzanilla, however much it may be eschewed in England, which being, fortunately, not a wine growing country, imports the very best of all others, leaving the inferior for native consumption.

One can only say that the town has changed beyond all recognition: nothing but its ancient beauty remains. Its greatest glory, though, is its wine. Manzanilla is a comparatively modern wine. In the very early days there is evidence that a form of malmsey was grown there. Later wines conformed to the normal sherry styles and there was also a red wine called *vino carlón*. Until well into the nineteenth century, much of the sherry prepared there was boiled down to make a dark colouring wine, or *vino de color*, used in blending. It is not known who first found how to prepare manzanilla, nor the exact date, but it probably happened as a result of a drive to improve the wine trade and commerce generally there in the last quarter of the eighteenth century. The first use of the word manzanilla is thought to have been in the bars of Cadiz, and there is an idea that when *flor* grew in the partially emptied casks of wine in the taverns people liked it. The first recorded mention of it is in an official document of 1781, but in a list of wines on sale in 1803 manzanilla was not mentioned, though probably some of those listed as *vinos finos de lujo*, or *de luxe* fino wines, were exactly the same thing. Esteban Boutelou wrote of manzanilla in 1807, but the name did not become common in commercial records until after the end of the Peninsular War in 1814. It first appears in the books of Barbadillo in 1827 and the wine was regularly sold from 1830. For the most part, however, it was sold in cask for local consumption until the coming of the railway in 1877 opened up trade in the Peninsula. In the middle of the century most of the trade from Sanlúcar was still in oloroso and colour wines sold to the shippers of Jerez and El Puerto de Santa María. They also became good customers for manzanilla, which they used for blending, and direct sales were neglected in their favour. By 1892 the production of manzanilla had become predominant but it was not bottled very extensively until the early years of the twentieth century. It was first introduced into England by Dr J. Gorman, of El Puerto de Santa María, a physician who abandoned the practice of medicine to spend the latter part of his life in the wine trade. By the 1920s the old trade in colour wines had disappeared.

The origin of the name has been the subject of much learned controversy. The following theories have been suggested: first, that it takes its name from the little Andalusian town of Manzanilla, not far from Seville; second, that it is derived from *manzana*, meaning 'apple'; third, that there was a vine of the same name; and fourth, that its flavour resembles that of *manzanilla* – the common camomile. The first theory is popular with tourists but with no one else. The wines made in Manzanilla hardly have even a superficial resemblance to those of Sanlúcar, and to derive the name by analogy with that of amontillado is obviously unjustified. It owes something to the writings of Charles Davillier, and is now discredited. The second is quite often heard in the sherry district, but the bouquet of manzanilla is so unlike the penetrating aroma of an apple that the derivation is too far-fetched to be taken seriously. The third, found in the dictionary of Ramon Joaquin Dominguez, can be dismissed at once, as there has never been a vine with a name even remotely similar. The fourth is almost certainly the right one, and the resemblance has frequently been remarked upon by those with the right kind of imagination. One wonders whether the name was first used as a jest to describe the newly created wine. The first reference I have been able to find to it is in a book written by Esteban Boutelou and published in 1807: '*De las uvas blancas aparentes como la listan, pisadas en Buena disposicion, y expedimas levemente, se obtenien vinos blancos sin el menor viso, que se distingen constantemente por su olor de manzanilla, y por su fragrancia exquisito que tanto aprecian los Gaditanos.*' ('From white grapes such as the Listan pressed in a good condition and gently you get white wines without the slightest colour, which are firmly distinguished by their aroma of camomile and by their exquisite fragrance, which is so greatly appreciated by those who live in Cadiz.') Listan is a synonym for Palomino. He goes on to refer to *vinos de manzanilla*; and it would appear that the manzanillas we know today date from about that time.

It is as well to utter a warning: in many of the Spanish hotels, if you ask for manzanilla, you are likely to get a cup of camomile tea, which is said to be good for the stomach. Even the aromatic resemblance, however, is unlikely to make it welcome. To add to the confusion, there is also the manzanilla olive, and the story is told of a prominent sherry shipper who sent a small barrel of them, preserved in brine, to one of his customers for Christmas. A very worried wine buyer telephoned and complained diffidently that his present of manzanilla had been tampered with: the wine tasted strongly of salt and it was full of foreign bodies.

Sanlúcar is not only distinctly cooler than Jerez but also more humid. These differences have a considerable impact on the metabolism of the *flor* yeasts, which grow there in superabundance. In this connection the microclimates of individual bodegas play an important part, and even different areas within the same bodega. There are also several minor differences in viticulture and enology. For instance, the grapes never were sunned, and excessive concentration is avoided by not pruning very short and by picking the grapes early enough for them to have ample acidity; but these practices are by no means unique to Sanlúcar and are, indeed, becoming normal throughout the sherry country. By far the most important difference lies in the way that the soleras are operated.

Manzanilla cannot be made as an añada: if casks of must are allowed to mature naturally over the years, not one develops as manzanilla, but all grow into the conventional styles of sherry, differing only very slightly from those matured in the other towns. The tendency to develop into a specific class of wine is naturally apparent in about six months, but after the must has been racked off the lees, it is fortified to a lower degree: generally to about 14.5° abv, and never more than 15.5°. After a few more months, musts that have proved suitable are added to the youngest criadera of a solera, and it is from then onwards that the principal differences are found. Instead of moving the wine in the solera every six months or so, it is drawn at intervals of one to three months, though in some soleras the pause may be no more than a fortnight. The quantity taken, however, is very much smaller: usually about three to five *jarras*, as compared with the ten in a typical sherry solera. Manzanilla soleras have more scales than those producing fino: never fewer than nine, and sometimes as many as fourteen. The casks are also kept emptier, leaving a large surface area in contact with the air, and hence there is a larger amount of *flor*. The soleras look different, too, because the bodega butts are mounted on stone supports, or *bajetes*, instead of wood. Sheets of cork are placed between the casks and the supports to prevent rot.

Manzanilla, of course, is a *flor* wine, and requires all the care bestowed on finos in the other towns: it must be regulated carefully, and the *flor* must not be disturbed, so a *garceta* is used for refreshing rather than a rociador. The *flor* grown by manzanilla looks slightly different from that of fino; it grows more profusely and for a greater length of time in the spring and autumn, and is thicker. If, through mismanagement, it goes away, the consequences are completely disastrous, and there is a saying in Sanlúcar that 'a bodega which does not flower is a bodega lost'. Manzanilla has been described as *el vino de la alegria* – 'the wine of joy', and so it is.

The alcoholic strength of the wine from a healthy solera lies between 15° and 15.5° abv. This is slightly weaker than fino, but manzanilla seldom deviates from these limits, as any less would put it in danger of spoilation, while a higher strength would reduce or even kill the *flor*, which gives the wine its natural protection. Until the 1980s it had to be fortified to 18°, even on the Spanish market, to prevent the development of *flor* in open bottles, but with modern filters all the yeasts can be taken out and it is sold throughout the world at its natural strength. It is also often bottled younger than it used to be as the modern taste is for pale, fresh wines.

The fino form of manzanilla, or *manzanilla fina*, is by no means the only one: all the other principal styles – fino-amontillado, amontillado, and oloroso – have their manzanilla equivalents, which are basically similar to those of sherry, but each of which has something of the sharp, penetrating and aromatic character associated with manzanilla. The fino form, however, is by far the most common and the adjective is invariably left out.

As with fino, when manzanilla fina ages, it loses its *flor* and gains in strength, first becoming *manzanilla pasada*, which is equivalent to fino-amontillado, and then *manzanilla amontillada* (though usually just called amontillado) when the strength may rise to as much as 20.5° abv. These latter wines are prepared by means of successive soleras, each being of greater equivalent age, and the wine in them is moved less often than that in the fina soleras. Palo cortado (here sometimes called Jerez cortado) and oloroso are also made in Sanlúcar, using the must that shows little or no tendency to grow *flor*. The method of preparation is similar to that of the other towns.

The date of the vintage and the working of the soleras are the two principal differences in the making of manzanilla, but there is a third factor that is entirely natural and vitally important: the climate. Sanlúcar, like El Puerto de Santa María, is by the sea, but unlike Puerto, it is bounded on the north by the wide mouth of the Guadalquivir and by the plains of the Marismas, which expose it to northerly winds. The climate could accurately be described as 'bracing' and, probably because it is so near the sea, there are fewer extremes of temperature than in Jerez. It is, in fact, delightful. It is rather more humid than the other towns, because the water lies very close to the surface of the ground, and a well can be made by digging only a few feet down. The higher water level in nearby vineyards does not appear to affect the grapes much, as some manzanilla is prepared from grapes grown in the vineyards near Jerez, while some shippers in Jerez have vineyards near Sanlúcar, and the must develops into normal sherry when taken to their bodegas. But while the climate is not sufficiently different to affect the vines, the wine is far more susceptible to small changes of atmosphere, and the temperature particularly influences the growth of *flor*. Manzanilla can only be made in Sanlúcar: attempts to make it in the other towns have produced only some strange finos, and when casks of manzanilla are taken to Jerez, or even to El Puerto, they rapidly turn into finos. After only six or seven months they are completely spoiled. For the same reason the wine had the reputation of not travelling well: when exported, it was often blended with fino, fortified and even sweetened. It remained an excellent wine, but it retained only a shadow of its natural elegance. But nowadays the real thing is available in Britain, almost as fresh and as elegant as in Sanlúcar. Modern fast transport and shipping the wine in bottles so that it does not get oxidized on the way, as it used to do when transported in cask, has transformed it.

Rather ruefully, the wine growers of Sanlúcar used to refer to their bodegas as the 'store-houses for Jerez'. Most of their wine was taken there, where it was blended for export. Some still is, as a little manzanilla can be blended in to add fragrance. In the past Sanlúcar always suffered first when there was any recession, as the shippers in Jerez avoided buying other people's wine when they could not sell their own. At the turn of the last century, when the demand for sherry slumped, many wine growers there were ruined utterly: they had no other markets, and their bodegas were abandoned; their wine, which had become worthless, was left to perish. Nothing at all could save them. The misery was repeated when the German blockade prevented shipments being made to Great Britain during the Second World War, and a grower with a stock of manzanilla normally worth half a million pounds found himself very hard up. But happily things are very different now. The leading Sanlúcar houses have become major shippers. This owed something to the rise of the Rumasa empire, which absorbed one after another of their traditional customers and gave the motive for the development of direct sales. Manzanilla, too, was becoming increasingly popular and suffered less than other styles from the current decline in trade. The Sanlúcar bodegas also developed the Spanish market, promoting their wines in the *feria* of Seville and are now enormously successful in that city.

In the cold, sunless English winter, a full-blooded amontillado or oloroso used to be favoured but, with the coming of central heating and a move towards lighter drinks generally, manzanilla has at last come into its own. More now is sold than ever before. Manzanilla is at its best, though, drunk in great draughts under the sun. When a nineteenth-century Earl of Derby was stricken with gout, his doctor forbade rich sherries and ordered him to try manzanilla. His wine merchant supplied a case, but he tried only one bottle. He sent the rest back, with a note saying that he preferred the gout. Perhaps we should be charitable and suppose that Lord Derby was sent an indifferent example, for manzanilla is so light, and so attractive, that it is almost impossible to drink less than a bottle at a sitting on a hot day. It is a soothing, apparently innocuous wine, but on no account is it a wine to get drunk on: the hangover is appalling and it gives one a stomach ache for a week. But taken in moderation it is a joy and a delight, a wine that stirs men to poetry. Manuel Barbadillo wrote a book about it, and his lyric *Canción de la Manzanilla* is as enchanting as the wine itself:

Manzanilla! Manzanilla!
Cantar de una seguidilla …
Revuelos de soleares …
Todo el cante de los mares,
de la sierra … y de Sevilla!

La caña en alto; la risa;
la ilusión como una brisa,
de verde y oro, en la frente.
Con tu aroma, alegremente,
la vida se immortaliza!

ICEWINE

In this detailed account, taken from his 2017 book *The wines of Canada*, Rod Phillips explores how a wine style that originated in Germany and Austria found its ideal growing conditions in Canada, leading to it becoming the country's signature wine.

Icewine, the wine that put Canada on the world wine map in the 1990s, is made from grapes that have frozen naturally on the vine in sub-zero (Celsius) winter temperatures before being harvested. By law, the temperature must reach -8°C or lower before the icewine harvest can begin. At this temperature the water in the grape pulp becomes ice crystals, and the only liquid released when the grapes are pressed is a small volume of juice that contains a high concentration of sugar, acids and flavour compounds, and that has a lower freezing-point than water. Alcoholic fermentation is slow and generally stops when the alcohol level is between 9 and 11 per cent by volume, leaving a high level of sugar in the wine – commonly around 200 grams of residual sugar per litre.

This means that icewine is extremely sweet, as well as richly flavoured and somewhat viscous in texture. Good-quality icewine is not simply sweet, however, but also shows intense and complex flavours and has well-balanced acidity. Icewines made from Riesling or Vidal are typically light to medium amber in colour and have flavours that can include tropical fruit, citrus fruit and honey. Icewines made from black varieties, notably Cabernet Franc, tend to be light red and show flavours of red berries and sometimes rhubarb. Yields of grapes destined for icewine are very low, and in many cases a single vine produces no more than one 375 millilitre bottle. For this and other reasons, icewine is more expensive than all but a handful of Canadian table wines.

Icewine has been made in Europe (mainly in Germany and Austria) for about two centuries, with the first icewine often said to have been made in Germany in 1794. The story is sometimes embellished as a narrative in which the monks of a monastery in Franconia made icewine unintentionally because they received permission to start the harvest only after their vineyards had been struck by freezing temperatures. There is no definitive evidence of this, and the first well-documented icewines date to Germany in the 1830s. The first time it was made commercially in Canada was in British Columbia in 1978, by a German immigrant, Walter Hainle. Ontario wineries began to make icewine commercially five years later, and the industry got a boost when the 1989 Vidal Icewine made by Inniskillin winery in Niagara Peninsula won the prestigious Grand Prix d'Honneur at the 1991 Vinexpo wine exhibition, in Bordeaux. Inniskillin skilfully leveraged this success to promote their icewines and many non-Canadians are more familiar with icewine from Inniskillin than from any other producer, even though some wineries, notably Niagara Peninsula's Pillitteri Estates winery, produce far more icewine.

Icewine is now much more closely identified with Ontario – especially with Niagara Peninsula – than any of the other provinces where it is also now made. British Columbia's wine regions have warmer winters, although temperatures in Okanagan and Similkameen Valleys fall low enough for icewine to be made on a regular basis, and between 15 and 25 producers (out of about 200 in those appellations) leave grapes on the vine for icewine production each year. In 2015, a year when icewine production in British Columbia was particularly low, only 16 wineries produced this style of wine. One winery, Lulu Island, makes about half the province's icewine and exports about 80 per cent of it to China. But British Columbia's icewine industry is a good deal smaller than Ontario's: between 2011 and 2015, Ontario produced an average of 850,000 litres of icewine a year, compared to British Columbia's 200,000 litres. In 2015, the value of Ontario's icewine exports was $15.6 million, compared to British Columbia's $2.5 million.

Icewine production is highly regulated. Canada, Germany and Austria have signed an agreement to standardize production methods, the main stipulation being that grapes for icewine must freeze naturally on the vine and be harvested only when the temperature in the vineyard falls to -8°C or lower for a sustained period. This convention aimed to distinguish icewines made only by this method from wines that were often called icewine but made from the juice of grapes that had been

Icewine grapes freezing naturally on the vine

artificially frozen. 'Icewines' of this sort have been made in places such as New Zealand and Australia. In 2014, Canada adopted additional icewine standards that regulated the labelling of icewines.

The stipulation that grapes must freeze naturally on the vine is fundamental to the definition of icewine, and it is a core definition of icewine in various international and national wine laws, as well as in the regulations in three of Canada's main icewine-producing provinces: Ontario, British Columbia and Nova Scotia. It was also in the regulations governing icewine production in Quebec until recently (see below). Because the yield from vines bearing grapes for icewine is so small (only a fifth to a sixth of the common yield for table wine), producers are permitted to use not only the grapes left on the bunches at the time of harvest, but also grapes that have fallen off between the time of the regular grape harvest and the icewine grape harvest. These individual berries are caught in nets stretched under the bunches and are collected, along with the intact bunches, during the harvest.

In 2015 the Quebec government adopted a different protocol at the request of some icewine producers in that province. Vines there need to be buried for protection from extreme temperatures during winter, when night temperatures often fall to between -30° and -40°C. Temperatures such as these would damage exposed canes bearing bunches of grapes. In addition, heavy snowfalls often reach to the top of vine trellises, and would bury grapes still hanging on the vines. Rather than resign themselves to the idea that icewine cannot be made in these conditions, some Quebec icewine producers requested permission to cut the bunches of grapes from the vines soon after the regular harvest and suspend them in nets attached to a wire at the top of the trellis. There they freeze and are retrieved for pressing once the vineyard temperature has fallen to at least -8°C.

The acceptance of this practice by the Quebec appellation authorities as permissible for icewine production in the province provoked loud criticism from the organizations representing icewine producers in the rest of Canada. They argued that harvesting grapes and leaving them in nets in close proximity to the vine is not the same as leaving grapes to freeze 'on the vine'. Icewine made this way, they said, was not only inauthentic but compromised the reputation of Canadian icewine as a whole. An organization of independent producers in Quebec, who make icewine from grapes that freeze naturally on the vine, argued that their wine demonstrated that this method was feasible in Quebec. But defenders of the method approved by the Quebec authorities argue that there is essentially no difference between using grapes that had been placed in nets and using grapes that had fallen from their bunches into nets, as is permitted in the rest of Canada.

The issue hinges on whether cutting bunches before placing them in nets on the trellis is tantamount to harvesting the grapes and whether there is a difference between grapes that fall from bunches without human intervention and grapes that are cut from the vine and placed in nets. While there are issues of definition here, it seems clear that cutting the bunches to put them in nets is more akin to harvesting them than later retrieving them from the nets for pressing. Icewine law in the other provinces also stipulates that harvesting and pressing must be done in 'one continuous' process, and this is certainly not the case in Quebec, where months might separate the cutting of the bunches from their retrieval and pressing. This dispute is an example of the difficulties the Canadian wine industry faces in creating a national wine law. In Quebec, icewine has *Indication Géographique Protégée* (IGP) status, a classification that does not exist in the rest of Canada.

As an aside, it is worth noting that in 2014 Quebec also gave IGP status to ice cider (Cidre de Glace du Québec), a beverage developed in Quebec in the 1980s and an increasingly popular product that is beginning to rival icewine. Ice cider is made by two methods, cryoconcentration and cryoextraction. Cryoconcentration, the more commonly used method, involves picking the apples in autumn and keeping them in cool-storage until the end of December. They are then pressed and the juice stored outside until most of the water freezes as ice crystals and only about a quarter of it – which contains concentrated sugars, acids and flavour compounds – remains in liquid form. This concentrated juice is separated from the ice crystals and fermented for up to six months before being bottled as ice cider.

The alternative method, cryoextraction, is less common and more expensive, and produces higher-priced ice ciders. It is used for varieties of apples that do not fall from the trees in autumn, and it is closer to the method used to make icewine in that the apples lose water and shrivel as they hang on the tree. They are harvested in December, January or February, when temperatures fall to about -15°C and most of the water remaining in the apples is frozen. The apples are then pressed and the small volume of concentrated juice is fermented for about eight months. In both methods, fermentation generally stops at about 10 per cent alcohol, the same as icewine. The result is a sweet apple wine that has rich, complex and definitively apple-centred flavours, high acidity and some viscosity. The similarities to icewine are evident, but ice cider tends to be a little lighter in texture and higher in perceived acidity. We might note that the two methods of making ice cider – leaving apples to freeze on the tree and picking them for freezing later – are analogous to the different methods of making icewine: leaving the grapes to freeze on the vine and picking them and allowing them to freeze in nets. The Quebec authorities seem to make a clear distinction in the case of ice cider that they blur in respect of icewine.

The IGP regulations control the production and character of ice cider. For example, the apples or juice must be frozen naturally (by being left outside in winter temperatures), not in a freezer, and the pressing must take place between 1 December and 1 March. The maximum level of residual sugar in the finished ice cider is 140 grams per litre (a little higher than the *minimum* level in most icewine laws), and the alcohol level must be between 9 and 13 per cent.

There are many more producers of ice cider than icewine in Quebec, but in other provinces the focus is on icewine. The notoriously cold winter temperatures in many parts of Canada, coupled with summers long enough to ripen grapes, produce ideal conditions for icewine production. In Niagara Peninsula the growing season is long enough to fully ripen many grape varieties, and the winter is reliably cold enough (that is, with temperatures falling at least as low as -8°C) that icewine has been made every year since it was first made in Ontario in the early 1980s. This compares favourably to Germany where more volatile winter temperatures do not allow icewine production every year and where climate change is leading to warmer growing conditions. In some years in Ontario, the threshold temperature of -8°C is reached as early as November, in other years as late as February and even March, but icewine harvests generally fall between late December and mid-January. British Columbia wineries typically harvest their icewine grapes a little earlier, in November and December.

It is not clear if there is any quality difference between icewines made from grapes picked earlier or later in winter. It is sometimes said that the process of alternately freezing and thawing that the grapes experience as they await the temperature suitable for the harvest adds complexity to their flavours. The chemistry of this is yet to be explained, but some tastings suggest that icewines made from grapes harvested late in the winter show more intensity than icewines made from earlier-harvested grapes. Icewine made from grapes harvested after 31 December is labelled not for the year of harvest but for the year in which the grapes grew. As an example, Henry of Pelham winery in Niagara Peninsula began harvesting its 2015 icewine grapes in early January 2016, and its 2016 icewine in mid-December of the same year. Labelling them 2015 and 2016, respectively, avoids having two consecutive vintages, each labelled 2016.

Icewine is a highly regulated style of wine, and the very word 'Icewine' (a single word with a capital I, rather than 'ice wine' or 'ice-wine') is a proprietary name owned by the Vintners Quality Alliance of Ontario (VQAO). Regulations are seen as desirable and necessary not least because producers want to ensure the authenticity of their icewine. So-called icewines made from artificially frozen grapes are produced in several parts of the world, and many counterfeit icewines can be found in some Asian markets, especially in China, where icewine is a luxury commodity. In British Columbia and Ontario, grapes intended for icewine production must be registered with the respective VQA authorities, and the grape varieties, acreage and estimated tonnage are verified by inspectors.

Only certain varieties of grapes can be used for icewine. In British Columbia and Ontario most approved varieties are *Vitis vinifera* varieties but icewine can also be made from Vidal, a French–American hybrid of Ugni Blanc and a Seibel variety. Most Quebec icewines are made from Vidal, while Nova Scotia wineries draw on Vidal, Ortega and New York Muscat. The icewine production process places particular demands on grapes and that reduces the range of varieties actually used. In general they must have sturdy stems so that they stay on their bunches, rather than fall off when they are ripe or when they are buffeted by winter winds – although, as we have seen, producers are permitted to hang nets under the bunches to catch grapes that do fall off, and to use the detached grapes in the icewine. Varieties suitable for icewine should also be late-ripening, have thick skins, and be relatively disease-resistant. High acidity to offset the high residual sugar is another advantage, which is why Riesling is a popular variety for icewine, but it is not essential because icewine can be acidified.

Icewine producers have recently expanded the range of varieties they use so as to make the icewine category more varied and interesting. In British Columbia, icewine is now being made from varieties such as Chardonnay, Pinot Noir, Kerner, Muscat, and Syrah, while Ontario producers are using Cabernet Franc (now the second most common variety used), Chardonnay, Cabernet Sauvignon, Gewürztraminer, and others. Icewines made from black grape varieties tend to be pale red in colour because there is no skin contact during fermentation and the only release of pigments takes place during pressing. A few producers are making sparkling icewine by a modified Charmat method: fermenting the juice in a tank and closing the lid towards the end of the process, thus trapping the carbon dioxide in the wine. The bubbles enhance the acidity in the wine and often provide better balance to the sweetness of icewine.

Vines intended for icewine production need to be netted to protect the sweet grapes from birds, and the crop is at risk of predators throughout the late autumn and winter. Not only birds but also deer, coyotes, raccoons and (in British Columbia) bears are attracted to the grapes as other sources of food diminish during the winter. As the grapes remain on the vine, they lose water and shrivel, and when they are ready to be picked, they are small, brown, raisin-like, hard berries, with most of their remaining water frozen. This leaves only a small amount of highly concentrated, very sweet juice in liquid form, with the level of sugar depending on the ripeness of the berries, dehydration and the weather in the weeks and months prior to harvest.

Although the harvesting threshold is -8°C, most producers wait for a stretch of temperatures between -10°C and -12°C. In British Columbia and Ontario, the juice from the pressed frozen grapes must meet a minimum average of 35° Brix for all the pressings destined for one bottling, with the juice from no single pressing falling below 32° Brix. Quebec and

Nova Scotia have established a lower average threshold of 32° Brix. In practice, the degrees Brix of the juice extracted in Ontario tends to fall between 35 and 40, but levels higher than 50° Brix have been recorded. The higher the sugar content of grapes, the lower the temperature must be to freeze the water, but at temperatures approaching -20°C, the water in the grapes freezes almost completely, and it is difficult to extract any juice. Juice extracted at a degrees Brix level lower than 35 (and second pressings of icewine grapes) can be used to make Late Harvest wines.

Icewine harvesting is usually done at night, when the temperatures are lowest, and although many small icewine producers harvest by hand – often using volunteers who enjoy the putative romance of picking grapes in frigid temperatures at night – larger producers machine-pick their grapes. Machine harvesting has the advantage of being more rapid, an important consideration when the picking window is narrow. The harvesting and pressing must, according to Ontario and British Columbia wine law, be done in a continuous process.

To extract the juice, powerful basket or bladder presses are needed because most of the mass is ice (the frozen water in the grapes) and it must be pressed hard to extract the relatively small volume of liquid juice. The pressing is usually done outside so as to maintain the temperatures of the grapes. The yield for icewine is about a fifth or sixth of the yield common for table wine: in Ontario the juice yield is about 150 litres per tonne of grapes for Vidal and about 125 litres per tonne for Riesling – far less than the 700 litres per tonne that is common for grapes harvested to make table wine. These low yields contribute to the relatively high price of icewine.

Sweetness is an essential quality of icewine but residual sugar levels in finished icewines vary widely. Residual sugar must be no lower than 100 grams per litre in British Columbia, 110 grams per litre in Nova Scotia, and 125 grams per litre in Ontario and Quebec, but icewines generally have about 200 grams per litre of residual sugar and some have more than 300 grams per litre. The sweetness in all icewines must result from the natural sugar of the grapes and chaptalization is not permitted. Because the juice from icewine grapes has such a high concentration of sugar, alcoholic fermentation tends to be slow and difficult. Studies at the Cool Climate Oenology and Viticulture Institute (CCOVI) in Niagara Peninsula show that juice that started at more than 42° Brix had difficulty reaching the 10 per cent alcohol that is common for icewine. In one case, Riesling juice that started at 46° Brix had achieved only 6.5 per cent alcohol by the time the yeast stopped working after one month's fermentation. The industry standard for icewine is 10 per cent by volume, and the typical range is 9 to 11 per cent, but the minimum alcohol is 7 per cent and the maximum is a staggering 14.9 per cent that is rarely ever approached. The high levels of residual sugar that are essential to icewine demand good balancing acidity, and acidification by up to 4 grams per litre is permitted. It is not generally needed for icewines made from naturally acidic Riesling grapes, but it is widely used for icewines made from other varieties.

Icewine is a luxury product and is usually sold in tall, slim 375 millilitre or 200 millilitre bottles made of clear glass that sell for between $50 (US$38) and $70 (US$53) in Canada. These prices reflect not only the low yields from vines dedicated to icewine production, but also the costs of maintaining vines for an additional period during winter, bird-netting, the loss of fruit to weather and predators, and the generally higher costs associated with the production of small volumes of wine. The retail price also factors in the value of the icewine brand because icewine is widely recognized as a luxury product. It is not intended for consumption on a daily basis, but on rare occasions and in small quantities, either with meals (foie gras and blue cheeses are often recommended), desserts or on its own. Its luxury status is reflected in the careful packaging, with many bottles sold in their own boxes or tubes.

Another factor adding to price is that half the icewine produced in Canada is exported and must bear the additional transportation costs. Total Canadian icewine exports have risen steadily in recent years, from 181,000 litres in 2011 to 235,000 litres in 2015. The price differential between icewine and table wines is graphically shown by the fact that icewine represents only 0.3 per cent of Canada's wine exports by volume, but 25 per cent by value. The main markets are China (which in 2015 accounted for almost a third of icewine exports), the United States (a quarter), South Korea and the United Kingdom (a tenth each), and Hong Kong (a twentieth). Three-quarters of all icewine exports go to these five countries. Within Canada much of the icewine is sold to Asian tourists at winery cellar doors and icewine is also found in many duty-free stores around the world.

Icewines made from artificially frozen grapes, and counterfeit icewines have become problems for the Canadian icewine industry, which also explains the reaction by producers in other provinces to Quebec's practice of 'pre-harvesting' grapes. Sweet wines made by artificially freezing grapes may be icewine in a broad technical sense, but Canada's icewine industry is keen for wine merchants and consumers to appreciate the additional demands posed by freezing grapes on the vine – demands that are expressed in the cost of production and that producers believe translate into higher quality.

Counterfeit icewine is another matter entirely, as it generally involves bottling artificially sweetened wine in the same style of bottles used for genuine icewine, and labelling them with labels that strongly suggest or explicitly state that the contents are Canadian icewine. Counterfeit brands for sale in China include Maple Dew, Silver Maple and Toronto Icewine, with the labels showing images of the Niagara Falls or Niagara Peninsula vineyards (sometimes taken off the internet). Images of silver and red maple leaves abound. Many counterfeit icewines are labelled 'Product of Canada/Produit du Canada', but many of them do not show a vintage or grape variety, both of which are always shown on Canadian icewine labels. As long as producers of counterfeit icewine call their product ice wine or ice-wine, rather than use the spelling of the protected name, Icewine, it is more difficult to prosecute them.

As with wine fraud more generally, counterfeit icewine often succeeds because consumers have never tried the genuine product or cannot distinguish counterfeit from authentic wine. Canadian embassies and wine marketing associations have hosted Chinese and other Asian wine merchants and sommeliers to instruct them how to recognize the sensory and chemical characteristics of genuine icewine and how to identify counterfeits. Individual icewine producers have adopted their own strategies to help consumers distinguish counterfeits from the real thing. Ontario's Pondview Estate, for example, has attached smartphone readable seals (called 'prooftags') to its labels. When the phone reads the seal, it links to Pondview's web site, which confirms that the seal is in its database.

Although there are occasional reports of the impending decline of icewine, it seems to be on a secure basis in terms of production and exports. In the important Chinese market, icewine is frequently given as a prestigious gift, and it is quite conceivable that each bottle is regifted many times. It is a good thing that icewine ages well and can be regifted for years. With high levels of sugar and acidity, icewine lasts for a decade or longer, and takes on not only darker hues but also more intensely pungent flavours that give the wine greater complexity and distract attention from the high level of residual sugar.

THE ENJOYMENT OF COGNAC

Here, the late, great Nicholas Faith offers a comprehensive guide to enjoying cognac, in his inimitable style. This extract from 2016's *Cognac* is both a cultural history of this iconic brandy and a guide to selecting, serving and tasting the contents of your (carefully chosen) glass.

The enjoyment of cognac, like everything else about this miraculous drink, is a complicated matter. It does not help that, as David Baker of Brandy Classics says with a sigh, 'today people are as ignorant about cognac as they were about wine thirty years ago'. Fortunately it is benefiting from the fact that people don't share their parents' tastes – which is the problem facing blended Scotch in many of its traditional markets. Helpfully, for today's younger generation cognac is a drink associated with their grandparents, so they are open to exploring its qualities.

Cognac's flagships are what Americans would call 'sippin'' brandies, essentially the XOs and above, though including some of the best VSOPs. In the words of Charles Walter Berry, for long Britain's greatest expert on brandy 'it is ideal after dinner; it cleanses the palate and its superfine qualities appeal to all that is best in the human mind'. The novelist Jacques Chardonne provides a wonderful and – for him – unusually precise description of one M. Pommerel. This master taster 'poured a drop of cognac into a cristal glass shaped like a half-opened tulip … he took the glass and then delicately between two fingers, he lifted it up without agitating it, breathing the fumes gently as if, through slow and silent exhalations. He was absorbing all its flavours.' A professional guide to tasting published in the 1970s states firmly that the sense of smell plays by far the most import role in sensory examination of a cognac.

In the past, and sometimes even today, the enjoyment of fine cognac has been bedevilled by its image. In a famous scene in his novel *Brideshead Revisited* Evelyn Waugh provided the tasting of old brandy as one example of the insufferable snobbery which permeates the whole book. The hero, Charles Ryder, is dining with the upstart Rex Mottram at a restaurant in Paris clearly identifiable as the Tour d'Argent. The cognac offered to them is 'clear and pale and it came to us in a bottle free from grime and Napoleonic cyphers. It was only a year or two older than Rex and lately bottled. They gave it to us in very thin tulip-shaped glasses of modest size.' Predictably, Rex does not like it: he 'pronounced it the sort of stuff he put soda in at home'. So 'shamefacedly, they wheeled out of its hiding place the vast and mouldy bottle they kept for people of Rex's sort … a treacly concoction,' which left 'dark rings round the side of his glass … a balloon the size of his head' (still often seen in pretentious surroundings the world over, but never in Cognac itself).

Waugh was being deliberately, outrageously snobbish. But he had clearly distinguished the separate markets which developed amid the cigar smoke and lush living of Edwardian England: the older, 'purer' tradition, of aristocratic sips of light, intense, delicate cognacs shipped early and bottled late, and the newer and more vulgar novelties symbolized by 'vast grimy bottles' and 'Napoleonic cyphers' – a phoney association which still survives. Indeed Christies' catalogues over the years provide numerous examples of brandies labelled not just with the name Napoleon but also with such associative names as *Grande Armée, Impératrice Joséphine and Maison de l'Empereur* fetching exaggerated sums at auction. As Charles Walter Berry put it with typical bluntness, 'Napoleon brandy is a snare and a delusion.' Virtually no cognac distilled before 1800 is drinkable as their storage over the centuries is suspect.

Waugh had also isolated a major element in the snobbery which deters younger drinkers, the glasses used. The vast balloons still regularly offered to diners not only lend an air of absurdity and snobbery to the drinking of fine brandy, but their very size precludes proper appreciation of the aromas. In the words of Georg Riedel, the glassmaker: 'with large glasses you have large surfaces and lots of evaporation and this means that the fruit disappears, so all you have left is the alcohol.' Basically you need a glass with a top that is narrower than the bottom to concentrate the aromas, but, unlike balloons of whatever size, is not too large to allow the flavours to be lost. I've even used a champagne flute, but the best is one used by professional tasters, the bulbous 'tulip' glass described by Chardonne which has a small chimney on top of the bulb. This has the desired quality of combining small quantities of spirits with the maximum capacity to entrap and concentrate the bouquet.

Riedel, ever the perfectionist, offers two types of glass – as well, rather shamefacedly, as a balloon for old-timers. His VSOP glass is taller than the usual tulip glass and is designed to play up the fruitiness of the brandy and minimize the fiery harshness, the burning sensation so evident in most VSOPs. The idea works, a VSOP nosed in this glass is warmer and less fiery than when tasted in the tulip-shaped glass used for older brandies. Because these should have lost their youthful harshness, the glass can be designed to maximize the power of the complex aromas of rich chocolatey fruitiness and nuttiness typical of the best cognacs. (Of course Riedel is not alone in offering well-designed cognac glasses, Baccarat and Jenkins, for instance, both offer similar ones.)

Chardonne's description of a glass 'shaped like a half-opened tulip' was confirmed in a fascinating session held by the BNIC in early 2009 for professionals from all over the world. Their preference was indeed for such a glass. The shape was found easiest to use, best for judging the colour but also, critically, concentrated the nose of the brandy because of its wide bowl and narrow neck and thus allowed the taster to understand the subtleties and layers of aromatic complexity in the brandy. Nevertheless, the traditional balloon was judged excellent for serving young cognacs, over crushed ice for example.

Of course the brandy should be at the right temperature. The ideal is about 18°C, since too warm a brandy evaporates too quickly and thus tastes too alcoholic. Better to start with a relatively cold glass rather than the warmed ones traditionally used – and if the brandy is already the right temperature, it's obviously sensible to hold it by the foot or stem to avoid overheating.

Tasters obviously have to rely almost exclusively on their sense of smell, for even the strongest stomach cannot survive the small sips ingested when sampling fifty or more cognacs in a row, especially freshly distilled or immature ones. They, like the rest of us, are judging on three criteria: age, *cru* and the general style which results from the combination of the age, the *cru* and the oak. They will instantly reject the harsh oiliness imparted to both nose and palate by the raw spirit used in even the best grape brandies. The *cru* is more difficult to distinguish. Most cheap cognacs are relatively anonymous, the better will, however, have a certain character. With less routine cognacs it is immensely enjoyable to look for the nuttiness provided by cognacs from the Borderies, and to try and detect the age of the cognac employed in different Champagne brandies.

Compared with wine, the colour of the brandy is of little import-ance, since most cognacs are coloured with caramel to provide the ele-ment of standardization important in maintaining the brandy's vital 'brand image'. Indeed in Cognac itself the tasters use blue-coloured glasses to eliminate the colour factor entirely. Nevertheless, it is pretty safe to say that brandies which are too deep in colour are overly viscous, containing too much caramel. I've not come across many dark cognacs which offer any elegance while all the best older brandies have a golden streak. You can also judge – roughly – the age of a brandy by the traces, the 'tears' as the professionals call them which fall down the inside of the glass, for the older the cognac the slower they fall.

Tasting cognac is a more complex matter than tasting wines – many wine writers simply refuse to taste brandies because they are so strong. Inevitably amateurs can cope with a far smaller number than profession-als. Personally I will taste five or six in a flight, accompanied by large doses of water – which I spit because swallowing would involve some of the brandy. I try not to do more than twenty in a morning.[1] Tasting for enjoyment should still be done in two stages to separate the more vola-tile constituents from the heavier ones. So the first impression should be gained by holding the glass still with the nose slowly approaching its rim. The glass can then be slowly rotated, rather than swirled, to capture the depth and variety of the more volatile elements which should be ema-nating from the spirit. This first 'nosing' should not be too near the glass or the strength of the flavours will be overwhelming. You then pause to catch your breath and put your nose into the glass to capture the more alcoholic components. Only then do you actually taste. Now the glass has to be twirled, just like a wine, to check for the individual taste com-ponents – the fruit, the balance, the length, the finish – which should be far longer than with wines.

Whatever the sensations, the drinker can generally be guided by the style of the house which blended the cognac. Most are commercial, for few blenders can afford the attitude of Alain Braastad, the former

---

1 My greatest achievement, which I hope never to have to repeat, was to taste thirty-two South African brandies – a few of which were excellent – in a morning. But I was much younger then.

Cognac comes in many colours, all appealing

chairman of Delamain, who says simply: 'I blend what I like.' These house styles are a strange mixture of the taste for which customers developed a fondness in times past, of the personal favourites of the blenders, sometimes of a deliberate, almost perverse complexity: 'The more you simplify cognac, the easier it is to imitate', said Robert Leauté of Rémy Martin. Once you rise above the VSOP level, the choice is almost infinite. As might be expected, Martell and Hennessy have very different house styles: Martell, as we have seen, is almost obsessionally dry and clear on the palate; Hennessy goes for a much richer, almost voluptuous, taste in its blends. The theme of richness, of a desire to extract as much of the grapiness as possible from the fruit, is also involved in Rémy's distillation policy.

'There are two snobberies associated with cognac,' says Bernard Gauthier who produces excellent cognacs in the Grande Champagne, 'age and new oak.' It was Warner Allen who provided the most accurate rant about old cognacs, which is just as valid today as it was sixty years ago: 'Too many unscrupulous dealers', he thundered, 'dress up a young cognac with sugar, darken it with caramel perhaps add a few drops of really old cognac to give it a purely fictitious date … Bottles with monograms mean nothing … Bottles of brandy that claim to have been in the cellars of the First Napoleon and his contemporaries may multiply themselves like the fragments of the True Cross, but the wise man will give them a wide berth.' Even then you should avoid the brandies strong and forceful enough to cope with the taste of cigars produced by a number of firms, even reputable ones like Hine.

Truly old cognacs, those that have absorbed all they can from the wood, are a class apart. But the most satisfying can often be as young – in brandy terms – as thirty-five years old when they have already developed their vital *rancio*. Indeed the idea of 'beauty before age' so far as cognac is concerned has recently received a major boost thanks to the universal, and deserved praise – and trophies – awarded to Frapin's Multimillésimes, which are composed of three cognacs none more than thirty years old. Whatever their age the best brandies 'expand inside the mouth'. Once they are fifty years old, the best of them have acquired an inimitable, golden-bronze colour and feel: a harmony achievable only with age.

Age can also bring with it a kind of anonymity, blurring the original distinctions between different styles, so some of the real golden old-ies, like Rémy Martin's Louis XIII and Hennessy's Paradis, resemble each other more than they do their makers' less distinguished offer-ings. Style applies more to younger, mid-range blends. The contrast between two widely respected cognacs, Frapin's Château de Fontpinot and Delamain's Pale and Dry, is striking. The Frapin is infinitely more woody; the oak, though dissolved and matured, is still emphatically pre-sent. In pre-feminist language, it is a 'masculine' cognac, where the in-finitely more delicate Delamain is 'feminine', all lightness and elegance. To my palate, the best balance is achieved by a single-vineyard cognac, that of the Fontvieilles from Ragnaud-Sabourin, which somehow com-bines the strength and delicacy of the two extremes. But a cognac like this is rare enough to prove the rule that the only way to establish a reli-able house style is to blend the products of many stills.

Beware, above all, the oldest cognacs. I've been lucky to sample some superb very old cognacs, but after fifty years quality depends on luck, chance, the skill of the producers and the care with which they have been stored. They may be very intense, very deep, but only too often they are not to my taste because there is no sign of fruity life. My com-parison is with drier tawny ports at forty years of age, as opposed to the delicious fruit-and-nut mix at twenty. I've now found support for my lack of enthusiasm for very old cognacs from Edward Bate, the co-gnac specialist at Berry's and Neil Mathieson who imports such delights as Ragnaud Sabourin. In any case some of these cognacs are far too woody, many may well have been blended with younger brandies, and the strength of some of them can have fallen to well below the statutory 40 per cent and some, of course, were never very good in the first place. Nevertheless, the oldest cognacs will have started as more concentrated spirits since they will have been distilled in much smaller stills – probably not more than 3 hectolitres, an eighth of today's normal size.

The older the cognac the truer these points. Cognacs bottled before 1857 had to be blended and sold without a producer's name and much was poorly aged. Even the cognacs from the Grande Champagne will not age for longer than about 70–80 years and must be taken out of the barrels to stop them deteriorating. Corks will also taint the cognac and need to be changed at least every twenty years, preferably more often.

There has always been a well-founded suspicion as to the accuracy of the ages given to cognac. In 1864 Charles Tovey put it bluntly: 'We place but little reliance upon the cognac shippers' declarations with regard to vintages; and the only security the merchant has is to get his vintage brandy over to England into his own bonded stores as soon after the vintage as is convenient.'[2] Maurice Healy described how some merchants operated a sort of *solera* system: 'Bisquit Dubouché offered to supply apparently unlimited quantities of their 1865, their 1834 and even their 1811. If a cask of 1811 brandy had got down to its last tenth, and was then refilled with brandy of a younger but sympathetic vintage, say 1834, the cask became, within a few days a full cask of 1811, the older vintage having endowed the younger with its quality, while receiving the strength and virility of the other.'

'Obviously', says David Baker, 'provenance is important,' but he's not only looking for their genuine date – though even carbon dating can only be accurate to within ten or twenty years. Mere age is not enough, he has to make sure 'that they are still alive', finding that too many of them are 'watery' or woody because they've been kept in casks too long. The worst are those from iconic vintages, above all the many allegedly from 1811, the 'Year of the Comet'. Taste is all. In the words of Charles Walter Berry: 'names and dates stand for little – the veritable article will speak for itself'.

And my own personal tastes? Like the locals – a long-lived bunch – I drink relatively little of it. For me a good or great cognac is more than the sum of its parts. I am looking for bitterness, its length on the palate and

2 Tovey, C., *British and Foreign Spirits*, London, 1864.

the finish – is it long? Too burny? In the end I am looking for the greatest possible impact from the fruit from which the cognac was made. This can be richer or leaner, for it is no more ridiculous to talk of the 'backbone' of a good Martell, the 'elegance' of a Delamain, the 'fruitiness' of a Hennessy cognac than it is to attribute the same qualities to clarets from Pauillac or Saint-Emilion. For the best cognacs have one advantage denied even to the finest wines, because of the sheer strength of the drink its qualities linger longer. You can taste for hours and still keep finding new depths, new flavours – even next morning when the glass has been empty the whole night long. But no one has put the experience better than the politician – and bishop – Talleyrand:

> *At the end of a sumptuous supper, one of the guests tossed down his glass of Fine Champagne in one gulp in the Russian manner. Talleyrand took the liberty of advising his friend quite quietly: 'That is not how you should drink cognac. You take your glass in the hollow of the hand, you warm it, you rotate it with a circular movement so that the spirit gives off its aroma. Then you carry it to your nostrils and inhale … and then, my dear sir, you put down your glass and talk about it.'*

INDEX

THE CLASSIC WINE LIBRARY

The Classic Wine Library is a premium source of information for students of wine, sommeliers and others who work in the wine industry, but can easily be enjoyed by anybody with an enthusiasm for wine. All authors are expert in their subject, with years of experience in the wine industry, and many are Masters of Wine. The series is curated by an editorial board made up of Sarah Jane Evans MW, Richard Mayson and James Tidwell MS. All the chapters in this book originally appeared in one of the Classic Wine Library books.

Amarone and the fine wines of Verona, Michael Garner
Biodynamic Wine, Monty Waldin
Cognac: The story of the world's greatest brandy, Nicholas Faith
Côte d'Or: The wines and winemakers of the heart of Burgundy,
    Raymond Blake
Fizz! Champagne and Sparkling Wines of the World, Anthony Rose
Madeira: The islands and their wines, Richard Mayson
Port and the Douro, Richard Mayson
Rosé: Understanding the pink wine revolution, Elizabeth Gabay MW
Sake and the wines of Japan, Anthony Rose
Sherry, Julian Jeffs

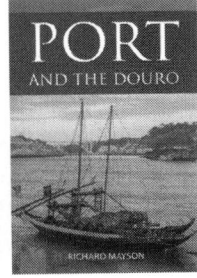

Spirits Distilled, Mark Ridgwell
The story of champagne, Nicholas Faith
The wines of Australia, Mark Davidson (pub. 2023)
The wines of Austria, Stephen Brook
The wines of Bulgaria, Romania and Moldova, Caroline Gilby MW
The wines of Canada, Rod Phillips
The wines of Faugères, Rosemary George MW
The wines of Chablis and the Grand Auxerrois, Rosemary George MW
The wines of Georgia, Lisa Granik MW
The wines of Germany, Anne Krebiehl MW
The wines of Great Britain, Stephen Skelton MW
The wines of Greece, Konstantinos Lazarakis MW
The wines of New Zealand, Rebecca Gibb MW
The wines of northern Spain, Sarah Jane Evans MW
The wines of Portugal, Richard Mayson
The wines of Roussillon, Rosemary George MW
The wines of South Africa, Jim Clarke
The wines of Southwest U.S.A., Jessica Dupuy
Wines of the Languedoc, Rosemary George MW
Wines of the Rhône, Matt Walls
Wine: A social and cultural history of the drink that changed our lives,
    Rod Phillips

Books are available from retailers as well as directly from the publisher.
Readers of this book can get a 30% discount on any title in the series
using the code READER30 at bit.ly/BuyClassics.